Winning Angels

THE FAST WAY TO USE THIS BOOK

Winning Angels was written to be used, and is organized so you can use it in three ways:

1 ● Pick a chapter or section that interests you and skim it for nuggets.

2 ● Use the table of contents or the index to find a specific issue that concerns you now.

3 ● Read *Winning Angels* for a comprehensive understanding of the seven fundamentals.

Here is a plan of action (POA) to get the most from this book:

1 ● *Read pages xii–xiii to see how we organized the book for your use.* Once you understand the format, you will see that *Winning Angels* is the best tool you have for making investments.

2 ● *If you are new to angel investing, complete the "Know thyself" assessment on page 5.* This will help you decide if angel investing is really for you.

3 ● *Actively participate in an investment while reading.* The most accelerated learning possible will come from making angel investments and reading *Winning Angels* at the same time.

Winning
Angels

The Seven Fundamentals of Early-stage Investing

DAVID AMIS AND HOWARD STEVENSON

Jocelyn Dinnin
Research editor and project manager

FINANCIAL TIMES
Prentice Hall

An imprint of Pearson Education

London • New York • San Francisco • Toronto • Sydney • Tokyo • Singapore • Hong Kong
Cape Town • Madrid • Paris • Milan • Munich • Amsterdam

PEARSON EDUCATION LIMITED

Head Office:
Edinburgh Gate
Harlow CM20 2JE
Tel: +44 (0)1279 623623
Fax: +44 (0)1279 431059

London Office:
128 Long Acre
London WC2E 9AN
Tel: +44 (0)20 7447 2000
Fax: +44 (0)20 7240 5771
Website: www.business-minds.com

First published in Great Britain in 2001

© Pearson Education Limited 2001

The right of David Amis and Howard Stevenson to be identified as authors of this work has been asserted by them in accordance with the Copyright, Designs and Patents Act 1988.

ISBN 0 273 64916 7

British Library Cataloguing in Publication Data
A CIP catalogue record for this book can be obtained from the British Library.

This publication is designed to provide accurate and authoritative information in regard to the subject matter covered. It is sold with the understanding that neither the authors nor the publisher is engaged in rendering legal, investing, or any other professional service. If legal advice or other expert assistance is required, the service of a competent professional person should be sought.

The publisher and contributors make no representation, express or implied, with regard to the accuracy of the information contained in this book and cannot accept any responsibility or liability for any errors or omissions that it may contain.

10 9 8 7

Designed by Claire Brodmann Book Designs, Lichfield, Staffs
Typeset by Northern Phototypesetting Co. Ltd, Bolton
Printed and bound in Great Britain by Biddles Ltd, Guildford & King's Lynn

The Publishers' policy is to use paper manufactured from sustainable forests.

DEDICATION

TO FOUR ANGELS WHO MADE A DIFFERENCE: O.H., TOM, AND MOM AND DAD

DAVID AMIS

TO MY MENTORS WHO GAVE WILLINGLY AND WITHOUT EXPECTATION

HOWARD STEVENSON

ACKNOWLEDGMENTS

We would like to extend a special thank you to the following angel investors, VCs and other professionals who contributed to this book:

Warren Adams, Tom Alberg, Betsy Atkins, Dave Berkus, Amar Bhidé, Jaap Blaak, Andrew Blair, Tarby Bryant, Craig Burr, Dick Buskirk, Lucius Cary, Faye Cone, Kevin Connors, Patrick Coveney, Tim Draper, Esther Dyson, Mark Eaton, Andrew Filipowski, SG, Josh Green, Carl Guerreri, Myra Hart, John Hime, O.H., Brian Horey, Mitch Kapor, George Kline, Frans Kok, Randy Komisar, Richard Kramlich, Frank Levy, Prince Heinrich von Liechtenstein, CL, Nigel Lovet-Turner, Audrey MacLean, James Mallinson, Tom Margrave, Paul Marshall, John McCallion, Steven McGeady, Jim Morgan, Dick Morley, Anthony Morris, Wade Myers, Jim Newton, Jeff Osborn, Mark Van Osnabrugge, Jeff Parker, Denis Payre, Peter Pichler, Cuno Pümpin, Robert Robinson, Michael Rockefeller, Ryan Schwarz, David Solomont, Cliff Stanford, Jeff Timmons, Howard Tullman, Bert Twaalfhoven, Reg Valin, Manny Villafana, Steve Walker, Darryl Wash, William Weaver, Tom Wharton.

Two special appreciations go to:

Jocelyn Dinnin, whose tireless efforts as the research editor and manager of this project were essential to its completion.

Bill Sahlman, who, as a teacher of David's and a peer of Howard's, has impacted our thinking in this arena more than anyone else.

Thanks also to friends, partners and Capitalyst team members who provided significant support:

Matt Ahern, Jen Amis, Kelly Amis, Jake Ben-Meir, Brit Blakeney, Kaitlin Conroy, Stuart Flavin, Dan Garner, John Glennon, Mrs. N. Hoegh, Rob Low, Amos Lu, Ogden Martin, Ryan Murphy, Michael O'Mary, Dale Pederson, Danny Tomeh, Errol Unikel.

CONTENTS

Acknowledgments vi

Foreword x

Part I The angel investor and investing strategy 1

1 The angel investor learning curve 3

2 Creating your angel investing strategy 5

3 The angels in this book 24

4 The seven fundamentals 26

   4 TAKEAWAYS 27

Part II The seven fundamentals of early-stage investing 29

Sourcing: 1st fundamental 31

5 Start section 33

6 Generating deal flow 35

7 Activities in detail 37

8 Things to think about 56

9 Winning angels 2000 61

10 Special sections 66

   4 TAKEAWAYS FROM SOURCING 71

Evaluating: 2nd fundamental 73

11 Start section 75

12 The Harvard framework 77

13 The expanded framework 79

14 Risk 105

15 Angel strategies for winning and speed 107

16 Rejection section 110

17 Things to think about 114

18   Winning angels 2000   120

19   Special sections   127

4 TAKEAWAYS FROM EVALUATING   142

Valuing: 3rd fundamental   143

20   Start section   145

21   The five approaches to valuation   146

22   The 12 methods   149

23   Interelate example   157

24   Four levers of early-stage returns   163

25   Things to think about   166

26   Winning angels 2000   168

27   Special sections   171

4 TAKEAWAYS FROM VALUING   177

Structuring: 4th fundamental   179

28   Start section   181

29   Two camps   183

30   Deal terms   185

31   The three fundamental structures   189

32   Future rounds   198

33   The VC perspective   202

34   Winning angels 2000   205

35   Special sections   208

4 TAKEAWAYS FROM STRUCTURING   222

Negotiating: 5th fundamental   223

36   Start section   225

37   Angels who don't negotiate   226

38   Angels who do negotiate   228

39   If you are going to negotiate   229

40   Winning angels 2000   235

41   Special sections   239

    4 TAKEAWAYS FROM NEGOTIATING   244

Supporting: 6th fundamental   245

42   Start section   242

43   The five participation roles   249

44   Value events   254

45   The four types of start-ups   257

46   Things to think about   264

47   Winning angels 2000   271

48   Special sections   276

    4 TAKEAWAYS FROM SUPPORTING   284

Harvesting: 7th fundamental   285

49   Start section   287

50   The seven harvesting methods   289

51   Negative harvests and other exits   299

52   Harvesting value events   303

53   Things to think about   306

54   Winning angels 2000   309

55   Special sections   313

    4 TAKEAWAYS FROM HARVESTING   323

Part III   Angels and other investors   325

56   Biographies of the angels interviewed in this book   327

    Bibliography   354
    Glossary   355
    Index   361

FOREWORD

Peter Crisp

Winning Angels is the first book to chronicle the activities of successful angel investors. Based on personal experience and interviews with over 50 angels, venture capitalists and entrepreneurs, it is a treasure trove of advice from knowledgeable angel veterans.

Not knowing the authors personally, I was not sure what to expect when asked to review *Winning Angels*. I was impressed by the breadth and depth of the book; the authors have summarized and organized the process of angel investing in a way that no one has done before. The book is a catalog of one anecdotal insight after another, bringing alive the fundamentals of angel investing.

The end result is that David Amis and Howard Stevenson have reduced the art of angel investing into a practice, and in so doing have opened the doors to those with little or no experience. But investors new to the early-stage arena should tread lightly as the authors warn, "angel investing is practically a profession now." If you are an aspiring angel, this book will help you improve your chances of navigating through the many difficulties of this exciting arena. If you are a seasoned pro, you will certainly find some new ideas and unique views of old ones.

Angels play a vital role in the US and European economies today; they represent the largest source of early-stage risk capital. It is estimated that over a quarter of a million angels invest between $20bn and $30bn annually in the US alone. With more investors joining the ranks of angels, and with more entrepreneurial activity than ever before, a definitive work on how to do it has been needed for some time. Both angels and entrepreneurs who read this book will see that there is a science to early-stage deals. The authors have identified 7 harvest methods, 19 sourcing methods, 5 supporting roles, and over 25 value events.

Above all, *Winning Angels* is a practical "workbook," which you can return to time and time again.

Peter O. Crisp is a founding partner of Venrock Associates, which was formed in 1969 as the venture capital arm of the Rockefeller Family. One of the oldest venture firms in the USA, Venrock maintains a tradition of collaboration with talented entrepreneurs and has participated as a founding investor in such companies as: Apple Computer, American Superconductor, Centocor, Intel, Millennium Pharmaceuticals and Thermo Electron. Peter Crisp served on the board of Apple for 16 years, and currently serves on the boards of numerous leading for profit and not-for-profit organizations, including the Memorial Sloan-Kettering Cancer Center. He has also held corporate directorship positions at several leading US corporations, including Hambrecht & Quist, The Rockefeller Insurance Company, and the US Trust Corporation. In addition to serving as a Senior Advisor to Cambridge Incubator, Peter Crisp is a member of the DFJ New England Fund's Investment Advisory Board and acts as a mentor to the fund. Peter Crisp holds a BA from Yale University and an MBA degree from the Harvard Graduate School of Business. He has been an angel investor for the last 40 years, and has invested in over 300 early- stage opportunities.

THE FAST WAY TO USE THIS BOOK

This book was designed with the active investor in mind. New angels should read it thoroughly before getting started, while more experienced investors may use it as a reference guide or to compare its ideas to their own.

Part II looks at all of the fundamentals of early-stage investing (sourcing, evaluating, valuing, structuring, negotiating, supporting, and harvesting), with the exception of the front and end parts. Part I includes the big picture view of both angel investing and of this book. Part III provides information about the angel investors who participated in our research.

Note that there is a "Takeaways" section at the end of each fundamental for those readers with limited attention spans (like many angels).

Finally, leave *Winning Angels* near your bed or in the library so you can continue to glean $100k ideas from its pages whenever you have a few minutes. Serious investors continue to learn enthusiastically, and this book is a goldmine of information. By the way, each time you save or make an extra $100k because of our book, send us $1,000, just to be fair!

Section	Normal length	Reader benefits
Start section	1 page	Introduction to the part and key points includes a quick view of the part as well
The chapter	3–15 pages	Overall understanding of the stage, key areas, relevant topics. How to approach it from strategic point of view
Winning angels 2000		
What do most investors do?	2 pages	Description of what most investors do at this stage, rightly or wrongly, brings you up to speed if you are new to the game
What do the winners do?	2–5 pages	Description of what winning investors do at this stage and how they do it
A few winning tactics	2–5 pages	Some of the best tactics from winning angels which you can apply immediately
Special sections	1–3 pages each	Extra insight into a particular area, or an excerpt from a particularly good interview
Takeaways	1 page	For experienced readers or those with limited time, we provide four takeaways

A few special symbols

POA

This is a book for doers and it is meant to be used. Some sections and subsections will have a **Plan Of Action**, giving you steps to take right away.

$$$

Certain tactics and strategies were so commonplace among winning investors that we designated them as having a particularly high likelihood of contributing to your success.

OK, KF, etc.

Some of our angel investors preferred to remain anonymous, and we we will use initials, not necessarily theirs, to quote and describe them.

Note: www.WinningAngels.com is a further resource for serious angels.

PART I

The angel investor and investing strategy

QUICK OVERVIEW

1 ● The angel investor learning curve 3

2 ● Creating your angel investing strategy 5

    I   Know thyself... 5

    II   Know statistical significance 15

    III Know expected value 18

    IV Know how much 21

    V   Set the strategy 21

    VI Two sample strategies 22

3 ● The angels in this book 24

    Advice for new angels 24

4 ● The seven fundamentals 26

    4 TAKEAWAYS 27

CHAPTER 1

THE ANGEL INVESTOR LEARNING CURVE

> After investing in a few companies, you begin to build up a
> sense of what can go right and what can go wrong. You
> learn to ask questions that you wish you had asked in the
> last unsuccessful deal you did.
>
> Bill Sahlman

If you are new to this game, one of your goals must be to climb up the learning curve as fast as possible. *Winning Angels* is designed to provide you with high-octane fuel for learning.

This book includes nearly every successful angel strategy and tactic that is currently being used in the US and Europe. If you are serious about angel investing, you will manage your progression up the learning curve. Figure 1.1 is an example of how one might progress from neophyte to competent angel.

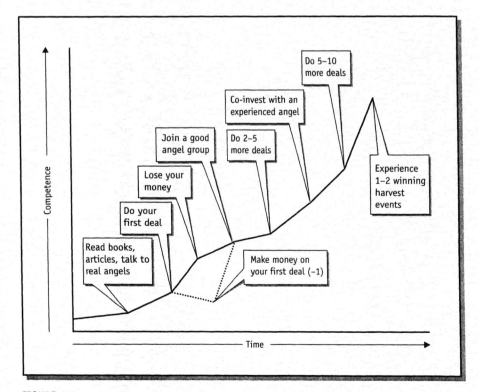

FIGURE 1.1

The elements in Figure 1.1 represent some of the major "aha!" moments of early-stage investing. Note that investors who make lots of money in their first deal are a bit like neophyte gamblers who win on the first hand of blackjack. From then on they lose but can't understand why!

Some of the best ways to facilitate your ascension of the angel learning curve include:

- Making investments.
- Investing with other angels who know what they are doing.
- Reading books, articles, etc.
- Starting a business or working directly for someone who is.
- Joining an angel group.
- Studying or teaching entrepreneurship.
- Working as a consultant, lawyer, or accountant on other deals.
- Attending angel conferences.

These are not in order of value, although actually doing is the best way to learn almost anything, and it applies in this case. The only exception might be that significant business and/or industry experience is probably critical prior to becoming an angel investor. If you don't have any business experience,

A COMBINATION OF DOING, OBSERVING, AND STUDYING WILL MAKE THE BEST ENGINE OF LEARNING

go work for 10 years. A combination of doing, observing, and studying will make the best engine of learning.

CHAPTER 2

CREATING YOUR ANGEL INVESTING STRATEGY

I ● KNOW THYSELF...

If you are new to angel investing, or if you would like to develop a thorough investing strategy, taking into consideration your net worth, time availability, background and relevant experience, then do the following:

1 Go through the angel inventory by answering the questions beginning below.

2 Assess your situation and decide or reconsider if angel investing is for you.

3 Plan your angel investment strategy in the next section.

As a result of this refined process you can accomplish in two hours what many angels spend years figuring out. You will learn the following: whether you want to do early-stage investments at all, how much, when, what role you might play, how it will affect your life, and how to maximize your chances of having fun *and* making money.

Angel investor inventory

Answer the following questions, *in writing*, then assess your angel situation using the outline on the following pages.

Financial

1 What is your net worth? (Don't count real estate unless you are prepared to sell if needed.)

_____

_____

2 How much do you think you want to place in early-stage deals?

_____

_____

3 Is this liquid now or how soon could it be liquid?

_____

_____

4 How long can you leave this money invested in the companies?

_____

_____

5 What are your likely earnings over the next five years?

_____

_____

6 Over the next 10 years?

_____

_____

7 Where are you in your salary-generating years? 25–29 (early), 30–34 (beginning of productive years), 35–45 (productive years), 46–60 (later productive years), 60+ (pre-retirement years).

_____

_____

Family and personal

1 Do you have support from your spouse and other significant people to make early-stage investments?

_____

_____

2 Is your personal life reasonably stable and likely to continue to be so for the next few years?

_____

_____

3 Do you think investing is fun?

_____

_____

Time

1 Are you working full time, part time, or not at all?

2 Are you starting a company?

3 How many boards, foundations, youth organizations, and other time commitments do you have?

4 How much time do you spend playing golf? *Civilization*? Traveling? And how much of that do you want to give up?

Experience

1 Have you started a company?

2 Have you started a company and sold it or achieved any other exit event where you and your investors generated 30% or better returns on capital?

3 In which industries have you worked?

4 In what capacities have you served?

5 What areas of business do you enjoy most? (Industry, role, function, etc.)

6 What kinds of companies do you think you would like to work with?

_____

_____

7 Ideally, what role would you play with a start-up company in which you made an investment, if any?

_____

_____

Other angels

1 Do you know any active angel investors?

_____

_____

2 Do you know any active angel investors who have achieved returns of 10–100 times?

_____

_____

3 Have you identified any angel groups in your area?

_____

_____

Risk (How much can you stomach?)

1 How much money have you lost in the past on risky investments?

_____

_____

2 Can you invest $xx and immediately accept you may lose it all? How much is that $xx?

_____

_____

▶

3 Will your spouse or other significant family members be affected if you lose $50,000? How about $150,000? How about $1,000,000? (Take a guess now and ask them later.)

_____

_____

4 Divide your answer to question #2 by question #1 in the first section. This will give you the percentage of your net worth you are thinking about investing. What is it?

_____

_____

5 What is the percentage of your net worth that is liquid or could be in 30 days without any significant tax implications?

_____

_____

Assessment

Financial

First, determine the percentage of your net worth that you want to place in early-stage deals. Net worth, liquid net worth, and earning potential should all factor into this decision. What do you think the number is? Keep in mind that you may want to retain some capital to invest in a second or third round.

_____% $_____

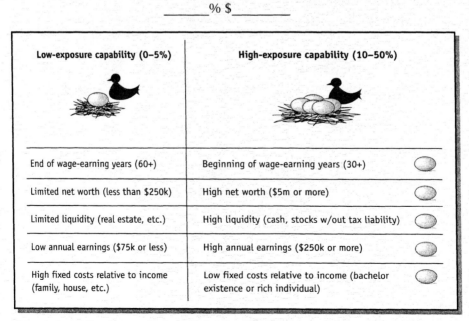

Low-exposure capability (0–5%)	High-exposure capability (10–50%)	
End of wage-earning years (60+)	Beginning of wage-earning years (30+)	
Limited net worth (less than $250k)	High net worth ($5m or more)	
Limited liquidity (real estate, etc.)	High liquidity (cash, stocks w/out tax liability)	
Low annual earnings ($75k or less)	High annual earnings ($250k or more)	
High fixed costs relative to income (family, house, etc.)	Low fixed costs relative to income (bachelor existence or rich individual)	

FIGURE 2.1

Now consider the nest egg chart (Figure 2.1). If you have low-exposure capability (one or two eggs and no more coming), you may decide not to invest at all. If your exposure capability is high (several eggs and more where they came from), you can invest not only more capital in total but a higher percentage if you have many wage-earning years to come. You will be able to replenish your cash accounts in the event you suffer losses.

Rate your exposure capability by checking each egg that applies to you and thinking through the implications of various investment strategies. You may want to invest smaller amounts in 10 different deals or you may want to invest in one but have capital for additional rounds.

Following are three examples of an assessment.

EXAMPLE 1

An older investor (58) who earns $50k per year should not invest anything in early-stage deals (other than time, see the start-up advisor and virtual CEO approaches on page 253). However, if she has a high net worth, say $2m and can comfortably live off the proceeds of $1.5m and only needs $250k tied up in her home, then she could risk up to $250k or so in early-stage deals. But this would generally not be wise since losing all of the additional capital reduces options.

> David's grandfather, at 88, has no business making early-stage investments, despite being a highly successful serial entrepreneur who built an airplane manufacturing plant and a Caterpillar dealership. He simply may not outlive the exit events, even though he could stomach the risk.

EXAMPLE 2

An investor (45) with a $3m net worth, an income of $200k per year and living expenses of $100k per year, could comfortably invest $100k–250k this year, and $100k each year going forward. If this investor has business experience he is primed for angel investing.

> Many of the angels in this book have significant financial resources, are aged from 45–60, and have extensive business, entrepreneurial and angel experience.

Dale Pederson, a founder of Amis Ventures, at one point had one-third of his net worth in early-stage deals while also providing for a young family of four and working in a start-up. This high-risk situation worked out for him. However, at 34, he had significant earnings potential so even if his investments had failed, he still had many years to rebuild his nest of eggs.

EXAMPLE 3

A young investor (32) with $50k in the bank and annual earnings of $150k, could invest up to 25% of his net worth, as he would likely recover from a complete loss.

Now, forget the logic for a moment, how much would you feel comfortable risking?

$_____

How much would you feel comfortable losing?

$_____

How much can you invest knowing you may not see it for many years?

$_____

(The answers to these three questions should be the same by the way.)

Consider all these points, and write down the approximate amount you are willing to invest in early-stage deals this year.

$_____

Family and personal

A lot of the family and personal decisions depend on the participation roles you may take on, described later in Part I.

If you intend to take on a controlling investor strategy, your time demands will be high. A silent partner has essentially no time demands, other than filling out paper work and making the decision while a reserve force strategy means sporadic needs of your time, sometimes significant.

Once you have decided on your participation strategy, and the amount of time you intend to invest, a healthy conversation with your significant other would be wise. State your case for why you want to invest, explain the risks (all of the money may be lost), and how much time and focus you will give to the process.

Finally, consider whether you will have fun doing this. If not, try playing Sid Meier's *Civilization*™, you can rule the world for under $50.

Time

There are actually three components to the time decision, although the third is reduced if you handled the first two well. You will need:

1 Time to source, screen, negotiate and do everything described in this book.

2 Time to support the entrepreneur in additional emergency situations.

3 Time to explain to your wife or husband why you just lost $100k and are going to do it again next week anyway.

Given all your current time commitments, how many hours per week can you devote to your angel investing?

_____hours / week

Risk

There is no chart or diagram to help you assess risk. The outcome of your investment could range from losing the money invested to a high level of return.

However, the amount of capital you can lose is a personal, financial, and family question. Do the appropriate thinking and talking to reach a conclusion.

Can you handle losing all of your investment(s)?

☐ Yes I can handle it.

☐ Are you kidding? I know my son-in-law will be very careful with my entire life savings, which is now invested in his hands-free, motor scooter cup holder business (which come in multiple colors).

Participation roles

Angel investors follow participation roles that vary based on their relevant experience, time availability, and preferences. There are five fundamental roles investors can play:

● **Silent partner**

Pure financial investor, takes no active interest in the company except to sign papers and hope for returns.

● **Reserve force**

Ready, willing, and capable to help as requested by the entrepreneur. Impact depends on relevant skills and contacts and also on being called at the right time.

- **Team member (full or part time)**

  Works in the company on particular projects or in a functional area. There is a risk here of micro-managing the entrepreneur if the investor has a significant stake or represents majority interest. Impact depends on relevant skills and contacts but also on the relationship with the entrepreneur (which is likely to be tested in this scenario). High to negative impact, depending on the relationship that develops between the investor and the entrepreneur team.

- **Coach**

  The highest impact investor who does not control the company. Meets with the entrepreneur regularly and provides support, advice, and any assistance as needed and requested by the entrepreneur. Consid-

  COACHES STAY ON THE SIDELINES

  erable experience in angel investing is a must. However, even new angels can have impact if they remember to act as a coach. Remember that coaches stay on the sidelines.

- **Controlling manager**

  Investor who really becomes the entrepreneur by taking control (outright or through conventions) and manages the company. High impact.

Please see the 6th fundamental, on supporting (page 245) and the biographies of some of our angels (Part III) to understand more about the various participation roles of angel investors.

To invest or not to invest?

Now that you have completed an assessment, it's time to make some decisions.

Financial

Do you have the financial wherewithal to make early-stage investments?

Unless you are going to invest time for equity, you probably need at least $25k to participate in any one investment. As you will see in the strategy section, it is highly recommended to do multiple deals, therefore, $250k might be a minimum amount of capital to commit to early-stage deals over the next 1–4 years, during which time you might do 10 investments (20 would be better). Some investors think that $50k or $100k is needed to be a serious participant and, in fact, some entrepreneurs require at least this much.

Winning angels typically invest less than 5% of their net worth into early-stage opportunities and will retain up to half of that for second-round investments. But strategies vary. Controlling angels (described later), may invest a higher percentage since they feel that they can watch their money closely.

Winning angels, such as Bill Sahlman and Howard Tullman, think that angel investing is not for everyone. *"I think this is not for many people a sensible financial decision,"* said Bill in discussing new angels. We asked Howard what he would do if he only had $250k, His answer? *"I would play the stock market, I would not do angel investing."*

Family and personal

Do you have the family support to make early stage investments?

Think carefully about whether this is a sensible financial decision for you and your family.

Winning angels, such as Dick Morley, separate their "investing activities" from the money reserved for spouse and family. Highly active or semi-professional angels know that family support is critical. John Hime, for example, has four children, a wonderful wife, and a time-consuming ranch. This all represents important commitments and time demands that must be taken into consideration.

Time

Given your intended participation role, number of investments, and how much time you will spend worrying, do you have the time?

Winning angels invest anywhere from one to 60 hours per week. Angel investor Darryl Wash invests *"an hour and a half a day"* and is currently in about seven personal investments. Dave Berkus spends that much time just reading plans since he looks at six per day,

BE SURE THAT YOUR PARTICIPATION STRATEGY IS CONSISTENT WITH YOUR TIME AVAILABILITY

and is a "semi-professional" angel. He, like others such as Lucius Cary and Steve Walker, spends all his time on investing.

Be sure that your participation strategy is consistent with your time availability, and be prepared for whatever time commitment you make to be doubled at a moment's notice, unless you are a declared silent angel and willing to take the losses without getting involved.

Experience

Do you have business experience?

If not, go get some before making angel investments or you may lose your money fast. If you have good experience be sure to use it: there are enough risks in early-stage deals. If you have entrepreneurial experience, even better: welcome to the angel club. You are the prime candidate to become an angel since you know what it takes to build a business.

Risk

Can you stomach the risk?

Early-stage investing is not for everyone. The risk is real and you may lose all your money. (Have we said that enough times yet?) This book is about how to do it well, which includes reducing the risks and maximizing the likelihood of getting a win, but you still need to look in the mirror on this one.

Go or no-go?

If, after all of this, you decide not to become, or to discontinue being, an angel investor, you have saved yourself years of heartache and probably, no, *certainly*, a lot of money. Angel investing is more of a profession now than ever before, and your heart needs to be in it.

ANGEL INVESTING IS MORE OF A PROFESSION NOW THAN EVER BEFORE, AND YOUR HEART NEEDS TO BE IN IT

If you still want to make investments, let's work on strategy and then we will tackle the seven fundamentals (sourcing, evaluating, valuing, structuring, negotiating, supporting, and harvesting).

II ● KNOW STATISTICAL SIGNIFICANCE

❝ If you're the best person going on these things, you'll hit it out of the park 10–15% of the time. That's one of the scariest things about angel investing. ❞

Howard Tullman

The first important question for setting your angel investment strategy is: how many investments will you make? You should do at least 20 early-stage deals or so to get a real winner, in our opinion, although angels have varying opinions and results. Some think that one out of five will be successful but most agree that it is a number larger than one. They also agree that the numbers improve dramatically as you move up the learning curve. Therefore, if you only invest in one deal, you are likely to lose your money, according to these experienced angels.

The theory of statistical significance supports this view. We are going to attempt to explain it in less than one page, so even non-mathematicians can understand it well enough to see how it impacts their investing strategy.

Let's say we are looking at several possible investments in lemonade stands where each has a 10% likelihood of succeeding or a 90% likelihood of failing.

The likelihood that one lemonade stand by itself will succeed is therefore 10%.

Now what happens if we do two or more deals? And how many deals do we need to do to get at least one winner?[1]

The likelihood that two lemonade stands will both fail is determined as follows: 90% * 90% = 81%. The likelihood that at least one will succeed is therefore 19%

(100% − 81%). There is an 81% chance that both will fail and a 19% chance that at least one will succeed.[2]

Now, let's go for some bigger numbers. If you invest in 10 stands, your likelihood of getting at least one winner is 65% $(1 − .9^{10} = .65)$.[3] If you did 20 similar investments your likelihood of getting at least one winner is 88% $(1 − .9^{20} = .88)$. If you did 30 lemonade stands, your chances increase to 96% that at least one will succeed. Keep in mind, that more than one may succeed. These numbers refer to the likelihood that at least one will succeed, and this is critical to your success as an angel.[4]

Why? Because most angel deals fail, and the way the winners win is to invest in opportunities that will pay so much if they succeed, that they will cover all the losers. So it is important to have at least one winner!

Here is Dick Morley's home-spun way of explaining it:

❝ When you have an ants' nest the ants go out and forage for food, but only one in a hundred ants finds food. Now, I have no way of knowing ahead of time which ant will find food, but if I only send out one ant to find food, he will likely not find it. My job is to send out lots of ants. If I send out lots of ants, I guarantee you one or two of them will find food. ❞

Both ants and lemonade stands help to explain the theory of statistical significance. However, in reality, experienced investors would not invest in only one industry.

Let's look at a real portfolio of investments. In June 1999, Capitalyst completed a study on 25 deals that raised money from VCR[5] angels three years previously.[6] One of the 25 was a serious winner, generating a return of 20 × the original investment, a few appeared to be 3–4 × winners, and several were failures.[7] However, many of the companies were less than three years old, and eight still had the potential to generate significant wins. The numbers from the Capitalyst study are presented in Table 2.1.

---

1 We will continue with the assumption that each opportunity has a 10% likelihood of succeeding. Our objective here is not to explore probability theory but to provide some hands-on insight that is useful right now. We are using binomial probability to simplify things.

2 If you are wondering what the likelihood is of two winners, it is 10% * 10% = 1%. Consequently, there is a 99% chance that you will not have two winners!

3 The formula is: 1 − (% likelihood of all failing) number of investments

4 There is one way to beat these odds: become great at sourcing, evaluating, valuing, structuring, negotiating, supporting, and harvesting! This will increase the likelihood of any single investment succeeding.

5 VCR stands for Venture Capital Report, Ltd, which was founded in 1978 by Lucius Cary. It has facilitated over 300 angel transactions and has a high level of expertise in this area.

6 All of the deals were done during David's tenure as Managing Director of VCR (1996–1997). VCR did not participate in this study or review the results.

7 Based on estimated values as of June 30, 1999.

TABLE 2.1

The status of 25 companies backed by VCR[8] angels in 1996–97 (as of June 30, 1999)

Industry	Investment	Status	Current/exit value of investor's stake
Software	$334,000[9]	Raising 2nd round	$1,322,640
Catering	$250,500	Imminent sale	$688,000
Computer security	$417,500	Doing well, no information disclosed	
High-tech	$465,930	Company value more than doubled. Raised further rounds	Not disclosed
High-tech	$33,400	No information available	
Property	$167,000	Raised more capital and began to roll out the concept	$500,000
Environmental	$100,000	No information available	
Mail order	$334,000	Sales doubling every month	Not disclosed
Computer services	$500,000	No information disclosed.	
High-tech	$76,160	No information disclosed.	
Coffee bar chain	$500,000	AIM stock market listing	$10.4m
Pathology testing	$125,250	Just raised $2.2m	$392,450
Clinical trials	$530,000	Company dropped in value	$220,440
Food and beverage	$125,250	Raised two further rounds, valuing company at $1.1m	Not disclosed
Biotechnology	$278,000	Raised follow-on capital, valuing company at $16.7m	$334,000
Internet	$16,700	No information available	
Domestic	$100,000	No information available	
High-tech	$167,000	No information available	
Antiques	$334,000	Valuation based on sales	$3.5m
Hotel	$308,950	No longer trading	
Internet consultancy	$167,000	300% sales growth in previous year	$350,700
Magazine	$167,000	No longer trading	
Web designers	$167,000	Company still going	
Security systems	$250,500	Valuation based on tangible assets and product rights	$668,000
High tech	$125,000	Raised several rounds, now out of business	

8 VCR was not involved in this study. Capitalyst completed the study solely through direct entrepreneur interviews.

9 These numbers were originally in pounds since they occurred in the UK. The British have been angel investing since before the incorporation of the East India Company.

The coffee bar chain was the one winner that paid for the rest. If this had been a portfolio from only one angel then the portfolio itself would already have generated an annual 41% return on investment.

Did we have only one big winner? As usually happens, theories have their limitations. In our real example of 25 deals backed by angels who subscribe to VCR, some were partial winners and some were still potential winners. How can we think about that?

Expected value is another concept that will help us to think about how a group of investments can contribute to a winning portfolio.

III ● KNOW EXPECTED VALUE

The concept of expected value (EV) can be helpful in early stage investing to understand the potential value of a portfolio of investments. Again, we are going to use a theory best left to mathematicians for a full explanation, but worthwhile for a quick look. EV will help us think about the potential value of a group of investments and further support our interest in doing multiple deals.

THE EV OF AN OPPORTUNITY IS THE VALUE YOU WOULD RECEIVE, ON AVERAGE, IF YOU REPEATED THE OPPORTUNITY MANY TIMES OVER

The EV of an opportunity is the value you would receive, on average, if you repeated the opportunity many times over.

So, let's say an investment opportunity in Cameron's Lemonade Stand has a one in 10 chance of succeeding, and it will be worth $1m if it does succeed. The EV would be 10% * $1m = $100k. So you would earn $100k, on average per investment, if you made many similar investments.

Before we look at a portfolio, there is one good question to ask: how much should I invest for that chance to earn $1m or an EV of $100k? The short answer is: less than $100k! Why? Because you would like to make investments that are rational, that will win over time. If the EV is always greater than your initial investment, and you make enough investments, eventually you will get the EV and make money! If the EV is lower than your investment, that is tantamount to investing on the premise, "If I repeat this many times over, I'll have less money for sure."

Now let's look at another portfolio of investments. Remember when we discussed 10 lemonade stand investments on pp. 15–16, we saw that there was only a 65% chance that at least one would succeed. With 20 such investments, the likelihood increased to 88%. Then, when we looked at 25 real angel deals, we found that there was one big winner, but several partial winners as well.

EV allows us to look at each investment, estimate the likelihood of success, along with the potential outcome, and come up with a potential expected value of the total portfolio.[10]

---

10 Any mathematician will recognize this as a crude version of expected value, since, among other things, confidence is not addressed. However, we think such a view is helpful for inexperienced angels and a good reminder for old ones.

Frank Levy, managing partner of Wasabi Fund I graciously shared his portfolio for our examination. This $1m fund, which he raised to make angel investments, placed $25,000–125,000 in 19 companies. Table 2.2 includes the amounts invested and the valuations. We have made estimates of the potential future value of each company along with the likelihood of occurrence. These estimates are unscientific but provide a useful look at what could happen with Wasabi Fund I.

EXAMPLE FASTRETURNS.COM **

Based on your evaluation of an opportunity in the developing return logistics industry, you believe that an investment in FastReturns.com has a 5% likelihood of succeeding on a significant scale.

The potential market is $1bn and FastReturns.com is one of only three companies now entering the market. Therefore, it may achieve a 4% (total guess) market share. Since companies in this industry are valued at 1x revenues, the company could be worth $40m in 3–5 years. Similar companies have needed over $10m in angel and venture capital, so you expect one more round of dilution at 50%, after an initial valuation of $5m.

You can invest $100k for 2% of the company at a $5m valuation. With the dilution mentioned earlier, you will own 1% before the company might sell. So your $100k might become $400k. (1% times $40m, which is the potential sale price.)

This would be a 4x return. Pretty good, huh?

Not if there is only a 5% likelihood of success.

5% * $400k = $20k. The expected value (EV) is $20k. It is less than your $100k investment! If you did this same kind of deal 20 times over and got one winner, you would invest $2,000,000 and get back $400k. (20*$400k*5%=$400k.) Not such a good deal!

Now, try the numbers with a 10% likelihood of success and a potential sale price of $200m (answers are below).

Once you examine the potential results of a deal that has a positive EV, you will see what kind of opportunity deserves your money.

Note: **If you have not seen this kind of problem before, have a look at the valuing section (p. 143) for more on dilution, valuing start-ups, and what to shoot for.

This example is purely hypothetical. It is used for illustrative purposes only and is very simplistic. The probability of success and the potential outcome are impossible to know upfront.

1 % (of ownership) * $200m (sale price of company) = $2m (your potential win)
$2m * 10% (likelihood of success) = $200k (EV)

Therefore, if you did enough deals for statistical relevance, you would earn about 2 × on your money, which would be a good portfolio return if earned in a few years. (26% ROI over three years.)

TABLE 2.2

Estimated EV for the Wasabi Fund I portfolio

Firm	Investment	Possible exit value	Likelihood	Expected value
ActiveSpace	$90,000	$250,000	15%	$37,500
AdVenta	$80,766	$500,000	25%	$125,000
BestSelf *	$50,000	$0	100%	$0
Bid4Assets	$50,000	$250,000	25%	$62,500
BookFace	$50,000	$250,000	25%	$62,500
Coolboard	$25,000	$200,000	40%	$80,000
EachNet	$50,000	$2,500,000	33%	$833,333
eCrush	$50,000	$333,333	33%	$111,111
eMode	$75,000	$250,000	50%	$125,000
Entregamos	$25,000	$350,000	25%	$87,500
ExpertCentral **	$25,000	$25,000	100%	$25,000
Foodline	$125,000	$2,000,000	25%	$500,000
GetConnected	$50,000	$500,000	25%	$125,000
GovWorks	$25,000	$250,000	25%	$62,500
ImageLock	$50,000	$300,000	33%	$100,000
Mambo	$50,000	$200,000	25%	$50,000
NetFreight	$50,000	$300,000	33%	$100,000
RevBox	$30,000	$200,000	50%	$100,000
VisibleMarkets	$100,000	$2,000,000	33%	$660,000
Total	**$1,050,766**	**$10,658,333**		**$3,246,944**

Notes: * Company has failed.

** Wasabi got its money back upon sale of company.

If these numbers are accurate, the fund will be worth about $3m and will return 3x or 32% annually if all the investments are liquid in four years.[11] The actual value will probably be between $0 and $10m. The primary benefit of this exercise is to get a sense of what could happen. This fund is likely to generate a few million dollars in capital gains if our predictions are within reason (and maybe even if they are not).

---

11 Bear in mind, that the investments are likely to become liquid over a period of several years. However, in order to find a rough estimate, a number between three and five years is reasonable since a significant number of early-stage companies will either sell, go public, or fail in that time frame.

Thus both statistical significance and expected value are friends of the angel investor if understood. Unless you plan to invest as a controlling angel and direct the outcome, it is highly recommended to do multiple deals.

IV ● KNOW HOW MUCH

❝ My typical individual investment can be anywhere from $50k–150k. If I am going up to $500k or approaching $1m, I'll be bringing in other guys. ❞

Angel CL, an investor in 20 deals, including two which exited via IPOs

The amount of capital you will employ in total and the amount per investment, on average, are also important aspects of your angel investment strategy.

Winning angels invest anywhere from $25k up to $1m. Of course, there are winning examples of $10k investments and investments of time, but most active angels will invest amounts that are significant to the entrepreneurs.

Lucius Cary, an investor in over 50 early-stage companies, has made investments ranging in size from $10k–$300k.

Also keep in mind that the total amount any one investor should place in early-stage deals should not be over 5% of their portfolio if they are nearing the end of their wage earning years and not over 25% if they are at the beginning.

WINNING ANGELS INVEST ANYWHERE FROM $25K UP TO $1M

What is the range of capital that you will place in any one deal? What is the total amount you intend to invest in this year or next?

Within each of the fundamentals of angel investing, there are strategic decisions to make. Will you implement a quantity sourcing strategy and focus on visibility activities, such as giving interviews and writing articles? Will you implement a supporting strategy that includes a reserve force role, only acting when called upon? Or will you become a part-timer in the business and watch your dollars more closely? Within each of the seven fundamentals, you will make strategic and tactical decisions that will determine your success rate.

V ● SET THE STRATEGY

Now it is time to set your investment strategy. Remember that your family should have some say and that the entrepreneur may need something other than what you planned. Also, you are likely to change your mind as you make investments, read this book, and move up the angel investor learning curve. So set a tentative strategy today and stay open to change. Your strategy should include decisions on the following, as well as specific ideas on each of the seven fundamentals.

Year One[12]

- Available capital for early-stage investing.
- Available time for early-stage investing.
- Possible participation strategies.
- Number of investments intended.
- Average amount intended.
- Follow-on investment reserve (if any).
- Summary of investment strategy.

VI ● TWO SAMPLE STRATEGIES

Sample strategy of an inexperienced but wealthy angel

My situation

55 years old; retired with 20–30 hours per week available for investing; $1.3m net worth – not counting real estate – which is primarily in treasuries earning 6% or $70k per year; severance pay that covers my family costs; a spouse who wants me out of the house and has her own money; so I can invest $50k annually and lose it without any change in my circumstances.

My preferences

With 30 years' experience in low-tech manufacturing as a CFO, and later president of my own company, I would prefer to invest in a familiar industry or possibly in something new and interesting, for a lesser amount. With the right entrepreneur, I could work a couple of days per week on projects, but I do not want significant responsibility.

My strategy

My first-year focus will be to learn as much as possible. I will join a local angel group and make one $25k investment alongside other angels, offering to help out the entrepreneur in any particular way that I can (i.e. reserve force). I will look for a couple of projects that allow me to learn more about the start-up process and to see it from the entrepreneur's point of view. I will invest in either my own area of expertise or make sure there is a lead investor in the deal. I will be prepared to put in another $25k if other investors do so. Meanwhile, I will attend some seminars, visit with other angels at least twice per month, and read all the books and articles I can find on the subject. In year two I will reassess my situation and perhaps look for more opportunities.

---

12 Keep in mind your plans for years two, three and beyond.

Sample strategy of an experienced angel investor

My situation

38 years old; working 40–50 hours per week as a managing partner of an accounting firm. $2m net worth – not counting real estate – which is one-third in the stock market, one-third in treasury bills, and one-third in eight early-stage companies. Two are looking pretty good, but none has exited yet. Annual income of $150k, which leaves, after family expenses, about $50k. A spouse who works as well so we can easily cover our family expenses for years to come, which include three children. I only have two to five hours per week, if that, but I can invest up to $300k more and would like to do so if I can find the right deal(s).

My preferences

I have already invested in seven high-tech deals and one financial services firm. My partners are some of the more active local angels and we usually do deals together. I want to continue to invest in whatever looks hot as long as there are some active investors in the deal. I will help out if needed but don't have much time or desire (i.e. reserve force role).

My strategy

I will continue to meet with my three partners every week to discuss our current deals and look at new ones. They usually do the due diligence and then I look over the numbers at our final meeting. I will place up to $300k in two to six more deals, if we find them, thus creating a portfolio of about 12 deals.

CHAPTER 3 THE ANGELS IN THIS BOOK

Although we have known and worked with hundreds of angels in our careers, for this book we completed 50 interviews specifically focused on the seven fundamentals of early-stage investing. Summary information about the angels, along with a closer look at a selection of the angels, can be found at the back of the book (p. 325). They include angels from Silicon Valley to Silicon Alley, from Austin to Boston and from as far away as London and Vienna.

IF YOU HAVE BUSINESS EXPERIENCE AND CAPITAL, YOU CAN INVEST WITH A REASONABLE LIKELIHOOD OF SUCCESS

Together our investors have done over 1,000 deals. Their combined knowledge allows us to turn angel investing into a science. If you have business experience and capital, you can now invest with a reasonable likelihood of success if you learn and follow the strategies and tactics in this book and do enough deals.

Here is what some of our winning angels had to say when we asked what advice they would give to new angels.

ADVICE FOR NEW ANGELS

❝ Early-stage investing is like drilling for oil... you can't do just one...❞

John Hime

❝ Invest in what you know. ❞

Randy Komisar

❝ Trust your intuition and judgment... it's fun and I encourage people who are in a position to do it, to do it. ❞

Mitch Kapor

❝ It's absolutely critical that people do multiple deals, it's critical that people figure out how the professionals do this business. ❞

Bill Sahlman

❝ Find other angels and watch them for a year, and only invest in areas that you understand fully that are not just financial opportunities, but are understandable by you. ❞

Dick Morley

❝ Target your network, and stay away from the financial players, meaning, angels who are ex-investment bankers, etc. Because the critical skill set is understanding the industry and the sector. ❞

Angel investor CL

❝ Don't do it alone, have others who have more experience, stick to investments within 200 miles, set a top priority for entrepreneurs, single or collectively, who run the company, have enough experience, and tie them to the venture so that they can't walk from it. ❞

Bert Twaalfhoven

Within these seven quotes are some of the most important themes in this book: do multiple deals; invest in things you understand; trust your own judgment; focus; and learn from the pros.

The angels were gracious in sharing their time and their secrets with us about how to win. Most allowed us to quote them directly and we have done this actively. If you know angels, you know they are bottom-line people who prize experience above all else. We have also liberally named the various tactics and ideas after the angels who brought them to us. Apologies to any investor who feels they developed the idea first, please write us.

DO MULTIPLE DEALS; INVEST IN THINGS YOU UNDERSTAND; TRUST YOUR OWN JUDGMENT; FOCUS; AND LEARN FROM THE PROS

Some of the angels preferred anonymity and we have provided this by using only initials (not necessarily theirs) to represent their thoughts and backgrounds. In this way you can still learn from them as some of the best angels intentionally avoid the press and any public recognition.

Short biographies containing background information about the angels who were interviewed for this book can be found on pages 327–334. There are also 15 detailed profiles that give further insight into the backgrounds and differing approaches behind some of the best angels, which can be found on pages 335–353.

If you know of an angel who should be in this book, send them to WinningAngels.com and we will try to interview them prior to the second edition. Alternatively, if you know of an entrepreneur who should be in our Winning Entrepreneurs book, please have them contact us as well (WinningEntrepreneurs.com).

Further resource

Our new website, www.WinningAngels.com will provide you with additional opportunities to enhance your learning curve, including information on angel clubs, investment opportunities, and newsletters.

CHAPTER 4   THE SEVEN FUNDAMENTALS

In looking for a way to structure this book and create a methodology that both new and experienced investors could understand, we settled on the seven fundamentals, because winning investors appear to be effective at doing seven things well:

- sourcing
- evaluating
- valuing
- structuring
- negotiating
- supporting
- harvesting.

In the *Winning Angels 2000 Study* by Amis and Dinnin, which led to *The Winning Angels Handbook*, the seven fundamentals were initially thought of as stages, but when we asked investors what they thought of these "stages," they invariably replied: "*Those are right, except I usually do several of them at once.*" Thus, winning angels tend to be aware of, and competent in, each of these seven areas, and deal with them in parallel.

NO ONE CAN PICK WINNERS WITH CERTAINTY NO MATTER HOW GOOD THEY ARE

In addition, when looking at the investment results of many deals, it became clear that failing to manage any of these areas often led to a predictable failure. Granted that no one can pick winners with certainty no matter how good they are, failure to understand the terms or the upside potential, for example, often meant no chance of getting a win no matter what happened.

Thus we have the seven fundamentals of early-stage investing. Learn and master them to succeed, or ignore them at your peril.

1 ● Treat angel investing like a professional.

2 ● Manage your learning curve.

3 ● Decide if you have the capital to stomach angel investing.

4 ● Do a lot of deals.

PART II

The seven fundamentals of early-stage investing

QUICK OVERVIEW

- **Sourcing:** 1st fundamental   31

- **Evaluating:** 2nd fundamental   73

- **Valuing:** 3rd fundamental: 143

- **Structuring:** 4th fundamental   179

- **Negotiating:** 5th fundamental   223

- **Supporting:** 6th fundamental   245

- **Harvesting:** 7th fundamental   285

Sourcing

The harder you look the luckier you get.

James Mallinson, Investment Director, ET Capital

QUICK OVERVIEW

5 ● Start section   33
Deal sifter   34

6 ● Generating deal flow   35

7 ● Activities in detail   37
Preparation activities   37
Networking activities   38
Visibility activities   43
Focus activities/tactics   51

8 ● Things to think about   56
Quality and quantity   56
The five-star entrepreneur   58
Referrals – Why are they so sweet?   59

9 ● Winning angels 2000   61
What do most investors do?   61
What do the winners do?   61
Winning tools and tactics   63

10 ● Special sections   66

   1 How many deals?   66

   2 Where did they come from?   67

   3 How angel investor Dave Berkus initiated his deal
      flow   69

   4 One-pager   70

   4 TAKEAWAYS FROM SOURCING   71

CHAPTER 5

START SECTION

Sourcing or identifying entrepreneurial projects of merit is the first step in the process of making early-stage investments. There are 18 sourcing activities provided in Chapter 7 which represent the most common and successful activities used in the US and Europe. However, some of the best sourcing activities are utterly unique, and unreplicable.

For example, Bert Twaalfhoven, a highly successful European entrepreneur and investor, is the founder of Europe's 500, the organization of leading entrepreneurs in Europe. Every year Europe's 500 brings many of the best new entrepreneurs to its annual meeting and Bert always figures prominently in the proceedings. The podium effect in this case is quite strong and strategic.

> SOURCING OR IDENTIFYING ENTREPRENEURIAL PROJECTS OF MERIT IS THE FIRST STEP IN THE PROCESS OF MAKING EARLY-STAGE INVESTMENTS

But you do not need to found a leading organization for entrepreneurs to generate high-quality or high-quantity deal flow. We will describe a number of replicable activities, which you can implement. We will also describe some that are not so easy to replicate, but which may engender an idea for an alternate activity that will suit you in particular.

"Sourcing is evaluation," said at least one angel. You should think along these lines as you develop and implement your sourcing strategy. If you are new to angel investing, generating numbers is probably a good idea, as you need to move up the learning curve. Experienced investors, however, tend to be more focused, as they know what they are looking for. In addition, since it is easy to burn up a lot of time in this stage of the process, strategic thinking will have a high, value-added impact.

The best way to manage sourcing is to think about it as panning for gold. You need to sort through a lot of rocks to get to the nuggets and it is best to do this with a series of pans, each with a finer screen. Sourcing, therefore, is all about filling the sifter. We have 18 activities for you to follow in addition to others that you may come up with on your own. As you choose your deal flow activities, you will want to think about both quantity and quality.

How you think about the various screens will depend on your experiences and chosen strategy. For example, angels who do not

> YOU DO NOT NEED TO FOUND A LEADING ORGANIZATION FOR ENTREPRENEURS TO GENERATE HIGH-QUALITY OR HIGH-QUANTITY DEAL FLOW

negotiate want to know quickly what the price is going to be. If it is too high, they will not spend any time evaluating the opportunity. Angels who do negotiate will thoroughly evaluate the opportunity before making an offer, since they already expect a negotiation on price and terms.

Price and terms are often treated separately from the other types of evaluation because of their high impact on the attractiveness of the deal, relative ease to understand, and the potential to change them by negotiation.

Sourcing and evaluating are the two major components in terms of time usage. The essential question is how will you invest your time in order to invest your capital?

DEAL SIFTER

Figure 5.1 shows how one investor might "plan for gold."

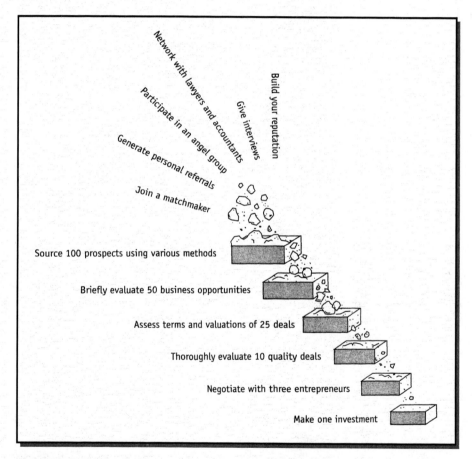

FIGURE 5.1

Note: Similar to a goldminer, you "pour" deals into the pans, and then sift them down, completing more assessments and refining your choices as you go. What you sift for will be based on your overall investment strategy in relation to the seven fundamentals.

CHAPTER 6 GENERATING DEAL FLOW

Although there are many ways to create deal flow, winning angels are more likely to do one of the 18 activities described here. Do these, or some combination thereof, and you will have more deal flow than you can handle.

Many of the best methods are based on the fundamentals, such as clearly and regularly communicating a target to your network, while others are based on an original twist of a common activity. For example, Darryl Wash uses his ties to African-American, Korean, and other minority organizations to source deals. He regularly communicates with his network and builds on it, but keeps a special eye on these communities. One of his best investments, StarMedia Network, came from such networking. Darryl's approach also represents a good example of one of the unique motivations of angels, he wants to *give something back."*

IT IS VERY EASY TO LOSE LOTS OF TIME IN SOURCING AND EVALUATING EARLY-STAGE DEALS

Some of the methods, such as teaching an entrepreneurship course, are not interesting options to most people. Still, their frequency and efficacy makes them worth observing. You will see that four of the 50 angels (including Howard) teach entrepreneurship. You might ask yourself, what is behind this strategy that may be replicable in other activities?

We have divided the sourcing activities into four groups to help you think about them as you strategize:

● preparation activities
● networking activities
● visibility activities
● focus activities.

Focus activities, by the way, are less "activities" and more of a disciplined approach. We have learned the hard way, as well as by observation, that it is very easy to lose lots of time in sourcing and evaluating early-stage deals. Focus activities can be worth their weight in plutonium.

If you are an experienced angel, you may be familiar with most of these activities. In that case, review them to see how your results compare, or jump to the section on page 61, "What do the winners do?".

As you review each of the activities in more detail, you might consider some of the following questions to help resolve your sourcing strategy:

● How many deals do you want to do in the next six months? In the next three years? And how much do you want to invest?
● How much time are you going to commit to this endeavour?

- How many deals do you want to review each month?
- What is more important: getting a good deal, learning how to invest, building a network, having fun?
- How much time and resources will you risk before closing a deal?

Table 6.1 provides an overview of the activities you can choose from, which is followed by descriptions for each with POAs.

TABLE 6.1

Summary of activities

	Impact on:	Learning curve	Quantity	Quality	Page
Preparation activities **Things you might do in preparation for** **generating and managing your deal flow:**					
1. Write one-pager	Med	n/a	High	36
Networking activities **Activities that develop and support your** **network:**					
2. Personal meetings with bankers, etc.	n/a	Low	Med	38
3. Participate in an angel group	High	Low	Med–High	39
4. Share quality deals	Low	Low	Med–High	40
5. Join an angel/entrepreneur matchmaker	Low	Low–High	Med–High	41
6. Reward your network	Low	Low	Med–High	42
Visibility activities **Activities that increase your visibility:**					
7. Give an interview	n/a	Low–Med	Low to high	43
8. Give speeches, publish articles	Low	High	Low–High	44
9. Teach entrepreneurship/angel course	Med	Med	Low–High	46
10. Write a book	High	High	Low–High	47
11. Make an investment (winner or loser)	High	Low	Low–High	48
12. Hire best lawyer and/or accountant in town	Med	Low	High	49
13. Co-invest with winning angels	High	Med	Med–High	50
Focus activities/tactics **Activities or tactics which narrow your** **focus to impact your deal flow:**					
14. Focus on your network	n/a	Low	High	51
15. Focus on 1–2 industries	Low	Low	High	52
16. Build a network in 1 industry	Low–Med	Low	High	53
17. Act in a syndicate	High	Low–Med	Med	54
18. Turn away all but...	Med	Low	High	55

CHAPTER 7

ACTIVITIES
IN DETAIL

PREPARATION ACTIVITIES

1 • Writing (and distributing) a one-pager

David Gladstone, in his book, *Venture Capital Investing*, suggests writing a *"one- or two-pager that describes what you are interested in and what you are willing to consider."* He suggests circulating it among bankers, attorneys, brokers, consultants, and at conferences and conventions. Angel investor John Hime, who has made 19 early-stage investments, has a one-pager, which you can see on page 70.

Consider the key elements of a potential investment and make your decisions now on the kind of deal you are targeting. Some of the key elements include: valuation, stage, industry, your investment size, size of entire round, status of management team, status of other investors and stakeholders, market size, market focus, and track record of the team.

NORMAL TIME TO RESULTS

- Working hours:
  1–2 hours to write it, 5–10 hours/month to distribute it.
- Calendar time:
  3 months to rethink and revise it, 30 days to distribute it the first time.

Result you can expect
Substantial clarity on what you are looking for and are not looking for. It will make you a better partner to both entrepreneurs and co-investors.

1 Discuss this with any active angels you know.

2 Get it out there, review your deal flow in so many months, then refine it again.

Recommended
Write a draft and share it with experienced angels. Ask what they are targeting. If they don't have a one-pager, ask them how much time they spend on investments they would have never done anyway.

NETWORKING ACTIVITIES

2 ● Personal meetings with bankers, lawyers, and venture capitalists

When David Berkus, referred to in *Inc* as a "professionalized angel," set out to become an angel investor, he started by meeting bankers and VCs. His pitch was:

> **Angel SG talks about his networking with VCs**
>
> ❝ If you're in the venture business for 17 years, you know all the venture guys. There are plenty of things they see that that aren't quite soup yet. They want to give a nice turn down to somebody friendly who's going to bring it back to them when it is soup. ❞

❝ Give me your tired, your poor, your hungry, your huddled masses yearning to break free ... The point was that I'd be a person they knew and trusted who was able to do the small deals that neither of them could do, deals that were too early stage for the bank and too small for the venture guys. So deal flow began immediately. ❞

Carl Guerreri, a Virginia-based angel, has told friends, bankers, and investment bankers that he is interested in investing. His deal flow is fairly consistent. Personal meetings are the traditional method of choice for an angel who intends to make a semi-full-time career out of making investments. Creating a network of referrers, if handled well, will result in consistent and good quality deal flow. It can be especially powerful to work with the "best."

NORMAL TIME TO RESULTS

- Working hours: 5–10 hours/month. This includes calls to set appointments, travel, appointments, and follow-up.
- Calendar time: 1–8 weeks+. They will need time to digest what you've said for an appropriate deal.

Results you can expect
1–5 medium to high-quality deals/month.

1 Complete a one-pager on your targeted investment.

2 Call up 5–10 attorneys, bankers, accountants, and other professionals you know and make appointments.

3 Show them what you are looking for.

4 Follow up often and creatively (e.g. send interesting articles, give a progress update). Promote the relationship and reward them for good referrals.

Recommended
Do some thinking on your targeted investment type and write a one-pager. This not only clarifies your thoughts but also makes it easy to communicate the kinds of referrals you want. If you don't have a target, you'll be like Alice in Wonderland asking for directions. Also, light and consistent follow-up will significantly improve the likelihood of referrals.

3 ● Participate in an angel group

Dick Morley, David Solomont, Jim Newton and many others have founded their own, or participate in, organized angel groups. Dick Morley likes to use the group as a screen. *"If they are strong enough in coming after us, then they get considered,"* he says.

Capitalyst angel group meeting in process

"The idea," says David Solomont, is to get the angels to think of *"group initiatives,"* as opposed to individual initiatives. This combines the strengths and weaknesses of members as well as creating the best win-wins for everyone concerned.

There are angel groups in nearly every US city now, and many cities in Europe and elsewhere. Some of these groups are tightly controlled and you can only join in if you know current members or have a unique reputation. Other groups are more open about membership. Some of the best opportunities are with groups that are just forming and have a natural deal flow source or draw for entrepreneurs.

NORMAL TIME TO RESULTS

- Working hours: 5–10 hours/month. This includes travel, the meeting itself, and an extra dinner or two, although ideally you will begin spending significant social or business meeting time with various members.

- Calendar time: 1–6 months. There are likely to be deals at your first meeting but it may take a few meetings to find a deal that fits your target and has the kinds of players with whom you would like to co-invest.

Results you can expect

1–5 medium to high-quality deals per month, an excellent learning curve, an enjoyable social event, and access to experienced angels.

 1 Ask around, read the papers, search the web for angel groups in your area. (Some key words might be: angel clubs, angel bands, breakfast clubs, and dinner clubs.)

2 Join.

Recommended

Find out what you can about the groups in your area and try to join the one with the most winners or the most promise. Consider their structure and see if it fits you.

4 ● Share quality deals with other angels

Betsy Atkins, an active New York angel who has made over 30 investments, always makes a point to share her best investment opportunities with others. In this way, she believes she generates additional, quality deal flow from angels that want to continue to be a part of her network. *"Be nice to people, they'll be nice to you,"* says David Solomont.

Angels flock and share – and for good reason. If you let me have some of your cake, I will share some of mine.

NORMAL TIME TO RESULTS

- Working hours: 5–10 hours to offer the opportunity to another angel(s).
- Calendar time: 1–8 weeks.

Results you can expect

1–5 medium to high-quality deals/month, and an opportunity to experience the investment process with someone else.

 1 Identify some winning angels in your area.

2 Show them the deal.

Recommended

If you are just starting out, take a minority position in the deal. Let someone else play the lead role.

5 • Join an angel/entrepreneur matchmaker

Andrew Blair, Audrey MacLean, David Solomont, and others belong to one of a few credible matchmakers that provide screened deal flow. There are hundreds of these organizations but only a handful that have significant deal activity.

Lucius Cary, Guy Kawasaki, and David, among others, actually founded match-makers to create deal flow for themselves and others. Reg Valin, a UK-based angel, likes his matchmaking service because *"the businesses are presented in a timely format and have passed a certain level of screening."*

NORMAL TIME TO RESULTS

- Working hours: 1–5 hours per month. Since the opportunities are pre-screened, significant time savings can be had. Many matchmakers also have angel groups which meet regularly.

- Calendar time: 1–4 weeks (deal flow usually starts right away). There are likely to be deals available right away but it usually takes some time to identify one that fits your interest. In addition, some deals get oversubscribed quickly.

Results you can expect

1–20 medium to high quality deals per month, an excellent learning curve, an enjoyable social event, and access to experienced angels.

1 Ask around, read the papers, scan the lists in this book, and search the web for matchmakers in your area.

2 Join.

Recommended

Understand their pricing and compensation structure. Compensation based on getting deals done, particularly when it includes equity, means the matchmaker is aligned with the investors and the entrepreneurs. Also, be sure to interact with a registered broker/dealer if they are taking commissions or contact the NASD to check them out.

6 ● Reward your network

Angel investor CL[1] includes people who have referred him in future deals. Since he is often the lead in a syndicate, he regularly controls part of the round. For referrers who are not investors, he might *"cut them a few thousand shares at the offering price just before the IPO."*

Simple things, like following up on referrals given, are also a way to reward your network. In one case, David called a co-investor who had made three good referrals

REWARDING YOUR NETWORK FOR REFERRALS IS AN EXCELLENT WAY TO CREATE A CONTINUOUS STREAM OF REFERRALS

to tell him what happened: *"One invested, one declined and one never took the call."* This company investor called again two days later with a few more referrals. This process repeated itself three times as the investor was motivated to help when he knew his efforts were working.

While this may seem obvious or easy to say, few people do it well. Rewarding your network for referrals is an excellent way to create a continuous stream of referrals. Rewards can include referrals for their business, pats on the back, and inclusion in some of the deals.

NORMAL TIME TO RESULTS

- Working hours: 2–3 hours per month.
- Calendar time: 1–8 weeks.

Results you can expect
1–5 medium to high-quality deals per month per referrer, generally well-screened and even more so the longer you work together.

 POA

1 Identify 2–3 methods for rewarding your network that are comfortable for you (i.e. 5 minute follow-up calls after each referral to share the progress, warrants in any deal you do, 10 minutes of thinking for each good referral on how you can help them out).

2 Do it, and make a habit of it.

Recommended
Giving good feedback on referrals has a much more significant impact than one might imagine. Feedback is like an information reward, so that the recipient knows he is helping. It also shows respect for the time investment and reduces any possible perception of reputation risk. Finally, it forces you to think through what is good about a referral and to communicate it.

---

1 We have used initials for angels who prefer anonymity (not necessarily theirs).

VISIBILITY ACTIVITIES

7 ● Give an interview

Reg Valin receives a *"large number of entrepreneur contacts"* every time he gives an interview. Audrey MacLean, a self-described "stealth angel" had her disguise blown when *Forbes* put her on the cover in 1999. *"Now every entrepreneur in Sri Lanka, Ukraine and South America thinks they must have me,"* she says with some regret. William Weaver was once described as an "arch angel." He received 300 plans in the next five months but wasn't happy about it. Some angels positively do not want additional press. In fact, several successful angels agreed to be interviewed for this book only if their real names would not be used.

IF YOU ARE ALREADY KNOWN OR CAN DO SOMETHING NEWSWORTHY YOU CAN GENERATE INTERVIEW OPPORTUNITIES

If you are already known or can do something newsworthy then you can generate interview opportunities. This kind of exposure increases your credibility and negotiating power, but it also means that lots of entrepreneurs, brokers, and others can find you.

NORMAL TIME TO RESULTS

- Working hours: 0.5–2 hours (to give the interview). This includes answering questions but not the time that it may take to get the interview(s) which can be 5–10 hours per month or the cost of a public relations agent.
- Calendar time: 1–12 months. This depends considerably on the quality of the article, the quality of the publication, and how you are represented. A special section in the *National Enquirer* on Space Angels would not be productive. Likewise, even a top business magazine might write something that is less than flattering.

Results you can expect

1–20 deals per month immediately after publication, continued trickle after that for each exposure or if the article is particularly good.

 POA
1 Do something newsworthy.

2 Hire a public relations agency or find other ways to get in front of the press (such as giving speeches at high-tech conferences).

Recommended

This is one of the sourcing activities that you can't just make happen. It requires the cooperation of a journalist. Therefore, create the environment for it to happen and be ready when it does.

8 ● Give speeches, publish articles

Many angels use the "podium effect" to create deal flow and credibility. Professor Cuno Pümpin, who can be seen speaking at the prestigious St. Gallen's University, Europe's 500 or in any other number of European events, gets most of his deals because of his reputation as a professor and as a well-known personality.

"Mostly, I do a lot of business schools," says Randy Komisar, who gets involved in early-stage deals as a Virtual CEO. Other investors, such as Steve Walker and Reg Valin give talks as well. Both Howard and David give talks on entrepreneurship, early-stage investing and other topics. In one event where David gave a talk on raising early stage capital to 230 members of the Harvard Business School Club of New York, over 30 entrepreneurs mobbed him after the event.

In another case David sent five faxes, made about 10 calls and practically begged, in order to give a talk at a European entrepreneur conference. Only four people showed up for his talk but one of them was a potential co-author and they later wrote a book together. This is that book.

Aside from the podium effect which, regardless of your experience, will raise the perception of your stature in early stage deal-making, each opportunity to talk to a large audience will generate deal flow although your control on quality is limited.

The only way to impact the types of deals by stage, industry, quality, or quantity, is to choose your audience strategically. For example, an angel choosing to focus on commercial applications of lasers might develop an expertise on raising capital for such businesses and write an article for the "Entrepreneurial Laser Section" of the annual High-Tech Fair Guide. Within that small community, she would become known as the angel to see, especially having done a deal or two. This will be especially true if there is no other perceived authority on the subject.

NORMAL TIME TO RESULTS

- Working hours: 20–30 hours to write, 2 hours to give. This includes doing enough reading, interviewing, learning, and practicing in order to develop some unique material. Depending on one's background, this process could actually be anywhere from 20 to 200 hours. In addition, getting the first magazine, paper or speaking venue to take you can require some networking and selling.

- Calendar time: 3–24 months. Dependent on one's background in relation to the area of choice. Developing the material, writing, gaining feedback, writing more, etc. are all significant time takers. Finding a publisher or avenue for speaking can take some time.

Results you can expect

5–10 deals per month immediately after publication or speaking, continued trickle after that and more for each exposure. If the presentation or article is any good, you can expect additional opportunities to present it.

1 Determine your preferred area of investing.

2 Look for expertise you have in that area and for areas where no one has demonstrated expertise in any significant promotion format.

3 Develop a speech or article, or both. Ask for feedback, refine, ask for more feedback, refine, etc.

4 Find an audience and get it out there.

Recommended

Start with something you know, perhaps in an entirely unrelated field, as a way to get published or speaking initially. Then move over to your new area of expertise. Also, being recommended by someone is always more powerful than trying to sell yourself.

If you can identify an interesting niche and develop some unique content, you can use that content in a variety of ways. Having it published or placed in front of an audience, such as a Rotary or other service club is do-able if you are a moderately competent public speaker. Any type of angel or business group will bring good results.

9 ● Teach an entrepreneurship/angel course

Howard, and a very few others, has developed entrepreneurship courses which they now teach. For example, the book, *New Business Ventures and the Entrepreneur*, written by Stevenson, Roberts and Grousbeck has become a staple of entrepreneurship courses in MBA programs around the globe. Rob Robinson recently created the Entrepreneurial Negotiating course at Harvard which puts him in touch with 40 aspiring entrepreneurs each semester that he teaches it. Audrey MacLean teaches entrepreneurship in the Stanford Engineering School where she *"meets a whole new generation of would-be entrepreneurs every quarter."*

Although this is an unlikely strategy for many angels, we have included it because there are hundreds of active angels who teach as a means to generate deal flow, have fun, learn, and give something back.

NORMAL TIME TO RESULTS

- Working hours: 4–10 hours per class during the course.
- Calendar time: 2–4 months (of teaching, it could be 1–2 years before you find a position).

Results you can expect

5–10 low to high-quality deals during the course and a few more for some time afterward. In addition, your network will expand with benefits that will accrue for several years. Additional visibility opportunities may arise.

 1 Develop a course and/or identify a teaching position.

2 Teach.

Recommended

There are several areas of entrepreneurship and new business creations that lend themselves to study. Some ideas include: angel investing, incubators, virtual CEOs, Internet start-ups, and matchmakers.

10 ● Write a book

Guy Kawasaki, the founder of Garage.com, wrote several books on marketing, evangelism and about his days at Apple Computer. When he started his company to start up start-ups, his high visibility gave him instant credibility with many VC's, angels and entrepreneurs. His book, *Selling the Dream*, is a must read for entrepreneurs.

The authors of this book

Publishing a book makes you an expert to many people even if they never read it. The book will often open up speaking and teaching opportunities that in turn create deal sources. If done well, it really will make you an expert because the hundreds of hours of thinking, writing, discussing, and interviewing will serve as an intensive course in the subject matter. You can't help but learn! Don't expect to make much money from writing a book and realize that it is primarily a credibility-building and research/learning event.

NORMAL TIME TO RESULTS

- Working hours: 1,000 hours easy.
- Calendar time: 12–24 months.

Results you can expect
- Speaking opportunities.
- Expectation of expertise.
- Real development of expertise (if your research and thinking is productive).
- Lots of uninteresting email.
- Some quality contacts.

POA
1 Find a narrow topic and write a book proposal. Get a publisher interested before writing the book.
2 Become a writer or hire one. Set aside a definite time each day to write.
3 Write chapters and articles. Have lots of people read them.
4 Write, rewrite, get your friends to write, write some more, then rewrite five more times. (If you like writing, it's actually fun.)

Recommended
Writing a book is a bear-sized project, only take it on if you enjoy writing and think you can really develop some interesting material.

Do research that will give you expertise whether you finish the book or not. Consider doing a white paper or a few articles instead.

11 ● Make an investment

Winning investments can lead to repeat opportunities, as with Darryl Wash, an investment banker turned angel:

> **Learning from losers**
>
> Look back to determine the lessons learned: sourcing, evaluating, valuing, structuring, negotiating, supporting, harvesting. What went wrong? What did you do wrong? What can you do next time to get a win?

❝ Much of my deal flow has come from existing investments, where we have supported the company and subsequently the entrepreneurs have encouraged other entrepreneurs to seek us out. ❞

Having said that, making a losing investment may be the best thing you can do on your first try. *"I would say that most of the learning process comes from losers,"* says Dick Morley:

❝ When you have a conference and the panel is full of winners, that's a waste of time. They may have been lucky. What we want is a loser's panel. ❞

Investing can be a networking and visibility exercise, as well as the chance to go to school. *Winners:* Success in early stage investing breeds success, as it does in most other endeavours. Entrepreneurs, angels, and employees looking for start-up jobs will seek you out when it becomes known you were an investor in a winning deal. *Losers:* This is the easier thing to do and it only takes minutes to get into a losing deal! However, if you pay attention, the learning curve is steep!

NORMAL TIME TO RESULTS

- Working hours: 50 to 100 hours to find a winner; 5 minutes to find a loser; 1–100 hours to deal with all of the problems from the loser, even if you are a silent investor.
- Calendar time: 1 month to 5 years (winners); 1 week (losers).

Results you can expect

- Winners: 1–5 low to high-quality deals per month for some time after the success. A high-profile deal may result in several months of 10–20 referrals.
- Losers: Experience and the capability to do better the next time, maybe hit the big one.

 POA 1 Read and use the strategies, tactics, and tools in this book.

2 Invest in many deals.

Recommended

As stated in this book, the best and fastest way to back a winning deal is to co-invest with experienced angels. Once you achieve a winner, look at the entrepreneurs, the lawyers and professionals involved in the deal, and your other angels to provide the best referrals. Winning is contagious and everyone who can say they were part of your deal is a winner by association; they will all attract more high-potential entrepreneurs.

12 ● Hire the best lawyer, accountant in town

"I insist they get one of four high-tech specialty law firms here in Austin and one of two accounting firms, and sign on as clients before I invest," says John Hime, who wants the entrepreneurs to have representation before he negotiates with them. Other angels agree. *"I think it is really important to get one of the major law firms involved,"* says angel Audrey MacLean.

In each city there are a few professionals known for being "the early-stage guy" or the "the best high-tech law firm". Find them out and get into their networks.

NORMAL TIME TO RESULTS

● Working Hours: 2–5 hours. If you can set up a meeting, it does not take long to pay someone money.

● Calendar Time: 2–4 weeks. The best are usually in demand and it may take some time to get in. An introduction will facilitate this considerably.

Results you can expect
High-quality deal flow if you can get on their radar. The best advice in town, which is probably more important in this case.

 1 Ask around to find out who the best are.

    2 Hire them.

Recommended
In bigger cities there are usually a couple of professionals focusing on each niche. You might use your quest for services as a way to meet all of them.

13 ● Co-invest with winning angels

Co-investing with a winning angel is, perhaps, the best tactic in this book. The benefits include: a higher likelihood of success, a steep learning curve, introductions to other winners, and credibility by association.

CO-INVESTING WITH A WINNING ANGEL IS, PERHAPS, THE BEST TACTIC

CL, an investor in two start-ups that went to IPO, and a full-time angel, says he had a very savvy mentor who *"taught me by example."* Dick Morley, Mitch Kapor, and many others also suggest partnering with successful angels.

If you do not know any major winning angels or cannot get their attention now, focus on learning the seven fundamentals and do some deals. You will either become a winning angel yourself or find an opportunity to get involved with one. You will become more attractive to the winner as you develop your knowledge and ability in early-stage investing.

NORMAL TIME TO RESULTS

- Working hours: 1–100 hours. This depends on whether you already know successful angels who will include you in their next deal or whether you have to go out and find them, show them you are real, convince them you will be a value adder and not a time detractor, and when the moment comes, write the check.

- Calendar time: 2 weeks to 1 year. Finding some winners will take a while if you don't know any now.

Results you can expect

Great learning curve, reasonable likelihood of success (remember that this is partly a numbers game), and an expanded network (winning angels will already have a network of referrers, professional service firms, and other people important to the cause).

1 Review your network to see if you or anyone in it knows some serious angel investors.

2 See them and ask candidly, "What would it take to get me involved in your next deal?" The great thing about working with angels is that the best ones are extremely straightforward.

3 If they can't or won't, ask if they know some other active angels you could meet.

Recommended

Seek them out to ask for advice and listen to what they say. Without bringing it up, they might think of you when the next deal comes in the door.

FOCUS ACTIVITIES/TACTICS

14 ● Focus on your network

❝ How do I interact with my network? I set up my network, as it turns out, largely driven by people I knew who were in the areas that were interesting to me. The distinction there being that they are people who are operating often in a web context in those industries, and specifically, the industry in my case is media and related technology, with a secondary interest in education. ❞

So says angel investor, CL.

Rob Low, a DC angel investor, has frequent dinner parties, which often include his two most active partners and other potential co-investors as well as get-togethers to discuss specific deals, and an annual skiing trip. Three of them have done a half-dozen deals together and now have an understanding of each other's strengths, as well as a camaraderie that allows them to be highly effective as an investing team.

This tactic is based on the outstanding angel and entrepreneur principle of focus. Within your network there are likely to be five individuals that could provide the most referrals, the best learning opportunities, the best additional networking opportunities, and maybe even the best advice on how to do it all.

NORMAL TIME TO RESULTS

● Working hours: 5–10 hours per week. This can include socializing and regular lunch meetings and is one case where choosing your golfing buddies or dinner club friends might make the most sense.

● Calendar time: 1–3 months. If it takes any longer, they aren't the angels or referrers you thought they were.

Results you can expect
1–3 high-quality deals per month.

1 Think through your network and whether there are some serious prospective major referrers.

2 Join new groups and network.

3 Narrow it down to 5 referrers and focus on them.

4 Find ways to reward them, have fun together (it helps if they are already friends or inclined to be such), and generally stay on their radar.

Recommended
Choose people you like and that will add value to your ventures.

15 · Focus on one or two industries

> **How Andrew Blair and his angels implement their concept of "selective industry targeting"**
>
> As a group they look at the background and experience of the business angels and then decide which sector they will go for. They call this technique "selective industry targeting." They may select 2–3 industries and then proactively go about finding suitable entrepreneurs.

Some, not all, angel investors restrict themselves to industries they understand. *"I only do medical deals,"* says Manny Villafana, one of the best known Minneapolis investors, who has invested in over 50 companies. Jaap Blaak, an entrepreneur and venture capitalist, is focused on bio-tech deals and spends a lot of time at the local universities, he says: *"What I have been involved in... is working with scientific institutes and universities to get technology there spun off."*

Other angels focus on the internet, on B2B, or on B2B supply logistics opportunities. Retail meat distribution, textile exporting, high-density materials are all examples of areas targeted by angel investors. Define industries broadly but choose one to two areas as your focus. It might be that you will identify a niche that has no expert or primary practitioner. This can be good. It works best if you have 20 years' experience in the industry, but can still be done even if the industry is new to you.

NORMAL TIME TO RESULTS

- Working hours: 5 hours per week.
- Calendar time: 1–2 years (1 month if you are already a well-connected expert)

Results you can expect

Improvement in every stage of the investing process. Credibility with entrepreneurs, angels, and other important stakeholders will enhance your ability to source, negotiate, and get into good deals. You'll be able to support and harvest better because you will know the terrain and the players. Finally, you will have a sense of the value of the deals with very limited time and energy.

1 Consider your background first and then look for an industry with the following: growth, a good revenue and profit model, interesting to you personally, local companies or an industry center nearby.

2 Study it, research it, network in it, etc. If you haven't worked in the industry, you might consider doing that for a year or more as well.

Recommended

Follow one of two strategies:

1 Choose the industry that will have the highest growth and subindustries to maximize your opportunities. Or

2 Choose an industry that no one cares about but that may still have some opportunities, and you will be one of the few pros (big fish in a little pond).

16 ● Build a network in one industry

Angel investor and venture capitalist Craig Burr suggests *"attending industry specific tradeshows and reading industry magazines"* in order to meet the people in one industry. David Solomont suggests:

❝ I just network with a group of people that bring deals to my attention... and I hate to say it, but it's not all about what you know, sometimes it's about who you know. ❞

Investing time in networking in one industry means a focus on *"know-who"* and learning through interactions. We define this separately from focusing on one to two industries because some investors will keep up on an industry but not actively network in it. They actively take referrals and screen, but do not pursue new contacts. This sourcing activity includes: attending association meetings, joining trade groups, consulting in the industry, socializing with industry professionals which can include managers, consultants, lawyers, members of the press, etc.

> **Angel investor SG talks about networking in an industry and in one company in particular**
>
> ❝ I've been doing business in information technology for 30 years. My investment focus is software, data telecom equipment, and internet related. I was the president for a period of time of the alumni association of a Massachusetts computer company (where I had worked previously). I maintained a thousand-name mailing list of people who went on to start companies. I mean hundreds of companies. That's been a great source of deal flow. I also ran the software and CPU development group. I had six direct report; five of them started companies and four of them went public. It was just a great source of people. ❞

NORMAL TIME TO RESULTS

- Working hours: 10 hours per week.
- Calendar time: 2 months +.

Results you can expect
Insight on the best deals and players in that industry. If you are well received and have something to offer, you will also get access to the best deals in that industry. If done well, you could have the industry's best managers coming to you when they get ready to start their own deals.

 POA

1 Choose an industry where you will have a competitive advantage or that is developing and/or growing fast.

2 Join everything in sight, read everything to find out who is doing what, show up wherever industry people hang out, and hang out with them.

Recommended
This sourcing activity works best if you naturally socialize with the kind of people in this industry. Are they mostly engineers or programmers? Is it about airplanes or transformers or web development? You'll have more fun if you already talk and think about the same things. Otherwise, it might just be a fantastic learning experience!

17 ● Act in a syndicate

Betsy Atkins rarely invests on her own. She shares the whole investment process with co-investors, including evaluating deals. This approach results in each key area of a business being evaluated by an investor/potential investor with expertise in the corresponding area. *"I think sharing responsibility is an incredibly useful practice which, in regards to sourcing and screening, everybody in the business community has an idiosyncratic set of characteristics about them,"* says Bill Sahlman.

SYNDICATES ARE POWERFUL IN THAT THEY SHARE RISK, SHARE RESPONSIBILITIES, AND ARE STRONGER CONTRIBUTORS WHEN ACTING TOGETHER

It is well known that angels often invest in groups, some of them forming their small groups or syndicates in advance. Two to five angels may decide to meet weekly or monthly to look at a handful of deals, often picking one or two in which to co-invest.

Syndicates are powerful in that they share risk, share responsibilities, and are stronger contributors when acting together.

NORMAL TIME TO RESULTS

- Working hours: 20–50 hours.
- Calendar time: 1–6 months.

Results you can expect

Some camaraderie and healthy peer pressure to get some deals done along with the benefit of different perspectives which start with aligned motives, not to be underestimated. In addition, you might have fun.

1 Choose two to five angels who you think will form a good social and working group.

2 Decide on one or two basic rules (e.g. any deal brought to the group will include each member who wants to join, everyone invests on the same terms or not at all, etc.).

3 Have your first meeting and start looking at deals.

Recommended

Have the following backgrounds represented if possible: angel investing, marketing/sales, technology development, management, finance, entrepreneur experience.

Choose your partners as carefully as you would choose full-time business partners.

Make sure your interests are roughly aligned in the following areas: amount of investment per deal, total amount to invest in the next 12 months, industry interest(s), stage of company development, geographic area and preferred participation strategy.

18 ▪ Turn away all but...

Reg Valin is so focused on his target preference that he searches the papers for additional opportunities in his sphere and calls them. Other angels who have seen 1,000 deals now know exactly what they want and refuse to hear about anything else.

Once you have completed your highly focused one-pager, refuse to listen to any deal or meet any entrepreneur with anything that is different. This will save enormous time and energy and allow you to make some quality investments.

NORMAL TIME TO RESULTS

- Working hours: −5 hours. Yes, this is such a time saver that we think of it as having a negative impact on your deal sourcing time. For new angels it may be better to look at a lot of deals and thereby learn by looking. Even many experienced angels will still want to see and invest in a variety of deals. But the exceptional investor, who is prepared to forgo other opportunities, can walk the shortest path to deal identification and success.
- Calendar time: n/a.

Results you can expect

Very limited but high-quality deal flow that you are able to assess quickly. In addition, some investors develop reputations for being the "one-industry" guy. This can be a powerful PR and negotiating tool.

 1 Choose an industry or part of an industry that you know well or can get to know well.

2 Let your network and all entrepreneurs and angels that you meet know that you only look at certain deals.

Recommended

Don't do this until you really know what you are looking for and can stand to pass on all of the other opportunities that will come your way.

CHAPTER 8

THINGS TO THINK ABOUT

QUALITY AND QUANTITY

When planning a sourcing strategy, angels should think about both quantity and quality as separate issues to manage. There is no golden number of deals per month winning angels see anywhere from five to 100. Given the different experience levels of angel investors and the variety of strategies employed, each individual angel should determine their own monthly sourcing goal.

Deal flow–quantity

There are two major factors that influence quantity: visibility and networking activities, which result in the approximate levels of deal flow as shown in Figure 8.1.

If you want to improve the quantity of your deal flow, do the action items listed in Figure 8.2 and read the tactics on pages 63–65. Consider both the results you want and the time you can invest when choosing where to focus your energies.

		Visibility	
		Anonymous	Famous
Networking activities	Educate and encourage network	Good and consistent 5–10 deals per month	Very high 20–100 deals per month
	Do nothing	Limited 0–5 deals per month	High but sporadic 0–100 deals per month

FIGURE 8.1

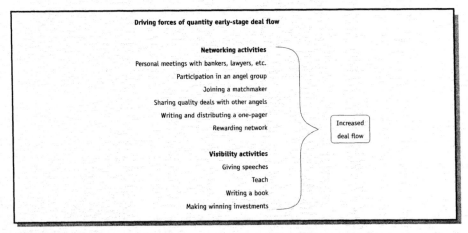

FIGURE 8.2

Deal flow–quality

There are also two major factors which influence quality: breadth of networking and breadth of opportunity consideration (see Figure 8.3). Basically, you have to decide if you are going to use the shotgun or rifle approach. Both strategies have their advantages. Investors new to the game might use a shotgun approach to maximize deal flow. Experienced investors may be more interested in protecting their time. Still, some of the most active investors want to invest in multiple industries and have their own screener who reviews opportunities for them (see Figure 8.4).

Usually new investors focus on quantity, and more experienced investors on quality. But, as noted, there are a variety of strategies. OH, a super-angel described in this book, once said, *"It's okay to be stupid, just don't be uninformed."* Your sourcing strategy should be based on fundamentals of good angel investing, regardless of whether you get it right the first time or not.

YOUR SOURCING STRATEGY SHOULD BE BASED ON FUNDAMENTALS OF GOOD ANGEL INVESTING, REGARDLESS OF WHETHER YOU GET IT RIGHT THE FIRST TIME OR NOT

		Search focus	
		Open	Tight
Networking	Targeted	Few deals received, all considered	Few deals received, even fewer considered
	Indiscriminate	All deals	All deals received, few considered

FIGURE 8.3

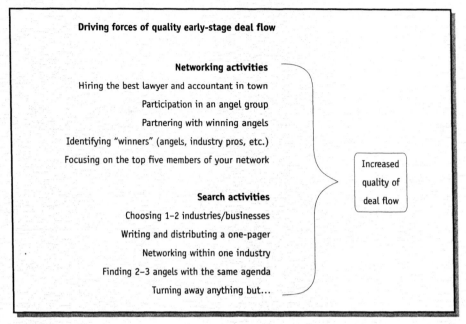

Driving forces of quality early-stage deal flow

Networking activities

Hiring the best lawyer and accountant in town

Participation in an angel group

Partnering with winning angels

Identifying "winners" (angels, industry pros, etc.)

Focusing on the top five members of your network

Increased
quality of
deal flow

Search activities

Choosing 1–2 industries/businesses

Writing and distributing a one-pager

Networking within one industry

Finding 2–3 angels with the same agenda

Turning away anything but...

FIGURE 8.4

In addition, everything you can do to improve your ability to identify winners and to understand the early-stage investing process will facilitate your ability to source and to communicate with your network. Study the seven fundamentals and practice them. Make investments and learn by winning or losing. Finally, review your sourcing strategy again in 6–24 months – and improve it.

THE FIVE-STAR ENTREPRENEUR

As you will soon see in the evaluation stage, the entrepreneur or the entrepreneurial team is the first key to a winning early-stage investment. Therefore, any sourcing

THE ENTREPRENEUR IS THE FIRST KEY TO A WINNING EARLY-STAGE INVESTMENT

method that brings good people is like a gold vein.

You will be a better angel if you have been an entrepreneur, and a better entrepreneur if you have been an angel. In the same way that natives of different planets have no problem identifying themselves, entrepreneurs are also able to identify other entrepreneurs.

Questions to ask

Here are some of the questions you will want to ask about the entrepreneur that are best answered by someone who knows them:

1 How well do they listen?
2 How well do they learn?
3 How well do they attract other people to work with them?
4 How honest are they?
5 How hard do they work?

These themes (that the entrepreneur is key and that the best angels have entrepreneurial experience) will surface several times in this book. You will want to have the quality entrepreneur in mind as you plan your sourcing strategy.

REFERRALS – WHY ARE THEY SO SWEET?

"The best opportunities come from personal contacts," says Denis Payre, the entrepreneur behind Business Objects, the first French software company to go public on NASDAQ, and an active angel investor.

Venture capitalists like to say that they, *"don't do deals over the transom."* Most winning angels will also tell you that they source most of their deals through referrals. Why? Because a quality referral from someone who knows how you think and who you understand equally well, will mean a whole host of questions and potential issues are already resolved.

First, the referrer herself is incredibly important. She will either be the most accomplished and successful angel investor in the area, or the shrubbery cutter, or somewhere in between. Obviously, referrals from people who understand the industry in question, know the people involved, or have done similar angel deals previously, will give the highest quality referrals.

The nature of your interaction with the referrer and how well you have communicated your objectives will also be instrumental in the quality and appropriateness of a potential deal. Assessing early-stage deals is,

How many deals?

There is no answer to this, as the best angel investors have deal flow that varies from 5 to 100 per month. However, for angels operating on their own without full-time jobs and whom have considerable experience, we have found that 5–20 per month is the number which they prefer and find manageable.

See Special section 1 on page 66 to see what a few angels had to say about their deal flow.

first and foremost, an assessment of the referrer, and the more you know about them and their thinking, the more you will understand about the parameters of the deal in question. Therefore, in the best case scenario, a quality referral means:

MOST WINNING ANGELS WILL TELL YOU THAT THEY SOURCE MOST OF THEIR DEALS THROUGH REFERRALS

- The first 20 questions have already been asked.
- The entrepreneur is trustworthy and capable.
- The people in the deal are not crooks.
- The opportunity is very good and will check out on all the key issues.
- Meeting the entrepreneur will not be a waste of time (meaning there are not any obvious reasons why you won't invest).
- The referrer has thought about you in terms of your investment interests, your risk profile, your preferred participation strategy, your personality, and considered this against the objectives, industry, personality, and overall opportunity presented by the entrepreneur.

CHAPTER 9

WINNING ANGELS 2000

The following excerpts from *The Winning Angels Study* © 2000, by David Amis and Jocelyn Dinnin: 'What do most investors do?', 'What do the winners do?' and the selected winning tools and tactics, are reprinted with permission. Highlights of this study were published in *The Winning Angels Handbook*.

WHAT DO MOST INVESTORS DO?

- **Network informally**

  Let their friends and family know that they are interested in early-stage deals. This generates some deal flow with varying quality.

- **"Advertise"**

  Some do this literally, others just let it be known in glowing terms to everyone they meet that they are an angel investor. Significant yet unfocused deal flow is often the result.

- **Do nothing**

  Some investors are so well known that they can sit back and receive tremendous numbers of quality projects. Other investors attract deal flow because they are known in their communities either for having money or for doing deals.

WHAT DO THE WINNERS DO?

- **Educate their networks**

  Martin Rigby of Egan & Talbot meets with those he wants to receive deal referrals from, and gives them the characteristics of the kinds of opportunities he wants. In this way both the investor and referrer save time, and the chances he will act on a referral increases, making the process more meaningful for the banker, attorney, or other who may be referring an entrepreneur.

- **Act strategically**

  Howard, an investor in over 80 early-stage deals, says that sourcing is your opportunity to get high quality. *"The rolodex is critical,"* he says. *"In addition, you need to find sources of deal flow that are naturally excellent."* Former students are one source of deal flow for Howard, as are business acquaintances from the last 20 years who understand his expectations and area of specialty in early-stage deals.

- Remain open to chance encounters

Although angel investor Mike O'Regan is a regular at social events and subscribes to a matching service, three of his 10 deals were found through chance

MANY WINNING INVESTORS ARE OPPORTUNISTS

encounters. He says that, again and again, a chance meeting leads to a contact and a new deal. Many other winning investors have voiced similar sentiments. They are opportunists.

- Set up their own operation

Lucius Cary, who has invested in over 50 start-ups, set up his own angel network, Venture Capital Report, in 1978 to channel deals and thus position himself in the middle of lots of activity. Venture Capital Report has around 800 investors, interacting with some 200 entrepreneurs a year. In 1998 David Solomont also founded an angel group, CommonAngels, which is located in Boston. Today they receive about 50 opportunities every month, and target closing about a deal a month.

- Source a good CEO

Andrew Filipowski, founder of PLATINUM technology, inc, says, *"find a good CEO and build the company around him."* This strategy, developed by VCs in the 1980s recognizes the major impact the right entrepreneur can have on a company.

- Manage public relations

Steve Walker gives talks at various clubs and organizations. *"Each one results in so many plans,"* he says.

- Join, or associate regularly with, an angel group

Rob Low, Amos Lu, and Larry Baucom, active angel investors in Washington, DC, organized their own group to meet frequently to consider deals. They also organized their own merchant bank that has participated in a half-dozen deals. The best one so far generated a 10 times return and another is staging an IPO in about six months. Rob Low is also a member of Private Investor's Network (PIN) and attends other angel events regularly.

- Use their relationships

"Get it from a known relationship," says Jeff Parker, CEO and founder of CCBN. *"This is a relationship business... 80% of my deals come from known relationships."* Audrey MacLean sources from, *"people I know and have worked with before."*

- Act supportively, even if they aren't going to invest

"I try to help out anyone who contacts me, even if I don't invest. This means I point them to other funding sources, give them feedback on their plan, their team, etc." John Hime is known as a good guy to call even if he does not invest. He has more calls than he can handle and does not need to do any active sourcing.

- **Invest in industries they understand**

  Some, not all, angel investors restrict themselves to industries they understand. *"I only do medical deals,"* says Manny Villafana. An equal number of angels invest in all kinds of start-ups, perhaps preferring to diversify. Howard Tullman saw an information appliance opportunity that he thought was pretty good, but his team did not see how they could bring any value to the deal in terms of *"expertise, connections or networking or resources,"* so they passed on the deal.

WINNING TOOLS AND TACTICS

Lost fountain of deals

As several of our angels have pointed out, developing your own source of deal flow is a high-value proposition. For example, Cliff Stanford, founder of Demon Internet, sold the company to Scottish Telecom for £66m. In the same month he set up Redbus Investments to provide financial, operational, and management support to British companies and individuals with new and innovative ideals. All new initiatives carry the Redbus brand and, in return, Redbus holds a portion of the equity. In doing so he has created a draw for entrepreneurs and an easy point of contact (www.redbus.co.uk).

A few things other angel investors have done include:

- developed relationships with incubator managers
- written a book
- set up a "band" of angels
- developed relationships with university scientists.

> Create your own unique deal flow source. Look for opportunities to develop exclusive relationships, generate unique credibility or name recognition, or find a source that no one has thought of yet. Alternatively, actively develop and refine your network of business contacts and turn it into a fountain of deal flow.

Develop a network

Betsy Atkins shares investment opportunities that come her way with an informal network of potential co-investors. She rarely invests on her own, choosing to invest with between six and nine other angel investors. If she has a good deal she feels it is *"rude"* not to share it with other potential investors. *"Why should they then invite me to invest in a potentially* **REFERRERS ARE PUTTING THEIR MONEY WHERE THEIR MOUTHS ARE** *good deal if I don't share mine with them?"* She believes that the advantages of co-investing run the whole way through the investment process, for example Betsy

Atkin's area of expertise is in the realm of marketing and sales, and she will thoroughly screen this aspect of potential deals, while the other angels in the deal will screen in the area of their expertise. It is an efficient way of receiving filtered, quality deal flow – in essence referrers are putting their money where their mouths are. Betsy Atkins has taken this theory one step further by setting up a fund, Net Angels, with a number of associates, which she uses as the vehicle for some of her investments. *"Building a network of angel associates and potential co-investors is an effective way of sourcing quality deal flow."*

> Build a reciprocal arrangement of quality deal sharing with angel associates. In this way, you will receive quality deals which through their sourcing have been partially screened.

Follow the leader

If you are investing for the first time (or in a new field), find someone who knows what they're doing and invest alongside them. Many experienced angel investors prefer co-investors. Angel CL had a "mentor" when he started out who taught him by example. They did several deals together and CL believes a fair chunk of his success is owed to the lessons he learned them. Co-investing with a winner will speed your learning curve through all the phases.

IF YOU ARE INVESTING FOR THE FIRST TIME, FIND SOMEONE WHO KNOWS WHAT THEY'RE DOING AND INVEST ALONGSIDE THEM

If you are going to co-invest with another angel, particularly one whose judgment you are going to follow, here are a few questions you might ask them:

- What industries are most interesting to you?
- Tell me about the investments you have made already. (It would be good to know how many, in what industries, and how much.)
- How much are you looking to invest in your next deal?
- What terms do you normally like to see? What terms did you have in most of your deals?
- What is your exit goal? How much and how soon?
- How have your previous deals worked out? What were the keys to success? (It would be helpful to establish that they have some kind of track record, if only one big winner.)
- How can I help other than by writing a check?

> Find an experienced angel investor and invest alongside them.

🎤 Make friends with a VC

VCs will receive deal flow which is not at the right stage for venture capital investment. Further down the financing chain they may want to become involved with these companies. VCs may be happy to refer such deals to angel investors, especially if they in turn will come back to them if venture capital is required later on.

William Weaver, an active high-tech lawyer and angel investor in Chicago, has relationships with several venture capital firms that often send deals to him they cannot do. In return they hope he will bring the deals back to them when they are ready for venture financing, so creating a reciprocal relationship.

VCS WILL RECEIVE DEAL FLOW WHICH IS NOT AT THE RIGHT STAGE FOR VENTURE CAPITAL INVESTMENT

3i, perhaps the best known UK venture capital firm, has an associate whose full time job is to develop relationships with angels in order to co-invest with them.

> Build reciprocal relationships with VCs to develop deal flow.

CHAPTER 10

SPECIAL SECTIONS

1 ● HOW MANY DEALS?

The quality of the deals you receive and the number of investments you would like to make in a year impacts your ideal rate of deal flow. Some of the investors we spoke to shared with us the types of numbers they deal with.

300–350 deals a year

George Kline, a well-known Minneapolis angel, looks at 300–350 deals a year. He has invested in 160 during the last 20 years. Two of his deals generated returns in excess of 100 x investment.

200 business plans a year

Lucius Cary is a well-known angel investor in the UK and therefore does not need to actively source his deals. He receives around 200 business plans through the course of a year, and has capital to invest in four to five deals. He has invested in 53 companies since 1978. Of his first 40 investments 20 turned out to be graveyards. These were predominately technology prototype investments, where around £30,000 was invested in each deal. His last 16 investments have been slightly later stage, and the investment size is larger – around £150,000 per deal, and since adopting this change of tack, he has had no failures and several winners.

THE QUALITY OF THE DEALS YOU RECEIVE AND THE NUMBER OF INVESTMENTS YOU WOULD LIKE TO MAKE IN A YEAR IMPACTS YOUR IDEAL RATE OF DEAL FLOW

10–15 business plans a year

Carl Guerreri sources his deals mainly via word of mouth. Only a handful of entrepreneurs approach him completely cold. He sees about 10–15 business plans a year, and in total has made four investments.

1,000 to 1,800 deals a year

Dave Berkus screens as many as 1,000 to 1,800 deals a year, between one and six a day. "*I invest in between six and eight a year between the three funds. And that is a number I can still control... most of them are here in Southern California.*"

One a day

Dick Morley looks at about 200 opportunities a year, or one for each working day. *"And we don't read them. Well we can't! I'm a guy, I don't have a company, I retired in 1964. I'm just a guy sitting here with a desk and a chair."*

120 deals a year

Darryl Wash looks at around 10 deals a month.

❝ I probably look at about 10 deals a month. The basic process of review is... either the executive summary or a full business plan to look at certain elements to determine whether it... warrants full consideration. ❞

6–12 executive summaries per month

Tony Morris, looks at executive summaries from between half a dozen and a dozen entrepreneurs a month. He generally invests in two businesses every year.

600 deals per year

John Hime has been investing for 15 years and has invested in 29 early-stage companies, five of which he helped to reach the liquidity stage (IPO, merger, acquisition). Around 50 entrepreneurs contact him each month. From these approaches he reviews 20 business plans and generally invests in one new deal a month.

2 • WHERE DID THEY COME FROM?

Here is how eight winning deals were identified by angels.

Amazon

Tom Alberg was introduced to Jeff Bezos through a Seattle-based angel who was also an attorney. Since Tom was working at McCaw at that time, they assumed he knew a lot about the internet, which was *"not exactly true,"* as he describes it.

Apple Computer

Richard Kramlich's previous business partner, Arthur Rock, asked if he knew about the Apple deal which he had just heard about. Richard called up one of the investors who was in the deal and asked if there was some additional room. Rock invested $50k out of a $400k round.

A few weeks later another friend of Richard's was visiting from England and asked what was hot. After Richard's description, he went immediately to see Steve Wozniak and offered to buy some of his shares (apparently Steve wanted to buy a house). Later he offered $45k of this to Richard who took half and gave the other half to one of his friends.

Lifeminders.com

Frans Kok backed the CEO of Lifeminders.com, whom he had known for seven years. He invested $100,000 for 1% of the equity. The subsequent IPO was in the $300m range, providing him with a return of 30 times.

StarMedia Network

Darryl Wash knew Jack Chen, the President of StarMedia from Goldman Sachs, where they had both worked, and through one of his co-investors who had known Chen in business school. So there were two connections.

A group of angel investors, including Darryl, invested approximately $500,000 in the company in three financing rounds. The company went public in May 1999.

Kozmo.com

Darryl Wash was referred from his previous investment in StarMedia. The company's President, Jack Chen, introduced him to entrepreneur Joe Park. Together with a handful of angels, he co-invested $100,000 (at a pre-money valuation of $18.9m) and $250,000 in a second round (at a pre-money valuation of $37.9m). The company is now valued at more than $600m based on its last financing rounds which included Amazon and Softbank.

Road Rescue

A friend of Howard's introduced him to a previous student of his who was doing a search fund. Howard invested $100,000 at a $2.7m pre-money valuation and a $5m post-money valuation. Last year $50,000 of debt equity was repaid and he sold back some of his shares for $270,000. A perspective exit via a strategic sale is on the table valuing the company at $300m, which would value Howard's remaining stake at $5.2m.

Inter Turbine Logistics

Bert Twaalfhoven had decided to shut down one of his many companies and fired the president. Almost immediately the ex-president asked if he could buy one part of the business that he thought he could make work. Having seen a very good business plan, Bert sold it for 500,000DM (about $250k). Then the ex-president now turned entrepreneur asked Bert if he would like to invest in the new company! He did and the company grew to $20m in sales in three years, generating a five fold return.

Netonomy

Denis Payre was approached by two American engineers who were working for the Business Objects in Europe, which Payre co-founded. He was there from day one, he was the first investor (putting in several hundred thousand dollars), and worked with them to create the company. Based on the last VC round by Fidelity, the value of his investment has grown by seven times in less than two years.

3 ● HOW ANGEL INVESTOR DAVE BERKUS INITIATED HIS DEAL FLOW

I have been angel investing since 1993. I have run two companies in my lifetime. The first beginning at the age of 13, which I ran for 19 years, and which put me through high school and college, literally. It went public in 1971, when I was 33, and then sold in 1974 during the gas crisis. I went into the computer industry at that time and ran a computer company that became the largest supplier of hotel reservation and front office software in the world. I sold it in 1990 and ran it for the buyer until 1993.

It was coming home from my last day at the office in 1993 that the concept of becoming an angel investor – we'll call it seed venture capitalist – occurred to me. So I was actually at work at my desk at home that afternoon. There had been no pre-planning is the point.

In the beginning of the operation I knew that I needed to get immediate deal flow and that I was unknown except for people in the Orange County, CA, area who had known me in my previous role. So that week I made appointments with two critical contacts. Firstly a key banker (who loaned and had relationships with the software companies, at that time there were no internet companies to speak of) and secondly with what I thought to be the pivotal VC company. I had lunch with the heads of both on subsequent days and in summary gave the pitch: "Give me your tired, your poor, your hungry, your huddled masses yearning to break free." The point would be that I'd be a person they knew and trusted who was able to do small deals that neither of them could do, because they were too early stage for the bank and too small for the venture guys. So deal flow began immediately. My first investment was three months later, which in fact came by way of a referral, it didn't come from one of those two sources.

So sourcing for me began with meeting two key contacts. It then went further, as the angel community began to evolve in the LA Southern California area, to include the Tech Coast Angels (a group now of 130, but at that time just 12 or 14 of us) who were finding deal flow as well. Those deals which they didn't like and I did became part of my deal flow. I used that as an alternate method of sourcing. One of the more successful methods of sourcing for me has been the directory of venture sources. If criteria for investing are carefully explained in the directory I have found that to be a very good source over time. So those are my three forms of sourcing. Direct contact with bankers and VC, angel groups, and directories. 〞

4 ● ONE-PAGER

Here is a copy of the checklist John Hime provides entrepreneurs with when he replies to their initial request for capital. This way, he minimizes deal flow which doesn't fall into his area of interest, allowing more time to focus on those that do.

John A. Hime
Investment Criteria Summary

Typical deal
- ❏ Internet focus: e-commerce related or "meta"-ware
- ❏ "Concept" stage: 2 to 4 people involved
- ❏ Rough draft business plan and lots of market research
- ❏ At least 2 potential major customers identified
- ❏ Demo version of product
- ❏ JAH invests $100,000 for 5 to 10% equity stake

JAH must-haves
- ❏ Match for JAH interest and experience
- ❏ Management team – CEO, sales/marketing, engineering
- ❏ Big market opportunity – rapid growth to $1B+
- ❏ Scaleable concept – $100M+ revenue in year 5
- ❏ Concise and convincing differentiation
- ❏ Compelling business model

JAH added value
- ❏ "Runway" money – to get company off the ground
- ❏ Advice on management team structure and hiring
- ❏ Advice on business strategy and marketing issues
- ❏ Guidance on writing business plan and presentation
- ❏ Introduction to VCs
- ❏ Counselling on VC terms and pricing

1 ● Find a sourcing strategy that works for you and gives you a competitive advantage.

2 ● Manage quality and quantity.

3 ● Use sourcing as an evaluation tool.

4 ● Look at 10–20 deals a month, and higher if new and learning.

Evaluating

Let me see if I've got this right, you want $150,000 to buy a boat to sail around the world, which according to every expert can't be done and on top of that you expect to find a new distribution route which will bring untold riches?

Angel investor Queen Isabella to Christopher Columbus, a man with no track record of doing these things and who later changed his business model from "new distribution route" to "new world"

QUICK OVERVIEW

11 ● Start section   75

12 ● The Harvard framework   77
A short lecture on entrepreneurial evaluation,
Harvard style   77

13   The expanded framework   79
Advanced course for those with longer attention spans   79
The people   80
The business opportunity   91
The context   99
The deal   104

14   Risk   105
Managing risk through investment decisions   106
Reducing risk   106
Moving risk to others   106

15 Angel strategies for winning and speed 107

Sharing the evaluation process 107

Develop (or use) your specialty 108

Practice going fast 108

16 Rejection section 110

The good, the bad, and the ugly of rejection 111

Rejection approaches 112

17 Things to think about 114

Time management 114

Reading business plans 115

1,000 questions 116

Adding value 118

18 Winning angels 2000 120

What do most investors do? 120

What do the winners do? 120

Winning tools and tactics 125

19 Special sections 127

1 Top 10 things Manny Villafana looks for in a medical start-up 127

2 What Tony Morris looks for in an IT or internet start-up 128

3 Must do, ought to do, nice to do 129

4 Angel investor John Hime's entrepreneurial letter 130

5 The entrepreneur's perspective 131

6 Interview with Mitch Kapor 132

7 Quotes on winning deals 133

8 Interview with Tom Alberg 135

9 Types of entrepreneur 137

10 "Losers" 140

4 TAKEAWAYS FROM EVALUATING 142

If you want to become good at early-stage investing, you need to learn how to size up the fundamental elements of an opportunity. Many investors use checklists or think of evaluation as a process of judging an entrepreneur, or an idea, or a particular set of facts. Based on our experience in doing over 100 early-stage deals, we believe that an

IF YOU WANT TO BECOME GOOD AT EARLY-STAGE INVESTING, YOU NEED TO LEARN HOW TO SIZE UP THE FUNDAMENTAL ELEMENTS OF AN OPPORTUNITY

investment opportunity has four essential elements, that, when brought together in the right form represent a high-potential opportunity to make money. If only one of the elements is out of sync, failure is predictable. The elements are represented by the Harvard framework (Figure 11.1), which was developed by William Sahlman[1] and Howard[2] and is described in Chapter 12.

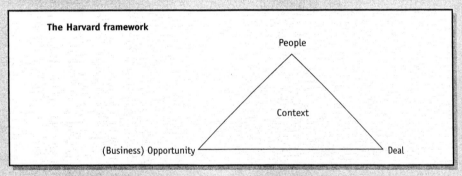

FIGURE 11.1

Good judgment comes from experience and experience comes from making bad judgments. So it is with evaluating early-stage deals. If you made a single investment in one of the big internet wins of the late 1990s, you may not know a thing about early-stage investing. By the same token, if you have had 10 failures in multiple industries, you may not know anything

IN BOTH ENTREPRENEURSHIP AND ANGEL INVESTING, THERE IS NOTHING LIKE DOING IT

either. But you will if you have been paying attention. Reading business plans, studying in business school or at angel seminars, learning an industry by working in it; these are all ways to develop expertise that will promote your success in investing. But in both entrepreneurship and angel investing, there is nothing like doing it. Nothing.

---

1 For more information, see *Some Thoughts on Business Plans* by William Sahlman (HBS Publishing, 1996, pp. 30–31).

2 Howard originally created a framework for real estate, which Bill Sahlman adapted for the entrepreneurial finance course at Harvard Business School.

The evaluation stage is the great time killer of all the stages and you will do well to manage your time carefully. Some angels think that evaluation starts with the first meeting and continues right up to the moment of writing the check. In order to structure this book effectively, we address evaluation as a single isolated entity, but bow to the correct idea that evaluation occurs throughout sourcing, valuing, structuring and negotiating. Given the potential time drain, the best angel investors are careful and strategic in their approach to evaluation.

THE BEST ANGEL INVESTORS ARE CAREFUL AND STRATEGIC IN THEIR APPROACH TO EVALUATION

Angels take a variety of approaches to this stage, with some doing substantial due diligence before a meeting (reading the plan, talking to people they know) and others granting a meeting without looking at the plan at all. Some angels rely on their intuition while others crunch a lot of numbers. Almost all angels source carefully, make good use of co-investors, and focus on the entrepreneur and team. Evaluation success will come from doing deals, emulating winners, and not making the same mistakes more than two, three or four times.

AOL: The one that got away, by Frans Kok

Frans Kok shares with us the story about his decision not to invest in America OnLine (AOL).

&& In about 1986 I was asked to take a look at America OnLine. My recollection is that they had about 10,000 subscribers at that time who were paying a little less than $20 per month. That gave them a running rate of $2.4m in gross revenues per year. I thought that that was impressive. In addition they were adding more subscribers every month.

The system was extremely complicated. Computers were not using the same operating systems so there were a lot of protocol compatibility problems. There were no databases that could be accessed. So the "nerds" would establish a connection and ask each other how "things" were and what was up. The connections were terribly slow. My reaction was "why don't these guys pick up the phone if they want to talk to each other?"

AOL was in the process of raising $5m on a $20m valuation. Based on revenues and subscribers I told them we could work with them and raise maybe $2m based on a $6–$8m valuation. AOL management was not interested and the rest is history.

Recently, I heard from a third party that at about the same time the technology guru at Alex Brown had the same reaction with respect to the superiority of the telephone. I guess I can stop kicking myself. &&

CHAPTER 12

THE HARVARD FRAMEWORK

> It is extremely important to do your own due diligence...
> there are a lot of people who can write a $100k check
> without thinking twice.
>
> **Audrey MacLean**

Rather than judge entrepreneurs or their business plans as winners or losers, it is most productive to look at the investment opportunity as an interconnected combination of four elements: people, context, business opportunity, and deal. The right combination, which is often manageable, means a high-potential opportunity. A bad combination, or the lack of any single element, is a recipe for failure. Most important, within any investment opportunity, there is usually some potential for a win, if only the right investor would join it, or if the right changes would be made. If you integrate this philosophy of investing into your thinking, you will be a far better investor.

A SHORT LECTURE ON ENTREPRENEURIAL EVALUATION, HARVARD STYLE

Bear with us while we explain the framework developed by William Sahlman[1] and Howard[2] at Harvard Business School. This is one of the areas in the book where you need to be mentally engaged and really look hard at incorporating this methodology into your evaluation process. At the very least, if you decide to discard it, you will do so having a much better awareness of your own framework.

You have seen the framework (Figure 11.1), let's review each of the elements:

- **People**

  The people in the deal, including the entrepreneur, team members, investors, advisors, and any significant stakeholders.

- **Business opportunity**

  The potential business opportunity, which includes the business model, the size (which implies the potential returns), the customers, and the window within which it can be seized.

---

1 For more information, see *Some Thoughts on Business Plans* by William Sahlman (HBS Publishing, 1996, pp. 30–51).

2 Howard originally created a framework for real estate, which Bill Sahlman adapted for the entrepreneurial finance course at Harvard Business School.

- **Context**

  The macro-situation, which includes external factors, such as: technology development, customer desires, the state of the economy, industry trends, etc.

- **Deal**

  The structure of the deal, its terms and pricing.

Not only is each element critical by itself, but the way they interact is also crucial. For example, in one opportunity at Capitalyst,[3] a web developer with $5m in sales was raising its first round of capital on a $10m valuation.

Two comparable companies in the marketplace were worth over $1bn each, despite having $300m and $20m in sales respectively. Most companies in the industry were valued at $1m per employee, and this company had 40. However, NASDAQ had just dropped about 20% (April, 2000), and voices predicting the end of the tech stocks' ride were appearing daily in the press.

Therefore, the context was that the potential existed to sell the company soon for a substantial return to one of its competitors. However, if the market turned in a big way, the potential valuation could come screaming down. The business would not fail, as it was choosing its customers and was already at cash flow break-even, but the investors might get stuck as minority shareholders if it became difficult to sell.

In this case, a deal structure with a note convertible to common would allow the investors to convert if the company sold or went public, thus getting their upside, or call the note after two years if the company was not able to exit but was generating positive cash flow. The deal structure can impact the attractiveness of an investment opportunity by addressing contextual or other factors.

INVEST IN COMPANIES THAT HAVE OUTSTANDING ELEMENTS AND YOU WILL HIT SOME WINNERS

Challenges with the business opportunity, or the time frame, can sometimes be addressed by finding a key member of management or an active angel who can help the company to move much faster through active use of their network.

Between people, opportunity, deal and context, there are a variety of multi-relational issues and opportunities. Invest in companies that have outstanding elements or at least good combinations and you will hit some winners.

---

3 Capitalyst can be found at www.capitalyst.com.

CHAPTER 13

THE EXPANDED
FRAMEWORK

ADVANCED COURSE FOR THOSE WITH LONGER ATTENTION SPANS

Each of the elements can also be further expanded to make it more useful (see Figure 13.1). Any of these elements could be the limiting factor of an opportunity and you do not need any limiting factors, given the already high risk of an early-stage opportunity.

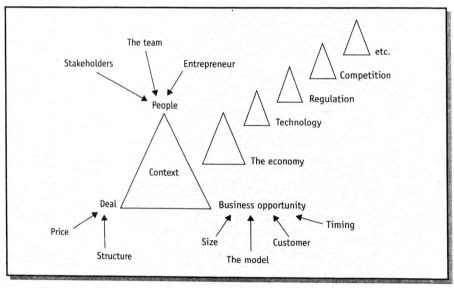

FIGURE 13.1

   Having said that, a solid combination is a recipe for success. Consciously or intuitively, winning investors focus on these factors.

   Several of these elements are the subject of one or more sections in this book, given their importance.

   Here are the places where you can read more about these elements of an early-stage opportunity:

The entrepreneur	Pages 80–86
The team	Pages 87–89
The stakeholders	Pages 89–90
The model	Pages 92–93
Customer	Pages 93–94

Timing   Pages 94–96
Size   Pages 96–99
Economy   Page 101
Technology   Pages 101–2
Regulation   Pages 102–3
Competition   Pages 103–4
Pricing/valuation   Page 104
Structure   Page 104

We will now examine each in detail. Again, if an opportunity has these factors in strength, your likelihood of success is good. If you do a lot of deals that meet the requirements of the expanded Harvard framework, you will almost certainly get some wins.

THE PEOPLE

There are three groups of people in any early-stage opportunity (see Figure 13.2) and each is critical to the success of the venture:

- entrepreneur(s)
- management team (often different from the above)
- stakeholders.

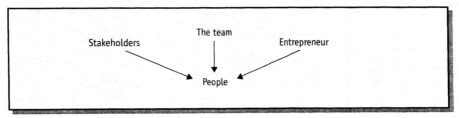

FIGURE 13.2

THE ENTREPRENEUR

"An A-quality man with a B-quality project, but not the other way around."

General Georges Doriot, the founder of modern day venture capital[1]

In the initial stages of a start-up, more rides on the shoulders of the entrepreneur than will at any other time during the history of that company. By the time the venture capitalists show up, the team or company is often developed well enough

---

1 In our opinion anyway. Also, the General would say "A quality man or woman" if he were around today. Women make great entrepreneurs.

to allow for the departure of the founding CEO. But in true early stage, most deals would likely collapse if the CEO/entrepreneur did not show up the next morning. In addition, the founding entrepreneur has more freedom to mess it up, save it, bring it to boil, or take it onwards, than she will ever have again.

Consider it from the entrepreneur's perspective for a moment. Not only are they doing many critically important things for the first time (such as raising capital or building the service) but they have to do almost all of them right! With limited resources, a major mistake will kill the company. Each new team member hire, each marketing decision, even each investor decision, has major ramifications, good and bad.

MOST EXPERIENCED ANGELS EVENTUALLY COME AROUND TO THE IDEA THAT THE INITIAL BET IS REALLY ON THE ENTREPRENEUR AND HER TEAM

So most experienced angels eventually come around to the idea that the initial bet is really on the entrepreneur and her team. There are still many major decisions to be made about the future of the company, and some of these will be critical to its success and longevity. Later, as most professional venture capitalists will tell you, it becomes the market and the management team. But in the angel round, it is the entrepreneur.

How to assess an entrepreneur?

"Honesty and strength of character have to be clarion."

Angel CL

Winston Churchill once said, "*Without courage all other virtues lose their meaning.*" In early-stage deals, if the entrepreneur lacks integrity, no single aspect of the proposal can be relied upon. So honesty, integrity, and reliability are sacrosanct. As Andrew Carnegie said, "*First honesty, then industry, then concentration.*" Without this first quality, there can be no relying on the intentions presented in the plan, the going forward updates, the use of resources, or even the actuality of a cash exit in the event of success.

IN EARLY-STAGE DEALS, IF THE ENTREPRENEUR LACKS INTEGRITY, NO SINGLE ASPECT OF THE PROPOSAL CAN BE RELIED UPON

Three bases

When assessing an entrepreneur, there are three "bases" to cover: their goals, their knowledge, and their capabilities (see Figure 13.3).

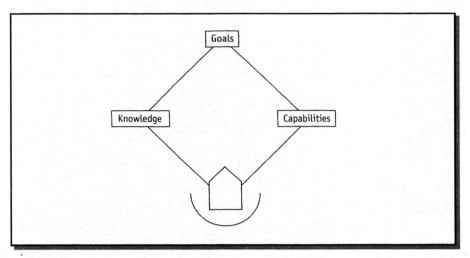

FIGURE 13.3

If these bases are not covered, you might find some unpleasant surprises after making an investment. For example, many investors have been left stupefied by entrepreneur decisions not to sell at an attractive price. In fact, these decisions probably supported the lifestyle business that the entrepreneur had dreamed about all along.

SOME INVESTORS, SEEK OUT WINNERS AND CREATE BUSINESS RELATIONSHIPS THAT RESULT IN A SERIES OF INVESTMENTS

Covering all bases, however, can result in identifying a homerun[2] hitting entrepreneur. In fact, some investors, such as Craig Burr, OH[3], and Arthur Rock, seek out winners and create business relationships that result in a series of investments.

So identifying a high-potential winner is as simple as covering the bases, except for a thousand or so variables. Here they are briefly.

---

2 For our non-American readers, we will try to include cricket, football, rugby and other sports analogies in the next version (we all know that football is the true world sport). In case you don't know what a homerun is, it is when you run around all three bases and then score a point! Some American angels will also say "hit it out of the park." This is a reference to hitting a baseball past the back fence of a baseball field, which is an automatic homerun, and the best you can do.

3 As mentioned previously, some of our angels preferred anonymity, so we will use initials (not necessarily theirs) to quote them.

Knowledge

Industry, market, technology, customers... the entrepreneur's knowledge of the opportunity is relevant to assessing their ability to evaluate the opportunity as well as modify it during implementation. Do they know enough to know what they are getting into?

The best way to assess knowledge is through direct conversations with the entrepreneur and by relying on other stakeholders who have relevant experience for assessing that knowledge (such as an old plastics entrepreneur for a new, temperature-retaining fast food container start-up). Potential co-investors and past associates of the entrepreneur can be quite useful.

Capabilities

Sales, management, product development... the entrepreneur's capabilities are relevant to their ability to implement. Can they make it happen?

Track record is the best indicator of capability. Most of the successful investments described in this book were led by entrepreneurs with winning backgrounds, such as StarMedia (MBAs with management and financial experience), idealab! (successful software entrepreneur who founded his first company while still at high school, and sold one company to Lotus 1-2-3), **TRACK RECORD IS THE BEST INDICATOR OF CAPABILITY** and RealNetworks (BA and an MA in Economics and a BS in computer science from Yale University, plus 10 years' experience at Microsoft). However, notable exceptions would include Microsoft (college drop-out), and Lotus (transcendental meditation instructor).

Goals

Career, financial, personal... the entrepreneur's goals are the undercurrent driving their actions and are relevant to big picture issues, such as when and how to exit. Does the entrepreneur share the investor's goals?

Indirect discussions and observations will reveal the most about the entrepreneur's goals. Do they think about strategic sales or salary?

As Howard describes one failed deal:

❝ The loss was a result of an egomaniac that refused to compromise or even recognize possible limitations to the market opportunity or to his talent! ❞

It is critical to get at the underlying beliefs and objectives of the entrepreneur as they will eventually win out or create a major break with some stakeholder group.

Here are some of the key questions for each reference point:

- **Goals**

  What are the underlying goals and are they relevant? What are they communicating indirectly about their goals?

- **Knowledge**

  Do they know what to do? Do they understand this business? Are they known and respected by others within this field?

● Capability

Can they do it? Can they get others to do it? Can they implement?

Winning angels who have learned to assess salesmanship, financial acumen, résumés, and business models, often miss by not identifying the underlying goals of the entrepreneur or by not realizing they are incapable of making things happen. Enough said (we hope).

WINNING ANGELS OFTEN MISS BY NOT IDENTIFYING THE UNDERLYING GOALS OF THE ENTREPRENEUR OR BY NOT REALIZING THEY ARE INCAPABLE OF MAKING THINGS HAPPEN.

A short note on checklists, personality tests, and structure evaluation
While there have been many studies and books on entrepreneurship and successful start-ups, most of the the work is of limited relevance.

Some of the studies that have been completed on entrepreneurs have been rather comical. For example, in one study, it was determined that 42% of highly successful entrepreneurs were first-born children. This seemed plausible and interesting until someone realized that 42% of all people are first-borns. Another study showed that successful entrepreneurs had lower than average education but failed to note it was a study of machine shop entrepreneurs.[4]

A few winning entrepreneurs who lacked...

Relevant background
Mitch Kapor had been a transcendental meditation instructor, among other things, before founding Lotus.

Strong education
Bill Gates was a college drop-out who spent more time playing poker than going to class.

Age
Colonel Sanders was retired, over 65, and on social security when he decided to open his first restaurant.

Sales ability
We won't name the entrepreneurs we know who couldn't sell heat at the North Pole, but some of them have been very successful.

---

4 With all due respect to machine shop operators, many successful entrepreneurs quit or fail at higher education.

So categorization has limited benefits. You can ask, however:

- Where is this person at?
- Do they know what needs to be done?
- Do they have a timetable to do it?
- Or do they almost know and need help with the timetable?
- Or perhaps, do they not know at all?

Determining what they are focused on, and the fact that they can focus, is perhaps a powerful way to zero in on their potential for success.

Track record is probably the only indicator of success you can measure: "*What men do, not what they say,*" as Andrew Carnegie admonishes us. If an entrepreneur has figured out what it takes to win in other situations, there is a reasonable chance he will do so here. One of David's bosses, Larry Etienne, used to say, "*I like winners because they know what it takes to win. Losers just know what it takes to lose.*"

IT COMES AS NO SURPRISE THAT MANY WINNING ANGELS WILL GO WITH THEIR "GUT" IN DECIDING ON AN ENTREPRENEUR

Given all this, it comes as no surprise that many winning angels will go with their "gut" in deciding on an entrepreneur, or they follow one of the decision making patterns described below or they use both:

1 Go with people they have worked with before.
2 Go with people they know in some other way.
3 Go with people that are known to someone they know.

If entrepreneurship is about the pursuit of resources, then the question for angel investors is, "*If we entrust her with some of our resources, will she do something sensible?*" An entrepreneur is going to make a million decisions during the course of the company's journey to success; will 550,000 of those be right?

One of the few impactful works on entrepreneurs was *Profiles of Genius: Thirteen Creative Men Who Changed the World*, by Gene N. Landrum, which looked at such entrepreneur wünderkinds as Fred Smith, William Lear, Steve Jobs, and others. Table 13.1 gives an overview of their characteristics of over-achievers.

TABLE 13.1

Profiles of male creative genius***
Behavior and personality characteristics found in great achievers

1 **Promethean** temperament (Carl Jung and MBTI) – INTJ, ENTJ, INTP, ENTP
   Intuitive – Perception of world (forest vs trees/macro vs micro)

2 **Competitive to a fault**
   Aggressive behavior where winning is more important than playing

3 **Innovator operating style** (Kirton's Style inventory)
   Preference for "doing things differently" vs "doing things excellently"

4 **Self-employed fathers** – Early vision for achievement outside establishment
   Fathers made their own way in the world as dentist, truck driver, or lawyer

5 **Big "T" personalities** (high in testosterone, thrill seeking – enormous risk takers)
   Big Ts—High in risk taking. Preference for uncertainty, unpredictability, variety, intensity, novelty
   Little Ts – Low in risk taking. Preference for certainty, predictability, simplicity, low intensity, familiarity

6 **Self-confidence/high self-esteem** – Built in early childhood – permissive parent allowing error and building sense of self. Arrogant attitude preferable to submissive one for innovative pursuits

7 **"Type A" behavior** (Meyer Friedman and Ray Rossenman) – Impatient and impulsive
   Impatient to a fault, obsession with winning, short attention span, multitasking personality types

8 **Charismatic** – The consummate salesman
   Enthusiastic, passionate, and inspirational leadership qualities

9 **Right-brain, qualitative "gut" decision makers** – qualitative vs quantitative
   They utilize macro vs micro, long term vs short term, qualitative vs quantitative, analogue vs digital, inductive vs deductive, and subjective vs objective operating styles

10 **Psychosexually driven** – Sublimated libidinal drives of insecurity and inferiority
    Intensely driven individuals with high sex drive and/or need to overcome innate fears of failure. Consummate overachievers

11 **First-born males** (Adler and Kevin Leman) – Morber the major influence
    Perfectionism, striving for superiority, and need to achieve. Natural leaders (12 of 13 innovative geniuses studied were first-born males, as were all seven of the Mercury astronauts)

12 **Personality focused and goal orientated** – Edison's aphorism "persistence vs inspiration"
    Persevering prevails in entrepreneurship. Individuals who never give up never lose!

13 **Transient childhoods** – Leading to consummate self-sufficiency
    Ability to cope in foreign environments learned early in life

*** From Gene N. Landrum, *Profiles of Genius: Thirteen Creative Men Who Changed the World*, Amherst, NY: Prometheus Books, 1993, p. 232. Reprinted by permission of the publisher.

THE MANAGEMENT TEAM

"As I get older, I pay less attention to what people say and more to what they do."

Andrew Carnegie

Having a team that surrounds the entrepreneur is important for three reasons:

1 The start-up is ready to go and can move forward with all due speed.

2 The presence of the team implies that the entrepreneur can attract talent, and probably knows something about selling or evangelizing.

3 Assuming the team members have relevant backgrounds, it is further evidence that the deal is do-able since they will have done their own assessment, and from a very personal standpoint.

While "quality, quality, quality" is as important with the team as it is with the entrepreneur, you can often rely on the kinds of people who will be joining if you have done your homework on the entrepreneur herself. However, there are also some specific things you need to see from the management team.

Relevant skill set

"Capability, desire, availability."

Wade Myers

Entrepreneur Wade Myers has a great chart he uses when planning for team growth. It includes a list of the positions, the most important tasks of each, the relevant skill set needed to complete the tasks, and, finally, the likely background and résumé. of a person who would have such a skill set. Table 13.2 is an example taken from Capitalyst's plan, giving the description for three positions.

In this way, one can build a team focused on the right people. Having the right skill set is also about speed. Time to market is a critical competitive factor and the management team will either effect rapid and strategic action or will spend their time getting up to speed and learning new skills. Which do you think is better?

TABLE 13.2

Targeted team member profile

Position	Description	Skill sets	Traits of an ideal candidate
Chief financial officer	Senior executive managing all financial functions	• CPA • Start-up experience • Capital-raising experience	• CFO in a start-up company • Started, or managed own CPA firm • Angel investing experience • Expert in entity structuring
Admin assistant	Office support for organization that markets to and supports entrepreneurs in raising early-stage capital	• Windows 98 • Office 97 • Internet • Bookkeeping • Scheduling events	• Worked as executive secretary or office manager for other professional service firm (three to five years' experience at a CPA, investment, or law firm)
Web manager	Responsible for day-to-day operation of the website, including functionality, content, and trouble shooting	• Internet expertise • Database expertise • Design experience	• Worked as a freelance web designer or for a small design shop

Commitment

"Bunk beds above their desks."

Josh Green

You can often see this in the way compensation is structured, in their résumés, and sometimes in the nature of any personal relationships. For example, when Dave recently hired a chief marketing and alliances officer, who was a multi-millionaire and had worked at Lucent and AT&T for over 30 years, it was clear that salary was not going to be the driving force of his compensation. So, equity and warrants were part of the deal, but still, did this really ensure commitment? Perhaps, but this chief marketing and alliances officer also invested in the company, brought in family members and friends who wrote checks, and let it be known that, *"He was doing this deal."* If for no other reason than to make sure his family and friends got their money back, and that he continued his track record of winning, it was reasonable to assume he would stay committed for some time.

Ability to win

"If you are going to be putting together a team, don't just measure their strength, watch them play."

Pierre Mornell speaking about recruiting football players

Pierre liked to see any potential recruit in 200 plays before he could make a recommendation. He felt this was necessary to know how they played.

Aside from having effective doses of capability and commitment, the team needs to know how to win. This is why so many angels will invest with people they know from past business experiences.

In addition, the team needs to be able to grow a business. If they are going from $1m in revenue to $25m in two years, there is a whole skill set of how to grow and manage such a rapidly expanding organization. Their understanding of the elements required for such size and growth will be instrumental in the company's future success.

THE STAKEHOLDERS

"Your actions speak so loudly I can't hear a word you are saying."

Dorothy Stevenson

The term stakeholder refers to anyone who has a stake in the success or failure of an enterprise. In early stage deals, this includes angel investors, advisors, board members, advisory board members, venture capitalists, customers, and suppliers.

Stakeholders are important because they can have a major impact on value creation and perception. It is worth repeating: both value creation and perception.

For example, in a recent opportunity reviewed by David, one of the original investors in StarMedia was already in the deal and Morton Goulder of the **STAKEHOLDERS ARE IMPORTANT BECAUSE THEY CAN HAVE A MAJOR IMPACT ON VALUE CREATION AND PERCEPTION**
New Hampshire Breakfast Club had decided to invest as well. Given this, one could expect that other angel investors would be joining in soon. The perceived value was now higher and it is likely that the actual value was also higher since the involvement of these angels could help the company succeed. However, if none of the angels had done their own due diligence, the deal could have been mediocre but suddenly made attractive by the unintended lead who thought he was *"just throwing in $50k."*

Tim Belton, the entrepreneur behind the turnaround of The Custom Shop, launched his concept of quickly delivered, digitally customized apparel with Express Custom Tailors. He obtained IT development financing from a major systems integration firm, which received no equity but a long-term contract commitment for Express Custom Tailors to receive its IT services from the firm. The arrangement was not unlike an IT outsourcing contract, only the client did not yet exist. The IT 'angel' providing $1.5m in systems development financing was one of the more powerful stakeholder demonstrations we have seen.

In another opportunity, Estée Lauder had signed an agreement providing $1m in services, as well as the use of some proprietary software. One of the top executives was going to join the board of the start-up. Such a commitment of time and resources from a major retailer represented strong stakeholder interest that was not only strategic but served as a 'stamp of approval.'

Some of the ways in which stakeholders can contribute include:[5]

- providing capital directly
- referring new capital providers (angels, VCs, bankers, etc.)
- helping to sell key accounts
- advising on company growth and strategy
- introducing and recruiting new talent
- raising the stature of the deal with their presence
- identifying and selling strategic partners
- providing functional, industry or entrepreneurial advice
- completing an evaluation based on their functional, industry or angel investing experience which other investors may rely upon.

The quality of the stakeholders says a lot about the quality of the investment opportunity, as well as the likelihood that it will meet future challenges successfully. By the way, stakeholders who have something at risk are much more valuable, as any angel will tell you.

5 For additional ideas on contributing, see the Supporting section, pp. 245–84.

THE BUSINESS OPPORTUNITY

"Monsieur Eiffel, we find your idea of a monstrous tower ridiculous and the suggestion that it will one day be a tourist attraction laughable."

French banker, 1889

Every angel, VC, and writer of entrepreneurship books has their own list of what they look for in an early-stage opportunity. Perhaps the most important agenda item is to make sure that you understand the fundamental business and that all of the big questions have been answered (see Figure 13.4). We believe this will be accomplished by looking at the four subelements of the business opportunity:

● model

● customer

● timing

● size.

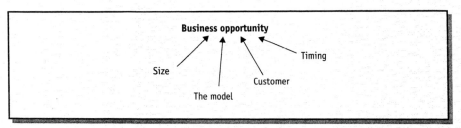

FIGURE 13.4

In addition, there are many ways to examine a potential opportunity, including some of the various checklists you will find in books, hiring consultants who may use analytical tools, such as Porter's Five Forces,[6] and investing hours to speak with potential customers, the management team, other investors, etc. We believe that in early-stage deals these four elements can be assessed relatively quickly, allowing for a timely decision, and will have the most significant impact on determining the potential, without regard to the people involved.

Another shortcut method to assess business opportunities is the classic new/old market, new/old product diagram. New product in an old market is a real opportunity. Old product in a new market is also a real opportunity. However, a new product in a new market has a fundamentally greater degree of challenge to creating success (see Table 13.3).

NEW PRODUCT IN AN OLD MARKET IS A REAL OPPORTUNITY. OLD PRODUCT IN A NEW MARKET IS ALSO A REAL OPPORTUNITY

[6] See *Competitive Strategy*, by Michael E. Porter, published by The Free Press, 1998.

If you can't comfortably assess an opportunty using Figure 13.4 or the four elements, then go ahead and ask 1,000 questions.

TABLE 13.3

	Old market	New market
New product	Opportunity	High variance
Old product	No profit	Opportunity

THE MODEL

"I like business models that are elegant, meaning as simple as possible, but also that have scale."

Angel investor CL

The business model is the short version of how the business will make money. It answers the question of why customers will readily part with their cash and thereby shows the fundamental business opportunity. Here is the definition of a business model:

Business model examples

A business model is the combination of fundamental factors that describe the business (e.g. developing and marketing patented incendiary devices to Alaskan gold rush prospectors). Look at the answers underneath to see the companies these models describe:

1 Do what you want on a computer.
2 AOL minus the ISP component in a new market.
3 24 hours a day weather information on a dedicated channel.
4 Hamburger cooked like you want it.
5 Multiple transistors on a single chip.
6 Low cost money management.
7 Electronic retail store for books.

Answers: *1* Apple, *2* StarMedia, *3* The Weather Channel, *4* Wendy's, *5* Intel, *6* Vanguard Index Funds, *7* Amazon.com

❝ The combination of factors that describe the business, including the market the business will serve, the perceived value delivered to the customer which determines profitability per unit of sale, and the sustaining factors which will allow the company to thrive over the long term.❞

Now here is a short version: "How you get customers, keep 'em, and serve 'em at a profit."

The business model is more important than the plan, which is always the first casualty of any start-up. It will be wrong, guaranteed. However, if the model is good, it means the entrepreneurs can make all kinds of mistakes and still make money.

How to tell if a model is good

Making investments in several models that go wrong is a big help. Otherwise, read, study, observe, and think. If the business model can meet the definitions pinpointed earlier and resembles other successful models, then you are probably on track. Remember that the biggest winners often have new models. Identifying winning models is one of the distinguishing characteristics of winning angels.

CUSTOMER

"I prefer CEOs who spend their days in the face of their customers."

Jeff Parker

Not all but most business people realize you need customers. "*The product in search of a customer*" or "*The widget with no market*" are old sayings used to describe start-up failures. In *The Origin and Evolution of New Businesses* by Amar Bhidé found that most of the INC 500 had been started by entrepreneurs who had left established companies where they identified a market niche the company didn't want to pursue. They typically had customers within two weeks. In early-stage deals, perhaps nothing is as unpredictable as the response of customers if no one has spoken to them. This is why winning investors and entrepreneurs focus on the customer before day one.

WINNING INVESTORS AND ENTREPRENEURS FOCUS ON THE CUSTOMER BEFORE DAY ONE

The value proposition demonstrated

"The graveyard of business failures is littered with the white, bleached bones of engineers who didn't listen to their marketing team."

Fred Amis

Demonstration of the value proposition is nearly as critical as the selection of the entrepreneur herself. The value proposition is whatever benefit the company is selling relative to its price. Demonstration means that a customer unequivocally shows they are willing to pay for the product at a price that will allow the company to earn a profit. Usually a check (i.e. money), a letter of intent, or a competitor's activity in the marketplace are the proof of the value proposition. The likelihood of success after the value proposition is demonstrated is about five times greater and this is why you will see a lot of venture firms hold back until a major sale has been accomplished. Even Amazon.com, when it raised its first million from angels, didn't get their checks until they had received some from customers.

Here are two examples:

1   When Wade Myers founded Interelate and began raising money, he had already completed extensive research and had sold and delivered several consulting and service engagements to Fortune 500 companies. This real-time research and customer interaction was the backbone of his marketing plan, with the company intending to repeat it hundreds of times over. The value proposition had been demonstrated.

A SALE DOES NOT MEAN THE BUSINESS WILL SUCCEED BUT IT RESOLVES ONE OF THE MAJOR BETS THAT ANY INVESTOR OR ENTREPRENEUR IS MAKING IN A NEW COMPANY

2   When Frank Levy approached StartUpFund I to invest alongside his other angels in FairAir.com, he had just completed an agreement with Northwest Airlines. This demonstrated the value proposition and substantially reduced the risk of the investment.

A sale does not mean the business will succeed but it resolves one of the major bets that any investor or entrepreneur is making in a new company.

TIMING

"If you think you have identified a real opportunity, then you better go like mad into the market."

Angel investor, OH

The business opportunity may be proposed 10 years too early or two years too late, both of which are equally as bad. Given the costs of running a start-up operation and the intensity of competition for new sectors (witness how many venture-backed start-ups enter a new market once someone has successfully argued the concept and begun proving it), you must rush to the marketplace. Timing can make or break the start-up.

Getting the timing right

As with most aspects of early-stage investing, you can save yourself from bad deals by asking a few questions to eliminate non-opportunities, such as:

- Is this business opportunity evolutionary or revolutionary (the first implies market acceptance and high likelihood of product success, the latter means much higher risk on both fronts)?
- Are customers ready for this product/service? Is there evidence that they will buy?
- What are customers doing now instead?
- Who else is doing this or is about to do it?
- What substitutes exist or might exist soon?
- Is there technology on the horizon that will surpass that of the company?
- Can we make money at this now?

Of course, having said that, all boats rise in a high tide, unless they have big holes. In new markets there is often room for several players and many investors make too much of the first mover advantage. *"It used to be first mover advantage that was a determinant of outcome. Now I think it is more a case of having the right business model,"* says Audrey MacLean. Timing isn't necessarily beating everyone else, but hitting the market when customers are ready to buy.

There is no scientific formula for checking your timing. Luck and intuition are your partners in this part of the game. For example, the timing of the start-up of Amazon.com was critical, as was the poor timing of Barnes&Noble.com. *"That was lucky,"* said angel Tom Alberg, an early investor in Amazon, describing the relative late start of Barnes&Noble.com.

Checking the customers, reviewing competition, and considering any contextual factors will help diagnose the likelihood of good timing. Otherwise, just go for it, there are plenty of examples of companies which appeared before their time, such as Apple – David Packard and

TIMING ISN'T NECESSARILY BEATING EVERYONE ELSE, BUT HITTING THE MARKET WHEN CUSTOMERS ARE READY TO BUY

other industry giants who had already stated unequivocally that there was no use for computers in the home; Pepsi – Coke was already dominant, had the first-mover advantage, and was known universally; Dell Computer – IBM and others were already dominant, and everyone knew that built to order would not work with computers anyway.

SIZE

"In early-stage deals, size does matter."

Enlightened angel investor

- What is the upside?
- How good can it be?
- How good can it be realistically?

If the likelihood of success is not high, then the potential needs to be substantial, say north of 10 x your investment or 50 x if the risk is outstanding. If the potential is smaller, then the likelihood of success needs to be higher for it to be worth your precious capital.

Of course, there are a variety of motivations to do early-stage deals and just as many early stage investment strategies. If you keep within your industry, you might do smaller deals because of your personal preferences and a higher likelihood of success. If the company will not require significant follow-on capital then a lower potential value might be worthwhile as well.

MOST SOPHISTICATED ANGELS ARE ONLY INTERESTED IN OPPORTUNITIES WITH KING KONG SIZE POTENTIAL

Most sophisticated angels are only interested in opportunities with King Kong size potential. However, risk and size (as it relates to potential gain) should be thought of together.

Big enough?

Let's say you have two potential $100k investments.

Investment A

The first is the purchase of Andrew's Grocery Store with positive cash flow and the potential to double in size (and value to $200k) through better management and the addition of a delivery service. You think the likelihood of success is 50% and the company could be sold in as early as two years.

Investment B

The second is the start-up of Nikki's Voice Recognition Systems for home security systems. No cash flow, but interested customers and technology that appears to work. The management is world class and they think they could build a company worth $285m in five years. So do other investors. You think the likelihood of success is 10%. The current valuation is $5m and there will probably be two more rounds of capital before an IPO.

How to decide between the two

In the first case, the likelihood of success is 50% and the potential return is double ($200k). The EV is $100k (50% * $200k). (See p. 18 for an explanation of EV.) In our estimation this is not interesting. Why? Because, even if we did enough deals to have a high likelihood of earning the EV, we would essentially break even. Buying US treasuries with a 5% interest rate instead may generate a better return for you with much less risk.

How about the voice recognition system? If the likelihood of success is 10%, the potential upside

WINNING INVESTORS DON'T DO DEALS THAT LACK THE POTENTIAL FOR SUBSTANTIAL RETURNS BECAUSE THE RISK OF LOSING EVERYTHING IS HIGH

needs to be significant. In fact, the EV should far exceed the investment amount of $100k. We would like to see 5, 10 or 50 x our money. Winning investors don't do deals that lack the potential for substantial returns because the risk of losing everything is high.

Given these two options, the first might appear to be less risky, but with some deeper analysis shows potentially subpar returns. Nikki Voice Recognition holds the potential for a better investment, as we will see below.

How big is big?

Let's take a closer look at Nikki's Voice Recognition. If the company expects two more rounds with 20% dilution each before going public and you are buying in at a $5m valuation, you will own 2% initially ($100k/$5m = 2% of the company), and 1.3% before it goes public (two rounds of dilution at 20% each).

If the company goes public and is worth $285m at exit, then your stake will be worth $3.7m ($285m*1.3%) which would give you a 106% return on your capital if it goes public in five years[7]. This is 37 x. This should be big enough. EV of the deal is 370k. Remember the 10% probability?

---

7 This is an ROI based on discounted cash flows where 100k goes to 3.7m in this case at 106% pa:

$$100,000 = 3,700,000/(1+i)^5$$
So: $(1+i)^5 = 37/100,000$
$(1+i) = 37^{1/5} = 2.06$
$1+i = 2.06$
$i = 1.06$

Another way to think about this is to consider it from a portfolio standpoint. If you did 10 similar investments and nine failed, on the one successful deal you would still generate 30% on your overall portfolio or 3.7 x!

THE BOTTOM LINE IS THAT IF YOU ARE GOING TO RISK LOSING ALL OF YOUR INVESTMENT, MAKE SURE IT IS WORTH IT

If you are not making any other investments, and are willing to accept the high risk of doing only one deal, then you still need to make sure its potential is big enough to make it worth it. In this case, 106% is worth doing a deal with a 10% likelihood of success,[8] as already shown.

What upside would it take to make the Andrew's Grocery Store deal worth doing? Write down a number by calculating or guessing, then read the answer at the foot of the page.

The bottom line is that if you are going to risk losing all of your investment, make sure it is worth it.

It's also important to consider second-round funding. *"The business has to be big enough to attract real venture capital,"* says Tony Morris, a coach angel who has made 19 investments. If you want a venture capitalist to follow you into the deal, then $100m+ potential is a requirement.

Scale and scope

There are two fundamental ways a company can grow and reap significant efficiencies. If a start-up does not have potential for either scope or scale, it will not be able to grow fast and significantly.

Scale

Scale, which is the preferred situation, means that the company can eventually deliver its services to new customers at insignificant costs. In other words, as it grows, there are either decreasing variable costs based on volume or it is able to spread major fixed costs over volume.

---

8 This analysis does not include partial wins. So, if there is a 1/10 chance of a great success, and a 2/10 chance of marginal success, then the numbers change. Regardless, make sure the upside is dramatic if the risk is high or pretty good; if the risk is significant. If the upside is not dramatic, just don't do the deal.

First, you have to decide what rate of return is sufficient for this type of deal. Let's say 20% is our number. We want to generate 20% on investments in expansion opportunities where the companies have positive cash flow already. There is a 50% likelihood of success if we do one deal, and that's not really good enough for sleeping well. So let's say you do at least two, which means there is a 75% likelihood of at least one winner (better to do several, of course). If you invested $200k in two opportunities ($100k each), you would need to earn 20% overall over the two-year period in question for a total of $288,000. If one fails (and let's assume all the money is lost) then the remaining deal must earn enough to cover both for 20% a year. $100k becomes $288,000 at a 70% return per annum over two years. So, you need the potential to earn about 3x (73% annual return) or more on your money in those two years for this investment to make sense.

Does this opportunity have scale?

- What resources would be required to increase sales by 1,000 times?
- Would we make more money for each unit sold or about the same?

One of the best demonstrated examples is Microsoft Word™. The cost to deliver a new copy of the software to a customer (who is willing to pay in the hundreds of dollars for it) is the price of the disk, the box, and some plastic covering.

As a new macro-development, the internet is the most fantastic scaling system ever devised for certain kinds of business. Electronic book publishers, for example, if successful on the internet, will owe their success partly to the fact that they can sell books to additional customers for essentially no cost. Customers print the book on their

AS A NEW MACRO-DEVELOPMENT, THE INTERNET IS THE MOST FANTASTIC SCALING SYSTEM EVER DEVISED FOR CERTAIN KINDS OF BUSINESS

own printers. There is no per unit cost, which is extraordinary when you think about it.

Scope

Scope, which is not always, but usually, the less preferred situation, means that the company can expand into other areas by nature of its business, relationships, brand positioning, etc. Amazon.com, has scale and scope. Its capacity for scale is that it can continually take on new customers for books using the same marketing and ordering systems (its website). It has scope because its brand is known for quality service through an internet ordering site and this has allowed it to expand into music, tools, movies, and other product lines.

THE CONTEXT

Context includes several factors that depend partly on the opportunity itself. The most common are: economy, technology development, regulation, and stage of the industry (see Figure 13.5).

For example, when David assessed an opportunity in the meat distribution business, some of the key contextual factors included the power and intentions of the major meat distributors.

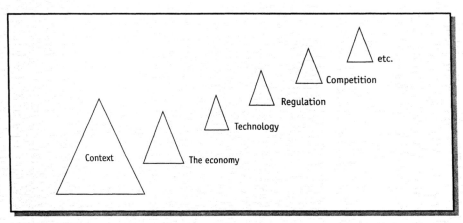

FIGURE 13.5

Here are some of the contextual factors that were considered:

- The overall economy was not as important since the business model would allow all parties to save money, in a price-intensive business.

- The internet and the development of powerful transactional software were important considerations in understanding why the window of opportunity had now arrived.

- The stage of the electronic meat distribution industry was at point zero, although one competitor had already tried and failed.[9]

So it appeared a quality, early-stage opportunity existed, considering the contextual factors as they related to the business model, the window of opportunity, and the overall size of the opportunity.

The simple way to identify contextual factors would include answering the following questions:

1 What macro-situation exists that supports or undermines the potential of this opportunity?

2 What economic, governmental, technological, or industry-related factors will expand or cripple the ability of this company to prove its business model?

3 Apart from entrepreneur and management team actions, what can hurt or help this venture?

A thorough contextual analysis would be too time consuming for this book as it is for any angel investor. Perhaps the best method for identifying and considering contextual factors is to first ask the entrepreneur what they think they are, to ponder that, and then to involve potential investors that know the industry, or its closest equivalent.

---

9 Two good questions for this entrepreneur would be, "Why did the first attempt fail?" and "How are you different?"

THE ECONOMY

Economic trends can have a major impact on the availability of capital, the acceptance of new ideas, buying preferences as they relate to necessities and luxuries, and the availability or likelihood of suppliers, competitors, customers, and substitutes.

For example, movie theatre attendance goes up in recessions, since people have less money for travel and need entertainment, perhaps more than in positive times. Real estate prices generally go down, although not as suddenly as that of internet companies!

TECHNOLOGY

"If it is not proprietary, forget it."

Harry Glazer, Greenberg Traurig, LLP

Any recent or expected technology development is an important contextual factor because it helps to explain why the opportunity is viable now, or why it might not be within a few months. There are always several driving forces that support the successful implementation of a new model at any point in time, and figuring these out is part of the intellectual challenge of assessing new deals. Technology is usually a driving factor as it impacts issues, such as per unit cost, new service or product development, new or more efficient use of "old" services or products, and elimination of entire industries.

ANY RECENT TECHNOLOGY DEVELOPMENT IS AN IMPORTANT CONTEXTUAL FACTOR BECAUSE IT HELPS TO EXPLAIN WHY THE OPPORTUNITY IS VIABLE NOW

Steven McGeady, angel investor and venture fund manager, and Vice President of Intel's Internet Technology until June 2000, had this to say about timing technology entrance into the marketplace:

> I would say that it is important to divorce the notion of a cool technology from one that is likely to be accepted by the market... As an engineer, I am often enticed simply because something is feasible, or because it is elegant. However... the best technology and the best ideas don't necessarily command the marketplace, at least not quickly. I have a strong belief in the difference between "leading edge" and "trailing edge" technologies. Trailing edge technologies might be quite advanced, but nevertheless don't get adopted by the market until late in the technology cycle, because they require extensive infrastructure, or have complex network externalities, or for a variety of other reasons. Often they simply deliver a function that is only marginally better than the function currently being delivered, or they deliver that function only after a substantial training or learning curve that might not be required for another device.

A good example of this is Pen-based computing from the early 1990s, versus the Palm Pilot. Pen-based computing was, and I would argue probably still is, a technology of the future. The notion of trying to put a fully functional personal computer with all of its applications in a form where one could interact only with a stylus was, then and now, a bad idea. On the other hand, a device with a simple interface, a small number of functions, and simple connectivity to existing PCs was more of a leading edge application. The Palm didn't require a bunch of pre-existing applications to be rewritten (it came with its own core set), it didn't require much infrastructure, and it didn't require a significant learning curve from the user. One sees many technologies that seem like good ideas, but they ultimately end up looking like the 1965 World's Fair Bell Labs PicturePhone – a perennially good idea that just never gets accepted by the market.**..........

Technology is a contextual factor that relates to why the opportunity exists at this time, what substitutes are or might be coming to the marketplace, and what might happen next in the industry.

Stage of industry

"The first <screen> is that the deal is a game changer somehow, that it either enables customers to do something they could not do before, or it dramatically reduces the cost."

Tony Morris

The stage of the industry relates to the number of competitors, the market acceptance of similar or related products and services, the acceptance of investors and other constituencies, such as suppliers, the labor pool, and many other factors.

THE STAGE OF THE INDUSTRY IMPACTS THE POTENTIAL RETURNS THAT ARE AVAILABLE

The stage of the industry, therefore, impacts the potential returns that are available, as well as the ease or difficulty of building a successful company. Unfortunately, this is not an area where investors can have their cake and eat it, as the best opportunities are "game changers", as angel investor Tony Morris says, and thus lead to the creation of new industries.

It is possible to be too early and too late. Rollerblade™ came along at the right time, even though they were not first in making inline skates. The stage of the industry should be understood by investors interested in maximizing their returns and in advising entrepreneurs in planning strategy.

REGULATION

Regulation includes any governmental rules, regulations, governing bodies or laws that impact the ability of a company to acquire, serve and keep its customers, while earning a profit. When operating in established industries with old rules, it is relatively easy to make business decisions and plans considering relevant regulations. In new industries it can be quite challenging.

For example, when the internet first started to gain acceptance, several companies, such as Priceline.com, applied and received business process patents. While some people argued that business processes on the internet should not be patentable, the company and its investors relied on the patents they had received in making investment and business planning decisions. As of 2000, there was considerable discussion on revising the process of issuing patents related to internet business practices. The result could be highly detrimental to the competitive position of Priceline.com, if its patents are critical to the company's success.

SOME PEOPLE ARGUED THAT BUSINESS PROCESSES ON THE INTERNET SHOULD NOT BE PATENTABLE

COMPETITION

"Typically there is not enough done here."

Craig Burr

It is far too common to hear from entrepreneurs that there is no competition. With the speed of new business creation in today's markets, there are always competitors. As one presenter at Europe's 500[10] declared, *"If there is no competition, there is no market!"*

Some angels will only invest in first movers while others are more focused on quality business models and teams. The impact of competition is industry specific as well. For example, there was only going to be one Microsoft Word™; everything about word processing points to a standardized product. Contrariwise, Web browsers were still being created and marketed successfully years after Yahoo! went public.

Aside from issues of market share, there is always a lot to learn from the actions of direct and indirect competitors, and any entrepreneur who ignores or can't see them is not dealing with reality in an effective manner.

WITH THE SPEED OF NEW BUSINESS CREATION IN TODAY'S MARKETS, THERE ARE ALWAYS COMPETITORS

---

10 Organization of the 500 fastest growing companies in Europe, founded by Bert Twaalfhoven.

THE DEAL

The terms of the deal can have as much impact as any other part of an opportunity. The deal includes two subelements, which are price and structure (see Figure 13.6). As you will see in the Negotiating section, some investors will negotiate the terms of a deal, while others will make *take it or leave it* decisions.

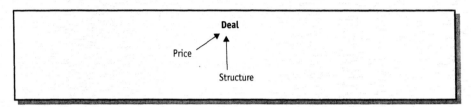

FIGURE 13.6

PRICE

Many investors ask about price in the first few minutes of a discussion with an entrepreneur because it is one of the easiest methods to eliminate a deal. If the investor has already decided he will invest in $1m to $3m valuations and no higher, then an over-eager entrepreneur who is looking for a $10m valuation, despite having no product or team, can be removed from consideration. (Review the valuing section for more detail.)

STRUCTURE

The structure of the deal, which includes not only the terms of the investment but also any other relevant factors, such as control of the board, or the limitation of management team salaries, directly impacts the likelihood and the size of the harvest event. Structure, which is dealt with thoroughly in the Struc-

THE STRUCTURE OF THE DEAL DIRECTLY IMPACTS THE LIKELIHOOD AND THE SIZE OF THE HARVEST EVENT

turing section, can have as much impact on the success of an investment as almost any other factor.

> I go in and invest my time to remove the risk that I know
> how to remove. And then I pass it on to the operating guys
> to take out the next level of risk.   **Randy Komisar**

It is not clear that risk and reward are positively correlated. First, it is possible to screen for opportunities with relatively less risk. Secondly, it is possible to help them manage their remaining risks. And thirdly, it is sometimes possible to move the risk that remains to other stakeholders.

What are the risks in an early stage deal? Let's review them:

- **Technological risk**

  The risk that the technology will not work, is irrelevant, or will be surpassed soon in a significant way.

- **Product/service risk**

  The risk that the company's product or service will not work.

- **Market risk**

  The risk that the market will not accept the product/service on a significant scale and the risk that the market will change.

- **Sales risk**

  The risk that the sales process will not work or will be too costly.

- **Competitive risk**

  The risk that one or several competitors will get an unapproachable lead or dominate the market early or take some action to create a barrier to entry, such as securing a business process patent which prevents the company from operating.

- **Financing risk**

  The risk that the company will not be able to raise further rounds of capital. Progress, management salesmanship, and the state of the economy all impact this.

- **Operating risk**

  The risk that management will not be able to competently or cost efficiently operate the company.

- **People risk**

  The risk that key people will either not perform or will leave the company. In most early-stage opportunities, the entrepreneur's absence would be fatal.

MANAGING RISK THROUGH INVESTMENT DECISIONS

Easy to say and hard to do

This is essentially a process of evaluating an opportunity by considering the risks we listed earlier, by a thorough review based on the strategies and tactics in this book, and by tapping into the investor's personal experience. One could say that this entire book is about reducing risk in early-stage investments. If you master the seven fundamentals of angel investing, you will know to reduce risk like a pro.

IF YOU MASTER THE SEVEN FUNDAMENTALS OF ANGEL INVESTING, YOU WILL KNOW TO REDUCE RISK LIKE A PRO

REDUCING RISK

Once you have made an investment, it is possible to reduce the risks in any given deal through supporting the entrepreneurial team and taking a number of actions. Here are some examples:

- Choose appropriate investors (such as an industry pro to reduce the market risk).
- Modify the business plan (such as a new market direction).
- Help to complete key value events (such as the product development).
- Advise on business issues (such as the vesting schedules to motivate employees to stay for four years).

MOVING RISK TO OTHERS

In some cases, it is possible to move or divide the risk in beneficial ways. For example, when the SBA grants a loan to a new start-up where private investors are present, it absorbs some of the capital risk, but does not take any of the upside. This is a good thing to have. In other cases, some investors might provide expertise for equity, in which case the capital risk is all placed on the cash-providing investors. In such a case, the cash-providing investors might think that the use-of-time risk is placed on the advisor.

IT IS POSSIBLE TO MOVE OR DIVIDE THE RISK IN BENEFICIAL WAYS

CHAPTER 15

ANGEL STRATEGIES
FOR WINNING AND SPEED

Each angel screens within their area of expertise.

Betsy Atkins describing her syndicate

Deciding what to look at is probably more important than how you look at it.

Here are some strategies for getting your evaluation process out of low gear and maximizing your chances to hit some winners.

SHARING THE EVALUATION PROCESS

There are several ways to spread out the responsibility and workload of the evaluation process. Winning angels do some or all of the following.

Stick with people they know

Aside from increasing the likelihood of winning, going with people you know reduces due diligence time. You don't have to check on their character, worry about whether they are honest, or question their motives as strenuously as you would otherwise. If you know how they think, you will know why they are doing the deal and how likely they are to succeed, almost regardless of the facts about the opportunity.

Join a formal angel group

There are groups in most major cities around the world. New groups are starting every day. These groups provide screened deal flow, a chance to co-invest, sharing of due diligence, and social opportunities. Some groups are filled or restricted to certain kinds of members. For more information on how to start or join an angel group visit our website at www.winningangels.com.

Form their own group of two to four angels to look at deals together

Some angels form their own small groups from people they know and like socially but with whom they can also have productive business relationships. Meeting weekly or monthly, they share the responsibilities of early stage investing from sourcing to harvesting.

Use a matching service

A more recent development in the angel world is the emergence of high-quality matchmakers. Organizations such as Venture Capital Report Ltd, which was founded in 1978, Garage.com, which was founded in 1998, as well as Capitalyst, which was founded in 1999, all provide high-potential deal flow to angel investors.

Hire a young MBA type to do the initial screening

Some angel investors hire a young MBA to do all their initial screening. This makes them look more like a venture capitalist and increases the time an entrepreneur has to invest in order to get a decision. But this system has its advantages, so long as the angel does a good job of communicating her target.

DEVELOP (OR USE) YOUR SPECIALTY

Angels, such as Manny Villafana, focus almost exclusively on one sector. In Minneapolis, he is known as the guy to talk to about medical deals. Manny is able to go faster and improve his likelihood of identifying real winners because he does not look at deals outside his scope of interest and his learning curve for start-up medical deals has been relatively steep. If you invest hundreds of hours doing early-stage deals in one industry, you will be able to move at lightning speed in comparison to other angel investors.

IF YOU INVEST HUNDREDS OF HOURS DOING EARLY-STAGE DEALS IN ONE INDUSTRY, YOU WILL BE ABLE TO MOVE AT LIGHTNING SPEED IN COMPARISON TO OTHER ANGEL INVESTORS

PRACTICE GOING FAST

The more business plans you read, the more entrepreneurs you meet (serials, high potentials, and wanna-bes) and the more deals you do will all help you move up the learning curve of how to evaluate early-stage deals. Speed readers, which anyone can become by the way, learn by doing. They read faster and faster, sometimes purposely losing comprehension in order to develop the habit of tearing through books. Later, they combine high retention with speed. Since some of your best learning will come from failed deals, there is an argument to get started fast, even if you do a poor initial job of evaluation. The sooner you start thinking and acting like an angel, the sooner you will develop the hunches and assessment tools that only the best angel investors have.

Angel investor SG compares his role in assessing new deals to that of a triage officer: *"Which ones can I fix, which ones will get better on their own, and which ones are going to die no matter what I do."* While this may seem a bit morbid, it is incredibly easy to get lost in sizing up deals. One initial conver-

SOME OF YOUR BEST LEARNING WILL COME FROM FAILED DEALS

sation is a solid hour and that probably leads to another, as well as some time spent on a business plan, and before you know it, it is Friday evening and you have looked at seven deals, none of which make it to your short list.

Save time and win!

Here are some additional evaluation stage time savers:

● Source carefully and strategically.

● Use a pre-prepared letter or template to respond to entrepreneurs, e.g. John Hime's letter (see page 130).

● Build your own website to clearly state what you are looking for (see some ideas at www.winningangels.com).

● Communicate a focused and targeted objective to your network.

● Communicate initially by email, then phone, then in person when warranted.

● Resolve your strategy, amount to invest, type of company, etc. upfront.

CHAPTER 16

REJECTION SECTION

> I think you are going to have a big win... I don't know if
> this is it and I've decided not to join you on this one. But I
> think we will ultimately do something together.

Craig Burr (talking to an entrepreneur about his decision not to invest)

Handling rejection well is the mark of a great angel or venture capitalist. We laud the approach practiced by John Hime who deals with the issue immediately and frankly. (See the special section containing his "form" letter to entrepreneurs on page 130.) He also refers or offers other kinds of help whenever he can. Craig Burr says, *"It is not about rejection but about leaving people wanting to deal with you in the future."*

HANDLING REJECTION WELL IS THE MARK OF A GREAT ANGEL OR VENTURE CAPITALIST

A fast answer is a friendly tactic

Aim to evaluate and make decisions about an investment opportunity in good time. Some angels and venture capitalists like to do the "venture capitalist dance." This involves putting the decision off, asking for more information, then putting it off again and again. They feel that saying no only hurts them and they should keep their options open until the end. Many entrepreneurs walk away from these experiences determined never to do business with "those people" again. The venture capital dance wastes valuable time and is emotionally draining. The best angels give prompt answers (by the way, they are entitled to change their minds) with constructive feedback or referrals.

THE GOOD, THE BAD, AND THE UGLY OF REJECTION
by David Amis

Having raised capital directly from over 100 investors and presented to a few hundred (which means more have said no), David has seen the highs and lows of no's. Here are a few examples from his experience:

The good

RS, a McKinsey partner, who was referred by a previous investor, showed great interest in the start-up opportunity at hand. In the first phone call he asked for an hour-long meeting by phone and all relevant documents. During the next phone call, he said, *"I think I'm in, can I let you know by the 17th?"* On the 17th he called in the morning and said, *"I can't decide today, can I let you know on the 28th?"* On the 28th his financial advisor called and said they declined to invest. Throughout the process he was respectful and timely, giving good clarity on what he was thinking and when he could decide. He took a very reasonable amount of time, perhaps even less than he should have, but gave the answer when promised, even pre-empting my call on the 17th. That is the way to do it. He will get 100% consideration for the next round if he wants it.

> HE WILL GET 100% CONSIDERATION FOR THE NEXT ROUND IF HE WANTS IT

The bad

JG, a venture capitalist at one of the premier Silicon Valley firms had committed to make an angel investment based on certain conditions. When the conditions were met (in this case a famous investor joining in), JG wrote in an email, *"Well that's it. Send the documents, I'm in."* This was repeated verbally as well and relied upon during the final weeks of capital raising. Upon receipt of the subscription agreements, JG got cold feet and claimed he wasn't really into angel investing at that time. The fund raising nearly missed its deadline because of his last minute cold feet and risked the entire round. If, as in other cases, there had been a major change in his financial situation, or a personal issue, a last-minute change might have been reasonable. But active investors need to decide what their investment objectives and boundaries are before giving their word on specific transactions.

> ACTIVE INVESTORS NEED TO DECIDE WHAT THEIR INVESTMENT OBJECTIVES AND BOUNDARIES ARE BEFORE GIVING THEIR WORD ON SPECIFIC TRANSACTIONS

The ugly

JP, a well-known European venture capitalist and early-stage investor, initially said, *"I like this deal and would like to invest significantly... probably joining the board as well."* After three promises for a decision date, two requests to hold pricing for another week, and almost four months of *"I'll decide by next week"* statements, he still had not decided what to do and continued to give the impression of being on the verge of investing. This is exactly how one should *not* treat an entrepreneur. It hurts the perception of investors in general, hurts the start-up by draining highly needed

TWO HOURS OF TIME OR $1,000 IN TRAVEL COSTS IS CRITICAL

time and capital (even two hours of time or $1,000 in travel costs is critical), and hinders the entrepreneur from pursuing others if he feels an obligation to hold open a board seat, for example.

One more good (but tough) rejection

BD, a highly active Dutch investor, had reviewed the initial business plan and said, *"I'm going to follow your progress, contact me again in a month or two."* The next time we saw each other was at a party and he asked me to send some more papers. I called two weeks later and he abruptly said, *"Don't waste any more time on me, you won't raise any money... okay?... goodbye."* While this may have stung for a couple of minutes, and I don't think BD remembered asking for more details and a follow-up call, it was still a clear rejection and much better than most. The "no" was definitive and no more time was lost. BD will also be invited back for the next round if he desires it. BD?

REJECTION APPROACHES

Overall, the best approach is probably one of a caring parent. It is important and okay to say no, along with the reasons. It is also important to

THE BEST APPROACH IS ONE OF A CARING PARENT

communicate that "no" does not mean anything personal about the entrepreneur. Following are the principles of friendly rejection.

Do it early and clearly whenever possible

Indecisive investors who keep their options open, often waste the time of entrepreneurs who are under severe pressure. Some investors start every conversation with, *"I won't be investing with you, but I'll look at your deal."* They believe this removes any expectations, although it might turn away some high-potential entrepreneurs. Other investors say they are not going to invest now but would like to be kept informed, and then later make a positive decision if the opportunity re-presents itself. The most important thing is to not leave the deal hanging, this can ruin any future relationship with the entrepreneur.

Be positive and supportive

"I think your project is good and that you will win, but it is not really for me because of X, Y and Z." Emphasizing that your decision to pass on a deal has more to do with the industry, stage of the deal, or because of your personal situation is wise. Many entrepreneurs will take the rejection personally. Keep in mind that they have a lot at stake, are trying to grow/save their baby, and are asking you for money all at the same time. It's a high-pressure situation and one that easily leads to bad feelings and rationalizations. Encouragement and positive reinforcement will be singularly meaningful to an entrepreneur at this moment.

Be tough with constructive criticism

We often advise entrepreneurs to seek out the best angels, get feedback on their deal, and act on it. Feedback from angels who know what they are doing is like gold. Consider this comment: *"Joe/Mary, this is a poorly planned deal and needs lots of work... your marketing segmentation needs to be clearer, your exit strategy is not consistent, and your team is lacking a financial officer."* If you have read a lot of plans and made a few winning invest-ments, this kind of feedback, particu-larly, *"I would do this deal if..."* may **FEEDBACK FROM ANGELS WHO KNOW WHAT THEY ARE DOING IS LIKE GOLD** sting the entrepreneur for a bit, but later, if they are smart, they will realize how much it benefited them.

If you have not done several deals or do not sense that you are qualified to give strong feedback, don't. Entrepreneurs have enough challenges already without getting misleading advice.

Giving tough, quality feedback is the best thing you can do for an entrepreneur, even better than giving them money in many cases.

Give them additional leads and contacts

If you know other investors that might be interested, refer them. If you do not think the start-up is ready for investment, refer the entrepreneur to some people that might be able to help and save you from more time drain. The SBA can and will support low-impact and lifestyle businesses that you don't have time for.

If you don't have time to do any of this, then do the next best thing: don't encourage the entrepreneur or take any more time. Getting ignored is not fun as an entrepreneur, but most will give up after three tries and even this is better for them than to be left thinking that you might invest.

CHAPTER 17

THINGS TO THINK ABOUT

TIME MANAGEMENT

The objective of this section is to convince you that evaluation can become a major time drain. If you are already convinced, jump to the next section or perhaps go straight to angel strategies for speed and success (on page 107). If you think 10 hours sounds like a reasonable estimate to close on an investment, read on.

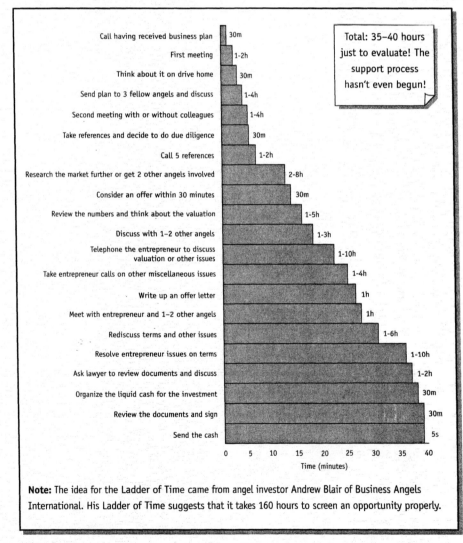

Note: The idea for the Ladder of Time came from angel investor Andrew Blair of Business Angels International. His Ladder of Time suggests that it takes 160 hours to screen an opportunity properly.

FIGURE 17.1

Figure 17.2 shows the steps one investor takes to make an investment decision. It does not include time to support or harvest the investment and it also does not include all the other opportunities that might have been reviewed to get just one to close. If you do not **IF YOU DO NOT MANAGE YOUR TIME WELL, YOU WILL BE HOPELESS AS AN ANGEL** manage your time well, you will be hopeless as an angel. Angel investor SG has made 50–60 early-stage investments as an angel and a VC over the last 20 years. Figure 17.2 shows how he reduces his screening time.

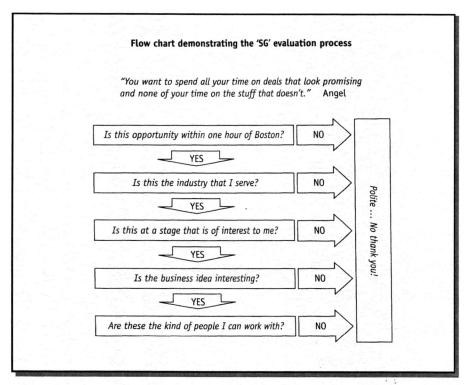

Flow chart demonstrating the 'SG' evaluation process

"You want to spend all your time on deals that look promising and none of your time on the stuff that doesn't."   Angel

Is this opportunity within one hour of Boston? — NO
YES
Is this the industry that I serve? — NO
YES
Is this at a stage that is of interest to me? — NO
YES
Is the business idea interesting? — NO
YES
Are these the kind of people I can work with? — NO

Polite ... No thank you!

FIGURE 17.2

READING BUSINESS PLANS

"Business moves so fast now that if you really stick to the plan, you will fail."

Howard Tullman

Today the business plan has become more of a management tool than a fund-raising device. As Howard Tullman advises, "*What you use a business plan for is to measure variance from what you thought was going to happen to what is happening.*" Many deals are now agreed based on slide presentations and investor referrals. Angels don't have time to read anymore.

From the investor's perspective, plans are useful for eliminating opportunities, and for understanding the economics and the various contingencies. The plan is a good check that the entrepreneurs have done their homework and that they understand the business model. It is a demonstration of their thinking and their knowledge.

Winning angels do not make investment decisions on business plans. They look at the people, the opportunity itself, which is best represented by the model, the

WINNING ANGELS DO NOT MAKE INVESTMENT DECISIONS ON BUSINESS PLANS

deal structure, and the context. Just ask the original investors in Sun Microsystems or Intel, where three page plans were enough to win the initial funding. In those cases, the quality and experience of management was so high that the investors could rely on the quality of thinking and planning to come.

New angels should read lots of business plans and figure out the differences between good ones and bad ones. They should also size up lots of entrepreneurs in relation to their plans, and follow up on their progress in order to see what kinds of people and what kinds of plans lead to success and failure. Experience cannot be replaced in this instance with any book or piece of advice (except, perhaps, to co-invest with winners).

Bill Sahlman, in his article *"How to write a great business plan"*, which we recommend reading, says:

&& A business plan should go beyond the basics of a solid product offering and revenue stream, it should also show how it can expand and create more revenue at attractive margins... The opportunity section of a business plan... must <also> demonstrate and analyze how an opportunity can grow – in other words, how the new venture can expand its range of products or services, customer base, or geographic scope. Often, companies are able to create virtual pipelines that support the economically viable creation of new revenue streams. &&

1,000 QUESTIONS

There are questions and then there are questions. Winning angels have personal styles that reflect both the types of question they ask and the way they ask them.

WINNING ANGELS HAVE PERSONAL STYLES THAT REFLECT BOTH THE TYPES OF QUESTION THEY ASK AND THE WAY THEY ASK THEM

Lucius Cary is an investor in over 50 start-ups, and asks questions in free form as a way of sizing up the person as well as the opportunity. Mitch Kapor and others rely heavily on intuition. Josh Green is interested in entrepreneurs whom he feels he can like and learn from on a personal level.

So none of these investors operates with a list of questions. Despite this, many articles and books give lists. There is one benefit: they are useful for learning what and how to ask about the business opportunity. David Gladstone has an excellent list of over 500 questions to use to assess venture capital deals in his book, *Venture Capital Investing*.

The list of 1,000 questions

There are, arguably, 1,000 questions that every business plan should answer. You will develop your own set as you go forward. Here are 21 to get you started:

THERE ARE, ARGUABLY, 1,000 QUESTIONS THAT EVERY BUSINESS PLAN SHOULD ANSWER

1 How will the business make money?

2 Who is behind it?

3 Who is the customer and what evidence is there that they will buy?

4 Is the profit potential adequate to provide a satisfactory return on investment of capital, time and opportunity costs?[1]

5 Has anyone bought the product/service yet? Are there any letters of intent or other proof of the value proposition?

6 How substantial is the market?

7 What follow-on opportunities exist for this company?

8 Can barriers to entry be created?[2]

9 Can the suppliers control critical resources and capture the innovative rents or profits?[3]

10 What skills, resources, and relationships does the entrepreneurial group already possess?[4]

11 What is really unique about the proposed business concept?
   - cost structure
   - technology
   - product features or quality, including augmented product definitions
   - marketing and sales channels
   - financial resources
   - focus
   - people.[5]

12 What are the major requirements for regulatory compliance?[6]

13 What are the key bets?

14 Are there enough resources to overcome unforeseen problems?

1 Harvard Business School Case, John R. van Slyke, Howard H. Stevenson, and Michael J. Roberts, *The Start-Up Process*, Harvard Business School case 394-067. Copyright © 1984 by the President and Fellows of Harvard College.

2 Same as above.

3 Same as above.

4 Same as above.

5 Same as above.

15 What are the potential problems or disasters that could occur?

16 What are the critical objectives of the members of the entrepreneurial team?

17 What are the critical objectives of the capital and resource providers?

18 Are incentives aligned?

19 How will the evolution of the entrepreneur's role be managed?[7]

20 Is there a specific mechanism for harvesting?[8]

21 Has the venture been structured financially and legally so as to maximize the after-tax yield from harvest?[9]

Some investors think of asking questions like shooting bullets. You take a number of shots at the entrepreneur(s) to see how they stand up; perhaps focusing on one area of the business to make sure the business plan has depth.

ADDING VALUE

Finally, you should consider your ability to add value to a deal as this may impact its attractiveness.

For example, Capitalyst Group, LLC, has over 100 investors in its funds and companies. Prince Heinrich von Liechtenstein, an early investor, is instrumental in making introductions to other serious investors. Tom Wharton, an investor who later joined the board, advises on strategy and management. Jake Ben-Meir invested and then joined the company full time as COO and President. Most of the early investors found their own way of contributing and adding value to the company.

Here is a list of short-term and long-term contributions angels can make to start-up companies depending on the role they prefer:

- **Silent partner**

  Invest.
  Lend use of name (by investing).
  Make three referrals.

- **Reserve force**

  Raise additional capital.
  Sell a customer.
  Sell a strategic partner.
  Advise on a project.

6 Same as above.
7 Same as above.
8 Same as above.
9 Same as above.

Closing supporter.
General advisor.
Functional advisor.
Introducer.

● **Team member (full or part time)**

Any operational role.
Short term full time.
Medium to long term part time.
Consultant.
Raise venture capital.
Sign up strategic partners.

● **Coach**

Mentor.
Daily advisor.
"Name" support.

● **Controlling manager**

CEO.
Chairman of the board (high activity and power).

Start-ups need a lot of help. The questions to ask are: where can you help, and where will the entrepreneur take help? Finally, can you help in a way that will improve the deal?

CHAPTER 18

WINNING ANGELS 2000

The following excerpts from *The Winning Angels Study* ©2000, by David Amis and Jocelyn Dinnin: "What do most investors do?", "What do the winners do?" and the selected winning tools and tactics, are reprinted with permission. Highlights of this study were published in *The Winning Angels Handbook*.

WHAT DO MOST INVESTORS DO?

- **Read the plan**

  Although we have known angel investors to make investment decisions in as little as five minutes, which obviously did not include reading the business plan, most angel investors spend 15 minutes to five hours reading and thinking about the plans they receive.

- **Ask 100 questions**

  Usually in a meeting with the entrepreneur, they grill him or her and shoot all the bullets they can think of to understand how the deal might not work. This productive process will send the "weaker" projects home and also test the mettle of the entrepreneur.

- **Focus on the downside**

  Considering all the things that might go wrong is good for testing the plan, but an inherent part of angel investing is looking for winning ideas and then implementing solutions.

- **Spend a lot of time**

  Huge amounts of time can be spent researching and assessing a potential deal. Developing an effective screening approach can curb time spent.

- **Meet the entrepreneur, perhaps several times**

  Evaluation of the key entrepreneurs is central to a positive investment decision.

- **Discuss with friends**

  Hearing an unbiased opinion is always helpful. If you have friends who have expertise in specific areas they may be better placed to comment on certain aspects of the deal.

WHAT DO THE WINNERS DO?

- **Recognize that sourcing = evaluation**

  One of the reasons that Howard is adamant about good-quality sourcing is that it is essentially an evaluation tool. With good-quality deal flow, he spends less time reviewing poor-quality projects, taking undesired telephone calls, and being talked into bad deals. He says, *"The better the quality of the source, the quicker the evaluation and the higher likelihood of finding a winner."*

Betsy Atkins, who has made 30 angel-type investments, also agrees with this observation: *"The referrers do the first level of screening."* Audrey MacLean starts the evaluation process by looking at the source: *"My screening starts in the sourcing channels."* And the first questions Brian Horey, founder of New York New Media Association, asks himself are: *"Who sent it? How did it get to me?"*

- **Focus on the model, not the plan**

"Plans are outdated at first enemy contact," said a famous desert tank commander. Entrepreneurial plans are likewise modified upon the initiation of operations and particularly on "contact" with the marketplace. Numbers are often off by a factor of two, three or 10, and the plan itself may change 100%. That is why winning investors know that the essence of any opportunity lies in the model behind it. If the model makes sense, a business can be built, regardless of execution mishaps.

> **EGO**
>
> **That big 3 letter word...**
>
> You need an entrepreneur with an ego because he needs to have self-confidence.
>
> However, egos have been known to ruin businesses and relationships. We have no idea how to manage this or screen for it.
>
> Good luck.

- **Emphasize the entrepreneur and the team**

As mentioned before, *"I will invest with an A-quality man with a B-quality project, but not the other way around,"* says just about every successful angel investor. General Doriot is often credited with this saying. He believed that a good entre-

WINNING INVESTORS KNOW THAT THE ESSENCE OF ANY OPPORTUNITY LIES IN THE MODEL BEHIND IT

preneur would figure out a way to win, despite the starting point of the project.

Winning investors choose winning entrepreneurs because they know early-stage deals rely more on the entrepreneur than anything else. Prince Heinrich von Liechtenstein, an angel investor in Austria, sums it up when he says, *"Entrepreneur, entrepreneur, entrepreneur."*

John McCallion, a UK-based angel, additionally likes to see entrepreneurs who have been through structured corporate training programs. His ideal candidate has a strong educational background, quality business training and a track record of performance in their chosen field. A determination to succeed is also a prerequisite.

Josh Green, an angel investor and attorney with Venture Law Group in Silicon Valley, also likes to know who has mentored the entrepreneurs. His primary focus in a deal is on the individual.

"*The ethics of the guy are the most important,*" Howard Stevenson tells his class at HBS.

Consider the following:

- Do people in the industry know him?
- Does he know his own weaknesses?
- Will he listen? If he will not listen, you are in deep trouble.
- If he is trying to figure out how to cut corners with somebody, he's going to cut corners with you.
- Are people running to things or from things? The latter is not a good sign.
- Are they realistic about the commitment required to succeed? Time, money, personal sacrifice?
- Is this the kind of person that other people want to make succeed? That first customer has got to like the person.

● **Exit, Exit, Exit**

"*Start with the exit,*" says OH. "*What is the founder's incentive scheme?*" Commenting on a fish distribution business that he invested $50,000 in: "*Every time I met that entrepreneur he talked about exits... that's why I invested.*" Given the difficulty of harvesting, winning investors know that entrepreneurs who are highly motivated to exit are more likely to get it done.

WINNING INVESTORS KNOW THAT ENTREPRENEURS WHO ARE HIGHLY MOTIVATED TO EXIT ARE MORE LIKELY TO GET IT DONE

● **What's my unfair advantage?**

Winning angels do not want level playing fields, they want opportunities where a patent, first mover, or other aspect gives them an advantage over any current or coming competitor.

● **Recognize that every entrepreneur is different**

"*In some of the best opportunities, the entrepreneur was rather foolish,*" says OH. "*No one would join in the second round; I did.*"

● **Use intuition backed by judgment**

Mitch Kapor started making angel investments "*before they had a word to describe it.*" He relies on a combination of intuition: "*Do I like this guy? Is this an interesting project?*" together with making a business judgment: "*is there a sustainable business proposition here?*" Lucius Cary is an example of an angel who often acts on a "*hunch.*"

● **Focus on deals where they know something**

"*Do I have experience in this area?*" is one question Jeff Parker asks himself. After she gets a referral, Betsy Atkins looks for projects that fall into her realm of specialty, i.e. marketing and sales. *"There are a lot of people that can write $100k checks without thinking about it... it's important to do your own due diligence,"* says Audrey MacLean.

- Add value

  "Investors must be value added," says George Kline, who has made over 160 investments. *"The entrepreneurs will look at you as mentors, the bigger the range of skills you (or your syndicate) can offer, the more attractive you become."*

- Invest with other angels

  Betsy Atkins can screen for marketing and sales aspects of a new opportunity, but she always invests with other angels, relying on them to screen the areas they know best.

Andrew Blair, a UK-based angel, always works as part of an investor syndicate of which he is often the leader. He also includes some virgin angels as well. In this way he can build generations of future value-added co-angels. The other benefit to the syndication approach is that individual angels can be assigned to different aspects of the business. For example, one of the angels will usually have extensive financial management experience, so this angel will be spending time with the CFO of the target company. Later, all of the angels involved in

> **Some things winning angels said about the entrepreneurs they invested in**
>
> ❝He is a geat chess player and always 10 steps ahead of anyone in the room.❞
>
> They have a high bar set... I feel personally challenged by them.
>
> I know they are going to win... it's just a question of what at.❞

What one start-up advisor looks for

Here is what Tom Wharton, who specializes in helping companies reach the next level, looks for in a start-up opportunity:

1 Quality, dedicated management that is passionate for what they are doing with industry experience and a willingness to test new ideas. If I walk away everything continues to move forward!!!

2 A business that is simple and has a clearly defined product and revenue model with clear customer benefits.

3 A reasonable time to market advantage, channel control, or technology advantage that creates some barrier to entry.

4 A scalable business that creates long-term customers and or a product that when generated can be sold in perpetuity to become marginally more profitable over time.

evaluating the opportunity will meet and give their recommendations and conclusive feedback.

In general, Howard only does technology deals when one of his co-angels who understands it deeply is involved.

- **Look for entrepreneurs who know how to use advisors**

"*I look for a willingness to take advice,*" says Lucius Cary, the founder of Venture Capital Report and an investor in over 50 early-stage companies, in describing his evaluation process.

"*Entrepreneurs need to get good advisors, and that's not their uncle,*" says Audrey MacLean.

- **Invest close to home (pre-internet)**

"*I only invest in companies within an hour's drive,*" says Lucius Cary. Lucius actively advises almost every company he invests in and wants to be close at hand.

- **Invest close to their knowledge base or with a lead investor regardless of the distance (post-internet)**

"*Focus 90% on the founders,*" says John Hime. "*The people part can't be emphasized enough.*" Manny Villafana, who has made some 50+ investments in the medi-tech industry, says: "*I stick to medical devices and stay in my field.*"

- **Hire their own screener**

David Solomont has a full-time associate who screens and helps to manage the deals he is in. Other angels also have a full-time associate who reads every business plan that comes in, making investment recommendations.

The Capital Investors in Arlington, Virginia, is a group of 20+ high-tech executives. The group has a full-time manager who reads all incoming plans and then recommends a few to a small committee of members.

- **Operate efficiently**

Winning investors use their time well. Most have already thought through the process and refined it based on their experiences. Here is how John Hime manages his evaluation process:

1 Entrepreneur contacts him by phone or email.

2 He replies with a request for an executive summary via email or fax and includes his form letter (page 130).

3 He reviews the executive summary.

4 If interested, he schedules a face-to-face meeting.

5 If not interested, he sends an email or fax saying so, being as specific as possible. He also sends a list of other people to contact.

WINNING TOOLS AND TACTICS

Red flags

There are a few things that entrepreneurs do which cause them to immediately lose the interest of serious investors, and for good reason. Consider these actions as red flags.

EXAMPLE **REDFLAGS**

1. Salary is utmost on their minds (they should be thinking about creating share value).
2. The business plan claims 10 revenue sources or products (early stage companies need to focus on one or two and make them work).
3. They say or do anything that is dishonest. (If they do not have a strong moral code, your money is history.)
4. They are not realistic about their own abilities (e.g. lacking any financial knowledge, the entrepreneur does not have "financial guy" on his list of to-dos).
5. They only "need 1% of the market."
6. They have not identified the first customer.

Three is company – set up your own group

Rob Low, an angel investor in the DC/Virginia area, has met with two other angels every month for almost 10 years. Together they size up opportunities, share the responsibility of further due diligence, and make investment decisions. "*Our best deal thus far returned 10 times and we have several more on track. The best thing is that we enjoy doing deals together*," says Rob Low.

Identify two other angels with whom you can have a lot of good times, people you will enjoy seeing and working with on a regular basis, and agree to meet weekly or monthly to start looking at deals.

Komisar's three stages

Randy Komisar breaks down the development of a company into three stages. His goal is to find companies in stage one and help them move into the second stage. By the third stage, he wants to be focusing his attention on the next venture.

Randy Komisar, known as the Virtual CEO, breaks opportunities into three stages:

Stage one
Purely Blue Sky: *"This is where you see if there is a potential business behind the proposed product or service... it's loosely bringing together the initial components to test the assumptions: the management team, some seed financing... some customers... and strategic partners, all to see if you can get it done."*

Stage two
Growth: *"This is where you aim at a market and really begin to focus the company and start to build the organization, refine the business model and create the foundation for future growth."*

Stage three
Managed Growth: *"Now it's an operating company, where your principal goal is to build predictable growth and manageable results."*

CHAPTER 19

**SPECIAL
SECTIONS**

1 ● TOP 10 THINGS MANNY VILLAFANA LOOKS FOR IN A MEDICAL START-UP

Manny Villafana is known in the Minneapolis area as the guy to see if you are doing a medical start-up. He has made investments in over 50 medical start-ups and agreed to share his list of what he looks for in this type of opportunity:

1 Is there a technical need for the device?

2 Is the technology readily available for the manufacturing of the device?

3 The management; composition of the team; previous experience of the management.

4 Capital requirements. Is the capital going to be raised in stages?

5 The make-up of the scientific advisory board.

6 The capitalization of the company. Is there fairness to the incoming investor? Is the valuation correct? Does the CEO have a meaningful investment in the company?

7 Does the CEO and do the members of the management team have a proper proportion of the ownership to make it worthwhile to invest their time and effort into this project?

8 The quality of the regulatory officer as a medical device company needs to have a top person in that field.

9 Are there any possible litigation factors?

10 What does my gut tell me?

2 ● WHAT TONY MORRIS LOOKS FOR IN AN IT OR INTERNET START-UP

Tony Morris has been involved in desktop computing and related IT industries since 1979 as an entrepreneur, investor, and consultant. So far he has backed 19 start-ups and early-stage companies, including idealab! which generated a return of several hundred times.

❝ I have looked at all the 19 deals I've done (of which there is only one loss), and tried to figure out what was common across them. I have identified five attributes:

1 The deal is a game changer somehow, i.e. it either enables customers to do something they could not do before, or it dramatically reduces the cost. With this comes an implied competitive differentiation, which is good, but can be a bad thing if it comes too early.

2 The business has to be big enough to attract real venture capital, so that the real money can come to the table.

3 I bring something to the table. This is where I can really understand the business and can figure out what is needed and go and help do it. I have been an active advisor in 18 of the 19 companies.

4 I feel good about the management. I am prepared to row the boat, but I have to at least respect the management. It is nicer if you like them, but you should at least respect them.

5 Follow winners. For example with the CEO Bill Gross (creator of idealab!), I have made four investments, and with another winning CEO I have made two. Essentially six of the companies from my private portfolio are attributed to two CEOs. The four investments where Bill Gross was the CEO were: idealab!, Intranets.com, TickMaster Online CitySearch, and Knowledge Adventure. All have proved to be extraordinary investments, with the only remaining outcome being for Intranets.com, and that is looking very favorable at this time. ❞

3 • MUST DO, OUGHT TO DO, NICE TO DO

OH, an angel investor based in Norway, has the habit of creating one-pagers like the following. He also does one-pagers for must avoid, ought to avoid, and nice to avoid when looking at early-stage deals. Here is an example list that might apply to early-stage investing:

Must have

- Match of interest and experience.
- Management team A++.
- Big market opportunity, rapid growth to $1bn+.
- Scaleable concept $100m in year 5.
- Compelling business model.
- Concise and convincing differentiation.

Ought to have

- 2 customers already identified.
- Draft business plan.
- Demo version of product.
- 2–4 people already involved.
- Entrepreneurs that know how to use advisors.

Nice to have

- Revenue.
- Track record in this kind of deal.
- Good advisors.

Must avoid

- Dishonest entrepreneur.
- Self-destructive ego.
- Lifestyle entrepreneur.

Ought to avoid

- Empire builders.

Nice to avoid

- Inexperienced CEO.

4 ● ANGEL INVESTOR JOHN HIME'S ENTREPRENEUR LETTER

John Hime, who has invested in 29 early-stage companies located in the Texas region, uses an efficient process for screening entrepreneurs. He responds to entrepreneurs who approach him with a standard email/letter, as follows. The letter includes information about what he is looking for in a deal so that entrepreneurs can self-screen to a certain extent. He then reviews the executive summaries to see if they match his criteria, and if they do he sets up a meeting.

> **Dear Entrepreneur**
>
> Please accept my apology for sending you this "form" letter instead of a personal response to your query. I would simply tell you that I have found this to be an effective and efficient way for both of us to determine the next steps (if any) of a potential relationship.
>
> I am often asked, "Why do you decide to invest in a company?" As a quick answer to this question, I have put together the attached summary of what I am currently looking for in my investment and advisory activities. I hope this helps you decide, at least as a first cut, whether or not I might be of help to you.
>
> An easier question for me to answer is "Why do you *decline* to invest in a company?" At this time, I am seeing, over and over again, two things that keep me from investing. First, is that I don't have the background or experience to feel comfortable that I can either add value to, or fully understand the deal. In other words, I just don't "get it." If this turns out to be the case with your deal, please don't take it as a negative. There are plenty of other investors out there with different interests and backgrounds than mine.
>
> The second major reason for my not investing is that the critical management team members, especially the CEO, sales and marketing, have not been identified. There is a tremendous shortage of management talent in the computer business these days, and rounding up a quality team with at least one "done-it-before" guy makes a difference of perhaps 10x in the value of a deal. I have a lot of personal contacts in the computer and software business, but I can assure you that all the good guys (and ladies) I know are already in deals that can potentially bring them great fame and fortune. And, they are working heads-down, 80 hours a week to make that happen. It also seems like there are 10 open jobs for every decent candidate that turns up. What this means is that finding a quality management team is probably the most difficult part of starting a company these days, and is the essential test an entrepreneur must pass before I can consider investing. For some good ideas on building your management team, see http://strategis.ic.gc.ca/SSG/mi05402e.html.
>
> In conclusion, thank you for your interest, and let's continue a dialogue (email is always best for me) if you think I can help you in any way. Although I have been financially successful in many of my investments, my biggest reward is when I can help smart, hard-working people achieve their vision.
>
> Good luck,
>
> John Hime
> jhime@austin.rr.com

5 ● THE ENTREPRENEUR'S PERSPECTIVE

Here is how Amar Bhidé, in his article, "Start-Up Strategies",[1] advises entrepreneurs to choose their concept:

Amar Bhidé

❝ The decision to launch a new venture rests on an assessment of its viability – whether it can earn a profit – and its attractiveness, as compared to other opportunities that could be pursued.

Analyzing a start-up's competitive prospects, though, is daunting. A complete analysis must take a great many industry participants into account: as Porter and other strategy gurus have pointed out, a start-up faces competition not only from rivals offering the same goods but also potentially from substitutes, suppliers, buyers, and other new entrants. In bidding for employees and capital, a start-up even competes with firms totally outside its industry. Complementing the external analysis of competitors, internal core competencies and weaknesses should be probed. Entrepreneurs must analyse their costs and access to capital, technology, distribution channels and so on...

THE DECISION TO LAUNCH A NEW VENTURE RESTS ON AN ASSESSMENT OF ITS VIABILITY

Therefore, a wealth-constrained, one-venture-at-a-time entrepreneur must use multiple criteria, favoring ventures with:

● Low capital requirements – ventures that can be launched with little external capital and have the profit margins to sustain high growth with internally generated funds.

● High margin for error – ventures with simple operations and low fixed costs which are less likely to face a cash crunch because of technical delays, cost over-runs and slow build-up of sales.

● Significant payoffs – ventures whose rewards are substantial enough to compensate for the future opportunities the entrepreneur can't pursue because of a commitment to see this one through.

● Low exit costs – ventures that can be shut down without a significant loss of time, money or reputation. Thus, for example, ventures whose failure is known quickly are better than projects that are not expected to make a profit for a long period and therefore cannot be reasonably abandoned in the interim. Similarly, short payback periods have value because the entrepreneur's loss of self-esteem, reputation, and, of course, personal wealth due to the closing of a venture are lower if it has already returned the investment made in it.

1 Amar Bhidé, "Note on Developing Start-up Strategies", Harvard Business School case 394-067, in William A. Sahlman, Howard H. Stevenson, Michael J. Roberts, and Amar Bhidé, *The Entrepreneurial Venture*, 2/E. Boston: Harvard Business School Press, 1999, pp. 122–124. Copyright © 1993 by the President and Fellows of Harvard College.

- Options for cashing in – ventures that can be sold or taken public. An entrepreneur locked into an illiquid business cannot easily pursue other more attractive opportunities and faces problems of fatigue and burn-out. Therefore, entrepreneurs should prefer businesses with a sustainable competitive advantage, such as a proprietary technology or brand name, which others would be willing to buy. 🙶🙶

6 ● INTERVIEW WITH MITCH KAPOR

Currently Mitch Kapor is a venture capitalist with Accel, a premier VC firm with offices in Palo Alto, California, and Princeton, New Jersey.

🙶🙶 I started to invest in what is now called angel investing – it wasn't called that then. It did not really have a name.

As to sourcing, I was just in the flow of things, meeting people, knowing people, because of Lotus I was somewhat visible. People tended to come to me, but when I would meet people at tradeshows and elsewhere I was curious and asked a lot of questions, initially relying on my intuition about things that I thought were highly interesting.

I was not self-reflective about this to begin with, but later on I tried to analyze my style. I would like things where technology could be used to make some sort of difference, to make something interesting that would have a positive impact on the user experience. So I particularly liked things that were whole new platforms because they were very powerful. I had a propensity to certain kinds of projects, some of which turned out to be big successes, a few of which turned out big failures.

So I wasn't being primarily driven at all by what was going to produce an attractive return. I was being driven by what I thought would be interesting to work on or be a part of. That also led to some failures in screening, where I would sometimes fall in love with projects and not see what were some of the obvious problems from the management point of view. That's the problem with intuition, "oh this is really interesting," "this is a smart guy," "I like this guy," and "I'll put a little money into it." Often times not applying business judgment was a problem. So ultimately I would always look to see if there is an investible proposition. Was there something that led me to believe there was a sustainable business proposition?

I probably learned more from my failures, such as GoCorporation, than from my successes, or at least as much...

In the kinds of high-tech deals that I do as an angel, I have seen companies valued at anywhere from $1m to more than $10m. It's a factor of many things, including: who's doing the deal, how far along they are, and how good their negotiating skills are. I was involved in those days in public policy issues about telecommunications. You remember the information superhighway and all that. So I was in and around Washington with people in the National Science

Foundation who were running the internet and that is actually how I found out about PSI and UUNET, the first commercial ISPs. I wasn't in an active investing phase at all but I thought they were really interesting companies in an interesting space and wound up persuading Rick Adams to take a small investment from me. Then after a period of some months the conclusion was reached to try to raise venture money. People I knew from the PC space were not interested but I had just met Accel, and had put a very small amount of money in as a limited partner. I called Jim Breyer and they had the great foresight to come and take a look.

If you could give advice to people who are starting to do angel investing what would that advice be?

I think pursuing angel investing with a combination of passion and discipline is a good formula. Passion about stuff you can get very excited about where you are willing to place a bet. Trust your intuition and judgment. I think that combined with a certain basic discipline about asking the fundamental questions, such as where's the management team and if it's not there where is it going to come from? And is there a sustainable business proposition in the face

PURSUING ANGEL INVESTING WITH A COMBINATION OF PASSION AND DISCIPLINE IS A GOOD FORMULA

of competition, and all those other questions. Asking these questions upfront saves a lot of pain later on. But it is fun, and I encourage people who are in a position to do it to do it. I think the angels are now an important part of the ecology of growing high tech companies. I've see companies now coming to Accel that have already raised $1–2m and in some cases $3m from angels and then we come in and do the next round which we still call early-stage. 🙶 . . . .

7 ● QUOTES ON WINNING DEALS

What angels had to say about evaluating their best winners.

Tony Morris

🙶 My biggest winner, though not yet fully liquid, is idealab! where the return is several hundred times. I would attribute that to following a winner, Bill Gross – he's different from you and me, he's just incredible. I am a so-called idealab! resource, so I have worked on a variety of idealab! companies. In exchange for that work I was permitted to be an original investor in the company and some other stock was made available to me, common stock, at a nominal cost. So I am extraordinarily fortunate. In actual fact, I see my investments in Contact Software International and SalesLogix as my trophy deals, because I can identify unambiguously my contribution to a big win with each. Although I brought something to the table in idealab! I do not see it as being replicable, there was a lot of luck there. Moving forward I will bet on what is replicable. 🙶

Angel investor CL

66 StarMedia basically was just duplicating AOL, minus the ISP component, in a new market. So it was very easy to see how that might work. And it was all a question of execution, not the viability of the concept, if you like. 99

Josh Green

66   Another couple that I think are absolutely going to lead to success are these two companies: Epinions and Tellme Networks. When you look at those guys they are the kind who have bunk beds above their desks and who are absolutely driven towards success and will accept nothing less. They are in those formative stages of their late twenties or early thirties when they still have the energy to do that kind of stuff and it is those people I want to be around. They are people that identify excellence at an incredibly high level. I don't know how to describe it or articulate it well for you. It is something where you get a very, very high bar established and you feel it. Carl Russo, the CEO of Cerent, is another guy who I hooked up with, where you absolutely sense this. I feel personally challenged by them. In other words I am learning from them when I am around them. When I sense that from somebody the bell goes off which says I want to be around that person, invest in them and spend my time with them. It is not only fulfilling on an intellectual basis but it usually leads to success financially as well. 99

Bill Sahlman

66 Almost all of the ones that have worked out have been great people, who've turned out to be even better than you thought they'd be. Good managers, good negotiators, good everything. 99

Darryl Wash

66   There are numerous indicators to show strong commitment. The most obvious is to look at what sort of financial commitment they have made relative to their own financial resources. The financial commitment can be looked at in two ways: relative to their own resources, net worth and cash availability, etc. and secondly to their own opportunity costs. What have they given up to start this business? Did they not have a job and decide therefore I'll start my own business. Or did they leave a relatively highflying job and really have devotion to succeed and be successful. Take StarMedia as an example, Jack Chen was a high flier at CS First Boston and had been at Goldman Sachs and basically was highly sought after. His partner, Fernando Espuleas, was one of the youngest managing directors of AT&T and had started its Latin American website, as well as having started an office for Ogilvy & Mather in Argentia and run its entire Latin American business. He could have done anything he wanted to do. So with those two individuals committing all of their time, energy, and resources to a business, you just had to believe that they were very committed. 99

8 ● INTERVIEW WITH TOM ALBERG

This is the story of angel investor Tom Alberg evaluating Amazon. Tom Alberg made the decision to invest $100k in Amazon's first round in 1995 and saw his stake grow in value to $26m. Since that time he has been part of a small group of professional angels, Madrona Investment Group, and they have put $15m in to 50 start-up companies.

❝ I had gotten a call from a lawyer in Seattle who had known me from my legal days. He had a small angel investment group, and they had met a young man that was going to sell books over the internet. He said that since I was at McCaw I must know a lot about the internet. McCaw wasn't really doing anything on the internet, it was doing wireless communications, but I've long known, if somebody said something like that, I'd say, "Well, sure."

BARNES & NOBLE WAS ALREADY TALKING ABOUT HOW THEY WERE SOMEDAY GOING TO SELL BOOKS ONLINE

I went to a meeting of four or five people, including a local venture capital firm, myself, and a couple of others. This was probably May '95 and Jeff Bezos was raising a million dollars from people in Seattle. In those days in Seattle there was some angel investing done, and there were two or three smaller venture capital funds, and the California funds would come up here and do some deals, as they got more mature. But there really wasn't a whole lot of activity and, of course, the internet hadn't taken off. So anyway, so I met with Bezos. We talked on the phone, I'd call him up with more questions, and this went on for a couple of months. I talked to the other investors and the actual investor who had referred it to me, his group decided that the valuation was too high. It was around a $4 million pre-money valuation.

The local venture capital firm did terrific due diligence. They looked into the book industry, bricks and mortar book industry, and the distribution chain, and everything that goes with how you traditionally sell books, and they concluded that, based on their due diligence, Barnes & Noble would kill Amazon, because Barnes & Noble had such huge volume purchases of books, and it was such a major factor that Amazon could never get to those kinds of margins, could never get those kinds of purchasing arrangements from the book publishers. In addition, Barnes & Noble was already talking about how they were someday going to sell books online.

I love bookstores, and we all said we like going to bookstores, that's a great experience, and thought about it a little bit more. But then they don't often have the book you want, at Christmas time there are these long lines... well, maybe there's a market here, and maybe the internet doesn't require everybody to buy all of their books online.

Jeff was impressive personally, but, you know, it's hard to measure people at that stage. He made a very strong impression, had researched the book industry very well, and seemed to know a lot about the internet. He had not launched his site, he didn't launch his site until July.

Believing that the internet was going to be revolutionary, it seemed to make sense to sell books online. It took Jeff from the spring until December to raise his million dollars, which is of course another commentary on how fast things have changed, that it really took him six months to raise a million dollars in Seattle.

ANOTHER COMMENTARY ON HOW FAST THINGS HAVE CHANGED... IT REALLY TOOK HIM SIX MONTHS TO RAISE A MILLION DOLLARS IN SEATTLE

One of the things that frankly influenced us all was that Jeff launched the site in mid-July and in late July, when I talked to him, he said *"Well, it's really amazing here. We've got orders from New Hampshire, Georgia, all over the country. Instead of getting one a day, we're getting a whole lot of orders every day."* And every week the traffic increased some.

His wasn't the only site, but it worked quite well. It wasn't super-duper, but it worked reasonably fast, and so people seemed to be buying books. He had, from day one, a huge commitment to customer service.

So the financing didn't close until early December, so that's a microcosm of what was going on in those days. I invested about $100,000, the other investment came from some local individuals and some of Jeff's family. I don't think there was a single institutional investor in that group. Some were as small as $25,000.

Making the decision to write the check came about as a combination of liking Jeff, I think he was a good entrepreneur and founder, liking the business model and then seeing some early revenue. I'm a big believer that revenue is very important early on, I'm less concerned about profit. They tend to think if you've got a lot of revenue, a good model, then you can get the profitability some day. That is certainly the Amazon story.

9 ● TYPES OF ENTREPRENEUR

Although there have been many studies on entrepreneurship, there is no single, high-quality source of entrepreneur typology that fits the angel investor's perspective. In addition, typologies have limited usefulness. People can change and grow, and entrepreneurs are especially guilty of being able to recreate themselves for success. Following are entrepreneur types based on the work of a few leading researchers, as well as our experiences in working with these dynamic types.

Serial entrepreneur

As described by Peter Kelly, who completed his dissertation at the London Business School, a serial entrepreneur is:

❝ Someone who has started up numerous businesses. Their key characteristics above anything else are that they know their role. As soon as the building is done, they know when to get out and I think that makes them a very special breed of entrepreneur. One of the most difficult things for an entrepreneur to do is say "I've taken the business as far as I can go and now it's time for somebody else to take it on."❞

While these entrepreneurs may represent the ideal target for an angel, it is characteristically hard to invest in them as they usually have a significant following of investors, associates, and professionals from past deals who are always ready to place some capital with them. We heard from several of our winning angels, "*Once you find a winner, stick with them.*"

ONCE YOU FIND A WINNER, STICK WITH THEM

Empire builders

According to active angel OH, empire builders are entrepreneurs that are interested in building large or multi-faceted businesses in order to run and grow them. They are not highly concerned with exits and selling is not a preferred strategy. Rather they want to build themselves an empire. Unlike lifestyle entrepreneurs, empire builders tend to build companies of significant value. The challenge is capturing the value.

Lifestyle entrepreneur

These entrepreneurs are creating a lifestyle for themselves. One German entrepreneur David met, in the Austrian ski resort Kitzbühl, had purchased a B&B halfway up the mountain. Previously he had been a trader in Frankfurt but now he managed the small hotel, along with the bar and restaurant, during the winter, skied and enjoyed life. During the summers he took his motorcycle and drove around the US or Europe.

Another entrepreneur, who David introduced to English angels, had set up a boating school on a tropical island. It was clear the returns would not shake the

ANGEL INVESTORS SHOULD AVOID LIFESTYLE ENTREPRENEURS AT ALL COSTS

world, but in this case the angels liked the idea of participating in such a venture, writing off their trips, and sailing with an expert.

Angel investors, unless wanting to participate in the lifestyle option, should avoid lifestyle entrepreneurs at all costs. Their motives are not aligned with return-focused angels.

High-potential entrepreneur

These entrepreneurs, who have not completed a major entrepreneurial win yet, have all the characteristics that winning angels look for and that are described in this book. A high-potential entrepreneur understands the investor's objectives, and builds the start-up with the exit in mind, although this doesn't necessarily mean a two-year window. Some angels and entrepreneurs want to build outstanding and substantial businesses, which will take 10–15 years to achieve.

High-potential entrepreneurs will stand up to the scrutiny of any angel, particularly one well versed in the industry. These honest, smart, tough, committed,

HIGH-POTENTIAL ENTREPRENEURS WILL STAND UP TO THE SCRUTINY OF ANY ANGEL

proven (as business people), and self-aware entrepreneurs have the highest likelihood of making their

business a success, even when things don't go as planned. In fact, they are model changers when necessary, adapting their companies to fit market-changing events on the go.

David Ronnick would be considered an example of such a high-potential entrepreneur. He started a company, which received financing from David and other angels in 1998. At the time of writing, that company was pursuing a VC round. However, what matters most is that David Ronnick is a straightforward and smart guy. He earned his MBA at Harvard,[2] and went on to start up Polo Jeans, a licensee of Polo/Ralph Lauren Corporation. He managed a $65m division of Tommy Hilfiger, where he doubled sales in an 18-month period. When he started his business, he recruited a full-time partner who had been at McKinsey and MIT. Six months after start-up, they realized their model was not going to hit in a big way. So they sold the assets they had created and focused on a similar opportunity that they had discovered in conversations with venture capitalists. Whether David Ronnick generates substantial success with the next development of his company or not, he is the kind of high-potential entrepreneur who will eventually get a major win, if he keeps at it. High-potential entrepreneurs have usually invested several months or years in pulling their plans together. Their financial, marketing, opera-

2 Earning an MBA or working at a blue-chip firm is not a prerequisite for success in entrepreneurship. In fact, the analytical process taught at most business schools kills some of the intuitive risk taking that successful entrepreneurs must have, in the opinion of David Amis.

tions and capital raising plans have been thought through. High-potential entrepreneurs do not have all the answers, but they have enough to know there is a solid opportunity and have a plan for seizing it.

Almost-there entrepreneur

These entrepreneurs are just shy of being high potential. However, they lack something that is critical, such as a key team member, a product development test, customer interest, capital raising knowledge, or a finalized concept and plan. These entrepreneurs generally need a hands-on, experienced angel or six more months working in the right direction. Depending on your investment strategy, they may represent excellent opportunities or time takers. You decide. However, this type of entrepreneur demonstrates why managing the entrepreneur interaction is important.

Wanna-be entrepreneur

The flying airplane pen, the solution without a problem, the programmer who cannot describe his customer, we have all seen these opportunities. In many cases, almost no amount of work would turn this entrepreneur into a high-potential entrepreneur. However, in some cases, if a professional manager can get control of the project, there might be something. David once invested in a brilliant German scientist who had the support of leading international cancer researchers. "*His approach must be supported,*" one of them wrote in a testimonial. David invested and helped to identify other angels.

Within two months, there were about four seriously interested angels, one international research institution and one government agency, altogether proposing to invest $1.5m as a first round. Unfortunately, this entrepreneur/scientist could not accept the terms or decide what he wanted. His demands on investor approval were extensive and slowed the process of meeting new investors dramatically. His need for information, since he was very smart and wanted to understand everything himself, was so great that he became a real time drain for any angel that talked to him. To this day he may still make it happen and we wish the best for him, but his situation lacked so many of the fundamentals needed for early-stage success that the project had made little progress after two years.

10 ● "LOSERS"

Not all angels are willing to talk about their non-wins, although most will say that it is where the real learning occurs. Our thanks to these angels who shared a non-win story with us.

Brian Horey

❝ Overall advice is focus on the people, because they ultimately make the business succeed or fail, particularly with very early-stage companies where there is not a business or customer base. Generally speaking, the people running the company have to live by their wits. The one that did not work was in part because they misjudged the market. The company was in a long development cycle and probably would have benefited from some marketplace testing earlier in life. The other issue was it raised venture capital from the wrong people – who pushed the company to spend money faster than it should have and made management changes that were ill advised in my view. ❞

Andrew Blair

❝ Woolsey Assured Housing plc. They invested £250,000 and then raised £750,000 under a BES share issue. Altogether they had about 300 shareholders. The object was to buy flats in East Anglia for furnishing and letting, but the problem was they over-geared.

They went to the bank and raised another £1m. They then had £2m of property. They found that the market was unexpectedly weak – they were simply not able to let easily. The team was badly led by a chairman who, although very experienced in commercial property, had no experience in renting flats, etc. We lost all the investors' money and the bank repossessed all the flats. We lost control through bad investor management and poor monitoring. ❞

Mitch Kapor

❝ I probably learned more from my failures, such as GoCorporation, than from my successes, or at least as much. ❞

Tony Morris

❝ A UNIX tools company. It was founded in September of 1993 and it was toast by March. I had a lot of respect for one of the investors that came in next to me, so I probably did not do the right amount of due diligence. However, the company had satisfied customers and a good product that worked. There just was a complete failure to execute. What happened was that the CEO brought in a senior marketing and sales guy from a huge software company, and discovered that the guy took the job casually and went sailing a few times instead of making calls. He fired the guy, but the CEO was so demoralized, he never recovered from that mistake. He got spooked. It was a competitive environment, there was a lot going on. What happened was that the CEO just went into scramble mode and never found a successor, and they began to run out of money. He negotiated an acquisition with an established software company. I don't know what happened, the company made the mistake of presuming that the deal was going to happen. Two days before the deal was due to be done, the acquiring company backed off. The CEO had not developed an alternative financing strategy and the company basically collapsed. So where did my screen go wrong: Well, it was sort of a game changer, it was pretty powerful, if it had got going it would have attracted venture capital. There were some limits to what I could bring to the table because I didn't understand that business that well. I just didn't do the due diligence. There were some attributes of the CEO that I didn't respect. Instead of making the calls on my own, I relied on my experienced co-investor, he and I invested together. I was following a winner. The truth is it scored okay on three of my five criteria, and I thought I was following a winning investor, but it turned out to be a weak CEO.”

1 ● It will take years to become good at this.

2 ● The Harvard framework, when applied, will screen out 98% of all start-up investment opportunities.

3 ● Evaluation is a time killer.

4 ● Co-investing with a winner is the best way to save time, learn, and win.

Valuing

It's tough to predict, especially about the future.

Sam Goldwyn

QUICK OVERVIEW

20 ● Start section 145
What is valuation? 145

21 ● The five approaches to valuation 146

22 ● The 12 methods 149
Quick and easy 149
Academic/investment banker 152
Professional venture capitalist 153
Compensated advisor 154
Value later 155

23 ● Interelate example 157
The 12 methods applied 157
What happened? 161
Which method is best? 161

24 ● Four levers of early-stage returns 163
1 Whether you choose winners 163
2 How the deal is structured 163
3 The price you pay 163
4 How much dilution occurs 165

25 ● Things to think about   166
 What to shoot for ...   166
 Options on the entrepreneur?   166
 The feel good factor   167

26 ● Winning angels 2000   168
 What do most investors do?   168
 What do the winners do?   168
 Winning tools and tactics   169

27 ● Special sections   171
 1 What numbers are reasonable?   171
 2 Winning deals: Initial valuations, and the investor
  return   173
 3 Visualizing risk and reward   174
 4 Greed   176
 4 TAKEAWAYS FROM VALUING   177

CHAPTER 20

START SECTION

> ... The value of an early-stage opportunity where angels
> invest almost doesn't matter within reason... these either
> work and are phenomenal in their returns or they don't work.
>
> **Darryl Wash**

WHAT IS VALUATION?

In early-stage deals, valuation is about placing a price on a stake in a company, based on a future, potential capital return. This price may include more than just cash. It can include the use of one's time, the use of one's name, and the opportunity cost of not doing something else. Likewise, the future return is not necessarily just a capital return.

VALUATION IS WHAT YOU ARE WILLING TO EXCHANGE FOR SOMETHING ELSE THAT YOU WANT

"*Contributing... having fun... giving something back,*" are phrases some angels use to describe why they invest.

Valuation is the only real numbers part of the angel investing process. It is often misunderstood and viewed with some suspicion. Early-stage finance tools are best used to eliminate or prioritize projects rather than for deciding how much one particular project is worth.

Many winning angels have derived shortcuts to make this process less painful and less time consuming. As you read through the comments from many of our winning angels, you will see that, almost universally, they think valuation is less important than, say, the stakeholders in the deal, or the quality of the concept. However, they do spend time on the numbers and have a variety of opinions on how to do that.

In Chapter 22 we will review every method we have identified that winning angels in the US and Europe are using. There are five fundamental approaches to valuing early-stage opportunities, which encompass 12 methods. Winners understand most or all of them.

Movie stars and cocktail parties

Investing in movies offers one the opportunity to meet movie stars and attend the cocktail parties. Investing in a Bermuda yacht school would have its own benefits as would owning part of Vail Ski Lodge.

There are several ways to get a "return" on employed capital. This book focuses on return of capital with appreciation and options on future opportunities.

CHAPTER 21

THE FIVE APPROACHES TO VALUATION

- Quick and easy

  Includes the methods developed by angels to resolve the challenges of early stage investing: the lack of information, the high level of unpredictability, the need to move with relative speed, and the need to garner a significant share of the upside. These methods include the $5m limit method, the Berkus method, rule of thirds, the $2–5m angel standard and the $2–$10m internet standard.

IN THE BEGINNING OF THE ANGEL AGE, THE MULTIPLIER METHOD AND DISCOUNTED CASH FLOW WERE USED TO TACKLE THE PROBLEMS OF VALUING EARLY-STAGE DEALS

- Academic/investment banker

  Includes methods long taught in MBA schools and used by investment bankers in valuing established companies. This approach includes the traditional financial tools that were originally created to value public and other substantial companies. In the beginning of the Angel Age, the multiplier method and discounted cash flow were used to tackle the problems of valuing early-stage deals.

- Professional venture capitalist

  Includes one method known as the venture capital method, which is built upon the traditional methods of multiplier and discounted cash flow. Venture capitalists have traditionally used this method and most still do. However, as VCs attempt to do earlier stage deals, they are finding it necessary to adapt to the quicker pace and often focus more on comparable deals or absolute numbers.

- Compensated advisor

  This includes a relatively new and unique approach to valuing a contributor's time. The "angel" is provided with some upside to become involved and usually has the opportunity to invest in the near future. The virtual CEO method and the start-up advisor method are included here.

- Value later

  This approach has two somewhat new, although effective methods, which include putting the valuation off until a further event occurs. The pre-VC method and the OH method deal in percentages instead of absolute prices.

The approach you select from this list will depend on your experience and your preferences. If you are new to angel investing, do not worry that there are many different approaches, and even more methods. After reading and absorbing them, a few will stand out as the most obvious for you. Being mindful of the basic range of methods and approaches will allow you to understand the perspectives of other angels as well as the team.

Many successful angel investors use the quick and easy methods. They can always be used as your fallback approach, in case results from other approaches do not make sense, do not feel right, or just take too much time.

SUMMARY OF APPROACHES AND METHODS

Quick and easy

- $5m limit
- Berkus method
- Rule of thirds
- $2m–$5m angel standard
- $2m–$10m internet standard

Academic/investment banker

- Multiplier method
- Discounted cash flow

Professional venture capitalist

- Venture capital method

Compensated advisor

- Virtual CEO method
- Advisor method

Value later

- Pre-VC method
- O.H. method

CHAPTER 22

THE 12 METHODS

In this chapter each of the 12 methods is looked at closely. Howard likes to pick two to three methods when he looks at an opportunity. David prefers the $2–5m angel standard, the pre-VC method, and the Capitalyst™ method.[1]

QUICK AND EASY

● $5m limit

"Angels don't have as much leeway to do due diligence that would get them comfortable with high valuations. They also have the risk of not being able to get additional financing to the table... so this is a good way to think about it."

Tony Morris

After years of analyzing, valuing, and investing in early-stage deals, Howard came up with a principle he sticks to *"at least most of the time"*:

Never invest in a start-up deal valued over $5m.

The reason is simple: how many entrepreneurs can really build a $50m (or greater) company? Let's say you invest at a $5m valuation. Then, a company worth $50m would generate 10 times your money when it sold if there was no further dilution. Whether you invest $100k or $1m doesn't matter, since the end value of the company determines your return as a multiple of the amount invested. So, if one out of 10 of your investments succeeds at that level and the rest fail, you have achieved a break-even on your portfolio.[2]

Pros: Simple and provides the necessary upside given the risk.

Cons: Even $5m is too high sometimes.

Time estimate: Less than the time it takes to read this sentence.

---

1 The Capitalyst™ method is non-published as of this writing.
2 If you are diluted by even 10% in your one winner, you do not break even.

● Berkus method

"I have had a unique formula that I built in the early 1993 period when beginning this business that I have never wavered from."

Dave Berkus

Dave Berkus created his own methodology for investing in early-stage deals. Typically he invests $200k and values the deal based on this simple formula:

For a sound idea	$1m
For a prototype	+$1m
For a quality management team	+$1–2m
For a quality board	+$1m
For any roll-out, sales	+$1m

Thus, the total value will be between $1m–$6m.

Pros: Identifies a clear relationship between price and tangible aspects of the opportunity. Simple. The result is always a reasonable start-up valuation.

Cons: The definition of these items may require lengthy discussions with the entrepreneur. Also, "quality" is deal specific and judgment requires industry and investing knowledge.

Time estimate: Thirty minutes to one hour to understand the qualifiers as they relate to the deal.

● Rule of thirds

"I find it usually comes down to this."

Lucius Cary

Despite all their calculations and premium educations, most VCs will admit that many deals come down to this. Lucius Cary applies this rule to the early-stage round, figuring that 1/3 should go to the founders, 1/3 to the capital providers, and 1/3 to management. He believes that the founders and management are usually not the same.

Pros: Simple and quick.

Cons: The line between founders and management is not always so clear and founders often have high personal value perceptions.

Time estimate: Fifteen minutes.

● $2m–$5m angel standard

"The initial valuations of my best deals have all been under five."

Angel investor CL

Most traditional angel investors invest at valuations of between $2m–5m, David Solomont says, "*$2.5m is the sweet spot.*" They have found that these are acceptable numbers for start-ups that have a reasonable chance of making it and where they don't play a controlling role. If the entrepreneur is asking for less than $2m, they are likely to be unsophisticated or lacking in significant progress. If they are asking for more than $5m, they either have dollar signs in their eyes or are quite advanced and really ready for venture capital.

Pros: Quick and easy, proven.

Cons: What exactly fits as "sophisticated" or "reasonable chance to succeed"?

Time estimate: Ten minutes (to check your gut).

● $2m–$10m internet standard

"A single digit is my general view of a seed round."

Audrey MacLean

The internet age has arrived which not only means a whole new development in business, but start-ups that can go at the speed of light to the public markets. The valuations of internet and some other high-tech start-ups have been operating in the $2–10m range. While these valuations will fluctuate more in the future, many high-tech investors have been successful, some even going to $20m in an angel round. Angel investor Brian Horey says:

❝ I tend not to like to invest in things that have more than a $10m valuation. Less than $5m is where I'd like to be, just because the law of large numbers compounding tends to catch up with you in time. ❞

Pros: Fast, which is needed in internet time.

Cons: Potential for company to overrun its valuation if it starts too high. If the second-round investors invest at a lower valuation, employee morale will suffer, early investors will be unhappy, and other types of fallout will require management time and focus. While this method may be in use, we do not believe the higher end is in the fundamental best interests of the entrepreneur, the investors, or the employees.

Time estimate: Fifteen minutes (to check your gut and take some Maalox™).

ACADEMIC/INVESTMENT BANKER

● Multiplier method

"One of the best ways is if the company is in a segment relating to established companies, either public companies or companies that have been financed recently."

Darryl Wash

Multiply a key number in the business plan times an industry standard, e.g. a nursing home start-up might project 2,000 beds and if $60k per bed is an industry standard for valuing a nursing home, the company could be worth $120m when it attains its target. That is how simple the multiplier method is, except for finding the right number to use, which is not so easy.

Pros: Looks at similar companies and the valuation process used by Wall Street bankers, or other knowledgeable investors.

Cons: Does not take into account the investor's risk, time, or cost of money, neither does it directly suggest how to price a deal now.

Time estimate: Fifteen minutes to eight hours, depending on your previous experience.

● Discounted cash flow

"It is a different language when it comes to start-ups and early-stage investing"

Andrew Blair who ignores *"academic"* valuation techniques, such as DCF

A financial calculation involving the concepts of present value, future value, interest, and periods of time. These calculations require some hands-on learning that cannot be addressed adequately in this book. Essentially, discounted cash flow means identifying a potential value of the company in the future, then "discounting" it by reducing it x% for every year between the future date and now. For example, if we think Tin-Tin's start-up will be worth $20m in five years, and our discount rate is 50% (the percentage we need the company shares to increase in value annually in order to make it worth our while), then the value of the company today in our opinion is $2.6m. $2.6m, generating 50% annually for five years, would be worth $20m. We could invest at a $2.6m valuation whether we were investing $100k or $1m. Carl Guerreri believes that you can't really base anything on the projections, as they are just not valid. He says, *"If you use DCF you are likely to overvalue the company."*

Pros: Risk and time are considered in determining the company value.

Cons: Complicated unless you have done it before or know how to use a financial calculator. Discounted cash flow also has the disadvantage of reducing the attractiveness of long-term projects that generate positive cash flow later, something an early-stage investor should not "discount" too quickly.

Time estimate: Two minutes to calculate, one to eight hours to understand and agree on the numbers involved.

PROFESSIONAL VENTURE CAPITALIST

● Venture capital method

This method builds on the multiplier and the discounted cash flow methods to determine how much of a company you need to own in order to achieve your financial return requirements, assuming some certain future value of the company. It sounds complicated at first but it is quite do-able. It works like this:

1 Determine the future value of a company using the multiplier method in a given year, say $25m in year 5.

2 Decide what ROI you need on your investment and calculate the future value to the same year. So if you are investing $100k and need a 50% return, in year 5, your investment should be worth $759,375 at that time.

3 Now simply divide the value you need ($759k) by the future value of the company ($25m) and that will tell you the percentage of the company you need to own. $759k/$25m = 3%.[3]

Pros: If the projections are accurate, the VC method is reasonably accurate. But, that is a big **1f**. More important, however, is that this method can demonstrate when a deal could never generate interesting returns, and therefore it may serve a better purpose as a deal killer.

Cons: Requires several calculations that are based on unsubstantiated financial projections.

Time estimate: Fifteen-thirty hours to really get into the numbers and make sure your calculations have more than a dart-throwing chance.

---

3 If you expect the company to raise a second round of capital and give up, say, 50% of the company, you would need to own 6% at the time of your investment.

COMPENSATED ADVISOR

● Virtual CEO method

"I essentially invest management time and experience."

Randy Komisar

This method includes providing significant support to a start-up in exchange for a percentage of equity. It is a method for pricing contribution, as opposed to a company. The virtual CEO almost becomes part of the team. Some things a virtual CEO would do include: guide the entrepreneurs to finish their plan, assist in closing angel investors, arrange for introductions to VCs, interview and hire new talent. Estimated percentages a virtual CEO takes range from 1% to 5% of the equity.[4] In some cases they may also charge $2k–5k per month.

Pros: No financial risk, you sell your time. Also, you are a stakeholder and your motivations are generally seen as being in line with the founders.

Cons: Creates a different kind of relationship, you may not be perceived as a true insider.

Time estimate: Fifteen minutes to set the number following dozens of hours to get to know the entrepreneur. Since the relationship will be very involved, substantial upfront due diligence and relationship building is necessary.

● Start-up advisor method

"The amount of equity is really insignificant compared to the value that can be generated by a serious advisor. For example, what is the value of an introduction to Draper Fisher Jurvetson that results in an offer?"

Tom Wharton

The advisor method is similar to the virtual CEO, except the level of expectation is significantly reduced. The angel agrees to provide some support to the start-up in exchange for some modest equity, 0.25% to 2%, sometimes with the intention of investing if the deal comes together. In some cases a monthly fee may be involved depending on the expected contributions of the advisor. This is more appropriate when the start-up is undeveloped and there is substantially more risk. "Advisors"

---

4 Common sense dictates that this depends on the amount of progress already achieved and the expected value added of the virtual CEO.

have been known to charge up to 10% in situations where there is just a guy with an idea. Committing to invest if certain, achievable events occur, further strengthens the angel's argument for upfront equity.

Pros: Allows a closer look at the company before investing by working in the business but insures some value for time. It also provides a way for a non-liquid but value-added investor to participate in an early-stage deal.

Cons: Without a track record, it may be difficult to convince the entrepreneur.

Time estimate: Several hours to get to know the entrepreneur. Since the relationship will be very involved, substantial upfront due diligence and relationship building is necessary.

VALUE LATER

● Pre-VC method

"Yes, but there are much bigger discounts that are reasonable and sometimes it's the opposite. It's not a discount at all. In some cases it is a premium."

Tim Draper when asked if 10–30% was a reasonable discount to a VC round

This relatively new method includes investing cash into a start-up without any shares exchanging hands and with no price set on any future transaction! It may sound absurd but it has become the method of choice for many sophisticated and successful angel investors. Essentially, the angel invests capital with the understanding that her terms will be the same as those in the coming VC round, but at a discount to that round. Discounts of 10% to 50% are possible. The initial agreement often takes the form of a loan note, payable in 12 + months.

The investors in PlanetAll used this method, and Warren Adams, the founder, describes the benefits:

❛❛ The reason we did that, was not so much to get a higher valuation, I think a bigger part of it is that it makes the initial investors' decision a lot easier. They don't have to worry about valuation. They know that someone who is professional, some way down the road, will put an appropriate valuation on the company. ❜❜

Pros: Avoids any value negotiation! Avoids any structure negotiation on equity. Assures the same terms as professional VC investors, but at a premium price.

Cons: Slightly complicated, with no control over the eventual valuation.

Time estimate: Five–ten hours if the contract needs to be negotiated.

● O.H. method

"When you are trying to get the money in quickly, leaving out the valuation question is helpful."

Warren Adams

This method, which comes from angel investor OH, is primarily for controlling angels. The entrepreneurial team is guaranteed 15% of the company after the final round of capital, which is protected by an anti-dilution clause. The investor usually provides all or the lion's share of the investment and is prepared to provide the next round or see that it happens.

Pros: The entrepreneur does not have to worry about dilution, assuming they accept the 15% number. Investor is in control.

Cons: Entrepreneurs might be less motivated, given the lack of control and the lack of impact of cost management on their compensation.

Time estimate: One to four hours to discuss and come to agreement.

CHAPTER 23

**INTERELATE
EXAMPLE**

THE 12 METHODS APPLIED

To demonstrate how the methods work in practice and the range of valuations that may occur in one deal, we have taken one of David's investments, Interelate Inc, and applied each of the 12 valuation methods.

In 1999 David invested in the angel round of Interelate, the first Customer Intelligence ASP which was launched in July 1999. The founder, Wade Myers, is a Harvard MBA who is an application outsourcing executive, and CRM subject matter expert. Wade Myers is a serial entrepreneur who has co-founded six new ventures. Interelate was later capitalized with over $25m from Goldman Sachs, Dell Computer Corporation, and several other prominent venture funds and individual investors. The company has more than 150 employees and is headquartered in Eden Prairie, Minnesota.

See how each of the valuation methods works and the results that are obtained when they are applied to Interelate as it stood in October 1999, when it raised its first round of capital. We will then look at what happened in two follow-on rounds.

Multiplier method

The multiplier method could be used in two ways, since Interelate has financial projections going out three years; a current-year valuation, and a 3rd year valuation. Since the ASP industry has several public companies with known revenue multiples, it is possible to value it by using a revenue multiplier. The relevant numbers would be:

> Interelate expected revenues in year one: $3m
> Interelate expected revenues in year three: $134m
> The appropriate revenue multiple for year one: 21x[1]
> The appropriate revenue multiple for year three: 5x

Estimated value of the company in current year, based on projection of $3m in revenues: $3m * 21 = **$63m.**

Estimated value of the company in year three based on projection of $134m in revenues: $134m * 5 = **$670m.**

---

1 Based on the valuation of comparable public companies, such as Usinternetworking, Breakaway, and others.

Discounted cash flow

According to the company financials, it expects a profit of $8m in its third year of operations. A purely financial investor would have to assign a multiple to this number, taking into consideration its expected longevity. If a multiple of 10 is used, then the value of the stream of cash flows is $80m in the third year. An investor would discount this back to the present by using the rate of return she expects, let's say 40%.

The relevant numbers therefore are:

$8m assumed cash flows in year three
Cash flow multiple of 10
40% required rate of return per year
3 years

Estimated value of the company in current year based on discounted cash flow method = $29,154,518.[2]

If we use a lower multiple, such as five, which would be realistic if no growth was expected and we were purely a financial investor/buyer, then the estimated value in year three would be $40m. The estimated value today would be $14,577,259.

$5m limit

This method is as simple as it sounds. It says, "*$5m or less is the value of the company.*" As long as the entrepreneur asked for less than $5m, the valuation would be okay. Since Wade asked for a $2m pre-money valuation, the price would be $2m.

Berkus method

Interelate had about half of its initial management team on board. The idea was sound and the plan was done. There were three board members and one initial sale, although it was a consulting sale and not a true ASP client transaction. So in some cases, we could give half credit. Here is how Interelate would score using the Berkus method.

	Berkus rule of thumb	Interelate score
For a sound idea	$1m	$1m
For a prototype	+$1m	$0m
For a quality management team	+$1-2m	$1m
For a quality board	+$1m	$500k
For any roll-out, sales	+$1m	$500k

Thus, the estimated value is $3m.

2 A financial calculator, such as an HP-12C, is helpful to determine this number. Discounted cash flow is too complicated to explain on one page. This is one thing you might want to learn if you don't already know it as there is always an implied DCF calculation. However, if you follow all of the fundamentals and invest at a reasonable price, you will do well anyway.

Rule of thirds

In its first round, Interelate raised $700k. So, according to the rule of thirds, the value would be **$2.1m** since 1/3 of the equity would go to the investors. ($700k divided by 33% = **$2.1m.**)

$2–$5m angel standard

Most angels will invest at a $2–5m price, which is often set by the entrepreneur. Wade asked for $2m, so the price would be **$2m.**

$2–10m internet standard

Interelate was not an internet company, so this valuation method doesn't really apply. If it did, the value would be $2–$10m.

The venture capital method

The venture capital method would take into consideration the future value of the company based on some expected liquidity event. If the market is valuing similar companies at 5x revenues three years out, then it would be reasonable to assume that such a price would be paid if the company went public. However, any VC would have some good way to reduce the $670m value (based on the multiplier method, the first method in this chapter), using analysts' multiples and/or company projections. They would, of course, say they don't think the company can achieve those numbers. So they might decide that $150m is a reasonable 3rd year valuation.

The relevant numbers[3] in this equation might be:

> $150m year 3 value of the company if sold
> $700k investment[4] considered
> 3 years to date valuation (or supposed exit event)
> 75% required rate of return

In order to earn 75% on $700k over three years, the value of the investor's stake in year three would have to be $3,751,562. This would represent about 2% of the company (3.7m/150m) and therefore, the total current value would be **$35m** ($700k/2%).

However, no VC would ever do that; they would come up with a number that gave them something like…33%. So, $700k/33% = **$2.1m.**

---

3 We have not included dilution to make this easier. We will discuss dilution later as it impacts any valuation using future projections.

4 Almost all VCs would invest more and at a later round. We will complete this example to show how it works.

What this example really shows (we hope) is that the venture capital method is based on big assumptions and is really more appropriate where larger dollars are concerned and a better estimate of the future can be completed. If, at the end of Interelate's second year, it has $10m in sales, it would be easier to project sales into the future and then use the VC method.

Pre-VC method

This method results in putting the price off until the next round. We don't want to spoil the story, but yes, Interelate did raise another round after this first one. The value of the company was $10m in the second round, so a discount of 30%, for example, would result, later of course, in a price setting of **$7m**.

OH method

Since there is not a controlling investor, the OH method is not relevant here. If the $700k had come from one investor, he would simply own 85% of the company from day one, but the entrepreneur would own 15% with a full ratchet, anti-dilution clause allowing him to keep his 15% until the company achieved an exit event. You could say the company was valued at $823,529 (700,000/85%), but that would not really be accurate since the investor will take not only his but also the entrepreneur's dilution going forward.

SUMMARY OF VALUATION RESULTS

Now here are the results in detail. Remember that neither the internet nor the OH methods are applicable and the compensated advisor methods are irrelevant, so we won't include them:

Method	Derived Interelate value
Multiplier method	$63m
Discounted cash flow	$29m
$5m limit	$2m
Berkus method	$3m
Rule of thirds	$2.1m
$2–5m angel standard	$2m
Venture capital method	$35m
Pre-VC method	$7m

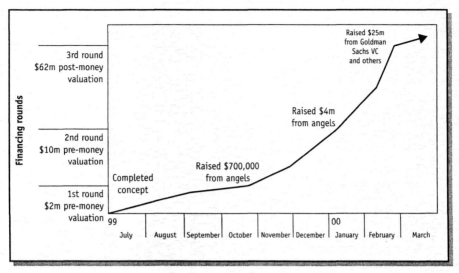

FIGURE 23.1

WHAT HAPPENED?

Figure 23.1 shows not only the first capital round and valuation, but the next two as well.

The first round was done at a $2m pre-money, followed three months later by a $10m pre-money round and then a $62m venture round.

WHICH METHOD IS BEST?

Choosing an early stage valuation method is one time when you can have your cake and eat part of it too. The complexity, and therefore time requirement, of a valuation method is not positively correlated with accuracy. In Figure 23.2, you can see the various valuation methods in relation to their accuracy and complexity.

CHOOSING AN EARLY-STAGE VALUATION METHOD IS ONE TIME WHEN YOU CAN HAVE YOUR CAKE AND EAT PART OF IT TOO

If you are providing capital to a high-risk venture, it is reasonable to share in the upside of that venture. The angel standard exists because most angels have realized that such a valuation, with the right deal structure, positions them to get a win. Anything beyond $5m limits your upside and may not make sense from a valuation standpoint.

Therefore, we think the angel standard is the most sensible.

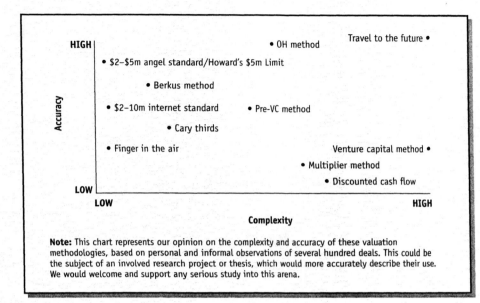

Note: This chart represents our opinion on the complexity and accuracy of these valuation methodologies, based on personal and informal observations of several hundred deals. This could be the subject of an involved research project or thesis, which would more accurately describe their use. We would welcome and support any serious study into this arena.

FIGURE 23.2

CHAPTER 24

FOUR LEVERS OF
EARLY-STAGE RETURNS

There are four significant levers of financial returns in the early stage. Think of them like switches on a current. They all have to be "on" in order to get a win. If only one is turned off, you will not succeed.

1 ● WHETHER YOU CHOOSE WINNERS

This is the subject of the sourcing and evaluation chapters in this book. The biggest lever of early stage returns is the deal itself, and if the company goes public and you own a percentage, no matter how diluted, no matter how high your valuation or ineffective your deal structure (as long as you do, in fact, own shares) you are likely to get some kind of a win. If you do a marginal job at each of the following and pick a winner, you will do exceptionally well.

2 ● HOW THE DEAL IS STRUCTURED

Poor structure thinking and implementation can result in a loss of the upside. So this switch, if not turned "on", can cause you to lose the value you deserve. For example, one angel we know once invested in an early-stage direct marketing company by signing a one-pager for 10% of the company in exchange for capital and time. When the company later raised a second round and finally distributed its shares, the entrepreneur had second thoughts about the deal and openly considered not providing the equity. In the end he did, and the company later went public. But the one-pager, which in this case didn't have sufficient legal force, meant that the investment was nearly lost by an entrepreneur's change of heart. The eventual upside in that deal? About $7m.

3 ● THE PRICE YOU PAY

Since ROI is a function of today's price and tomorrow's price (present value and future value to financial people), the valuation at which you invest is a significant lever of future financial gain. Consider the following example, where you might invest $100k in GreatDeal.com which later goes public for $100m and you sell out (Table 24.1). Your initial valuation determines your ROI and your final cash out.

TABLE 24.1

Your investment	Initial valuation	Exit valuation (in 5 years)	Your cash out[1]	Annual ROI
$100k	$1m	$100m	$10m	151%
$100k	$2m	$100m	$5m	119%
$100k	$4m	$100m	$2.5m	90%
$100k	$5m	$100m	$2m	82%
$100k	$10m	$100m	$1m	58%

Mathematician alert! It's non-linear! Although it may not be obvious, the initial valuation at which you invest has a non-linear effect on your TOTAL ROI. For example, if you invest at a $10m valuation and the company is soon worth $20m, you made 2x your money, or 100% total return (assuming no dilution). But, if you invest at half that, say a $5m valuation, you will get 300% on your money, not·200% as one might suppose. Half the valuation means triple the return. Take it further, if you invest at one-fifth of the originally proposed $10m valuation or a $2m valuation, and the company still becomes worth $20m, you will make 900% on your money not 500%. Each decrease in valuation has a non-linear impact on your total return. Remember that a low price does not make a good deal, but a high price can make a good deal a bad investment.

> **Total ROI versus ROI**
>
> Remember that ROI (return on investment) normally refers to the annual return on capital. If your savings account pays 4.1%, that is the ROI. TOTAL ROI is the total percentage increase over the life of the investment.

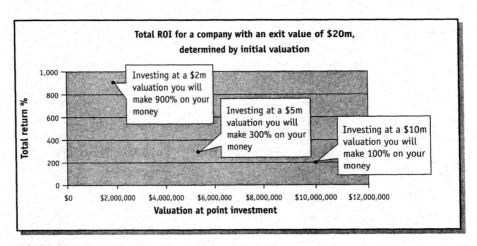

FIGURE 24.1

---

1 Be careful! Dilution is not taken into account here.

4 • HOW MUCH DILUTION OCCURS

This is not entirely within your control, except to the extent that you choose deals with relatively smaller, ongoing cash needs. Every time another investor or group of investors joins the company, your percentage of ownership is decreased, unless you invest additional capital to maintain it. Consider Table 24.1 again to see how dilution impacts your cash return and ROI. Compare this with Table 24.2.

TABLE 24.2

Your investment	Initial valuation	Additional rounds	Exit valuation (in 5 yrs)	Your cash out	ROI
$100k	$5m	None	$100m	$2m	82%
$100k	$5m	1 at 10%	$100m	$1.8m	78%
$100k	$5m	1 at 50%	$100m	$1m	58%
$100k	$5m	1 at 30%+ then 1 at 30%	$100m	$980k	58%
$100k	$5m	1 at 30%+ then 1 at 10%	$100m	$1.3m	66%

Companies with smaller than average cash needs have the following characteristics:

- A frugal CEO.
- Products/services that are far along in the development cycle (i.e. ready for sale).
- Little need of hard assets, such as custom buildings, manufacturing equipment.
- Limited competition (competitors can change the landscape at short notice).
- Relatively early exit potential, ability to create perceived or real value within 1–3 years.
- Favorable working capital cycle (subscription versus R&D).
- Limited or no inventory.
- Customers who pay in advance, upfront or quickly.
- Suppliers that give favorable credit terms.

CHAPTER 25

THINGS TO THINK ABOUT

WHAT TO SHOOT FOR...

"At this valuation, even if it's the most successful product, company, etc., you'll never get your money back."

David Solomont, talking about an over-priced deal

Angels shoot for anywhere from a 30% to 100% annualized ROI and more. Others describe it in multiples, such as 5x or 10x. Depending on the perceived risk, they need to know they have a shot at earning a significant return.

"Five times my money... 50% annually or better... a whole lot," are some of the ways winning angels describe their expected upside.

If you are going to risk losing all of the capital you place in an early-stage deal, and this, despite what anyone might say, is exactly what you are doing, then the potential returns must be dramatic.

IF YOU CAN CONSISTENTLY EARN ABOVE 30% ACROSS YOUR PORTFOLIO, YOU WILL BE SUCCEEDING LIKE MOST OF THE BEST ANGELS ON THE PLANET

Remember EV (expected value) as we described it on page 18 If you buy into the portfolio approach to angel investing, and we hope that you do, then you know that you must invest in enough opportunities with positive EVs, so that your final capital returns will be good.

If you generate 20–30% across all of your investments, which means you might have several losers but one or two that pay 100% or more, then you will be performing at a level that is successful given most of the other opportunities in the marketplace. If you can consistently earn above 30% across your portfolio, you will be succeeding like most of the best angels on the planet.

OPTIONS ON THE ENTREPRENEUR?

There is another, often over-looked, aspect to value in early stage deals: options on future opportunities.

In some cases, once you have invested in a company you will gain access to: unique expertise, new deals, follow-on investment opportunities, and contacts. These "options" can be worth far more than the upside of the original investment. Consider the following:

● **An option on the entrepreneur**

If the relationship is positive and the interaction is meaningful, you will be likely to have additional investment opportunities with this entrepreneur.

● **An option on the industry**

By investing in a developing industry, you may gain unique insight into the industry and the developing markets, which will allow you to make other investments in early- or later stage companies with a competitive advantage.

● **An option on future financing rounds $$$**

This option is sometimes part of the subscription agreement. For example, a preemptive right grants the investor the option to maintain her relative position by providing new capital. Regardless of the legal agreement, if investors maintain a positive dialogue with the entrepreneurial team, they will often have the opportunity to place additional capital since it is usually in everyone's best interest.

● **An option or exposure to additional relationships**

Making an investment can open doors to new co-investors, new entrepreneurs (which may come from the management team in the future), and other types of relationships, such as attorneys or strategic partners.

THE FEEL GOOD FACTOR

"Nice and low."

Angel investor CL

The feel good factor should not be underemphasized. Regardless of the calculations, comparables or logic of the situation, both the entrepreneur and angel are likely to have a feel good number, which will make them feel... good.

Jeff Parker, when asked about selling one of his companies, or investing in a new deal, says he uses the "feel good" number to make final decisions. Once all the analysis is done you simply need to decide, *"Do you feel good about the numbers?"* Mitch Kapor has different words for dealing with value: *"Go by instinct,"* he says. Mitch prefers to see someone else negotiate the deal, then he can decide if it works for him.

IT IS IMPORTANT TO MAINTAIN YOUR FUTURE RELATIONSHIP WITH THE ENTREPRENEUR

It is important to maintain your future relationship with the entrepreneur, as Craig Burr, a Boston investor, once said to an entrepreneur: *"I don't know if this is going to be your big win. But I do believe you will have one and I would like to participate in that."* Craig is a believer in identifying winners and sticking with them. Hard negotiation on value might muddy the waters for the next deal.

Other investors have similar viewpoints. When they find a quality entrepreneur, they want to join them and stay with them. So consider that even if the valuation does not seem ideal, it may be worth participating in view of other opportunities it will lead to.

HARD NEGOTIATION ON VALUE MIGHT MUDDY THE WATERS FOR THE NEXT DEAL

CHAPTER 26

WINNING ANGELS 2000

The following excerpts from *The Winning Angels Study* ©2000, by David Amis and Jocelyn Dinnin: "What do most investors do?", "What do the winners do?" and the selected winning tools and tactics, are reprinted with permission. Highlights of this study were published in *The Winning Angels Handbook*.

WHAT DO MOST INVESTORS DO?

- **Calculate a lot of numbers**

  Reading the financial section thoroughly, they look for numbers that may not be believable. Then they do their own calculations, trying to discern how much money can be made.

- **Focus on the plan or the market**

  They decide that either the numbers in the plan or the total potential market should be used to decide what potential profits can be made. For example, a new automobile anti-theft device may take 10% of the $120m market of anti-theft devices therefore generating $12m in sales eventually.

- **Follow other investors**

  Many angels (particularly when they come later to the party) will just accept the valuation to which other investors have already agreed.

- **Use a combination of methods**

  Apply various valuation methods, which results in a range of value options.

WHAT DO THE WINNERS DO?

- **Use numbers to discount or kill**

  In Bill Sahlman's Entrepreneurial Finance class at Harvard Business School, students use future value expectations to eliminate opportunities. For example, if a new restaurant concept (Lynn's Lasagne) required $750,000 to start-up, but the best similar restaurants in the area had selling prices of only $1m and incomes of $100,000, it would be impossible to generate more than 15% on your money. A poor return for a true start-up investment and therefore not deserving of your money. Whenever you can use numbers to knock out deals without the potential to generate real returns (50% or greater), you have saved your capital to fight another day.

- Go to Harvard (and realize that they don't know either)

  There are limits to how exact one can be in valuing early-stage deals and the winners know this because they made a point of getting the best information available. The result of their hard earned experience, there is nothing exact in early-stage deals. *"If you are going to use analytical tools, choose tools that are appropriate to the investment... the older the business is – the more detailed the analysis,"* says Lucius Cary, who has been known to value early-stage deals on a third of a piece of napkin.

  WHENEVER YOU CAN USE NUMBERS TO KNOCK OUT DEALS WITHOUT THE POTENTIAL TO GENERATE REAL RETURNS, YOU HAVE SAVED YOUR CAPITAL TO FIGHT ANOTHER DAY

- Look for low-capital, large-market opportunities

  It is usually fairly discernible in an early-stage deal whether the capital requirement will be closer to $500k or $5m. It is also possible to see whether the revenues are more likely to be $1m, $100m, or $1bn. Winning investors source and evaluate lots of projects to find those with less capital requirements and larger potential markets. *"I like low capital requirement, high potential deals,"* says angel JT, an angel investor in such notable companies as Cellular One.

- Pass by it quickly

  Given the inexact science of early-stage deal valuation, many investors adopt simple rules in order to quickly get to a reasonable number. The thinking here is a small piece of a larger pie is preferred to no pie and that is what you will have while people are arguing about valuation.

- Leave it to the lead

  John McCallion says that if the entrepreneur has his price set up and it feels about right, he would rather go with it and avoid the aggravation of spending huge amounts of time on such a small deal. If he was the lead investor and putting in large amounts of capital, then he would do it differently.

WINNING TOOLS AND TACTICS

These two tactics, while explained earlier in the chapter, are worthy of further explanation.

$5m limit $$$

As an early-stage investor, you need an opportunity to earn greater than five times your money in so many years. Consider Table 26.1. A company valued at $10m needs to be worth at least $50m in five years. How many companies can realistically manage that? Therefore, if you focus on companies with present valuations of $5m or less, you are more likely to earn five times your money in five years.

TABLE 26.1

Invest in companies with valuations of close to or less than $5m

Company value today	Multiple	Company value in 5 years
$5m	5	$25m
$10m	5	$50m
$20m	5	$100m

✗ Berkus method

David Berkus, who has founded and run two companies, began angel investing in 1993. He developed a methodology for valuing companies from which he has not wavered since. He starts off by giving $1m of credit for a sound idea that he would like to invest in and builds from there. Typically he invests $200,000 per deal. Here, he·describes his valuation methodology:

> I give $1m credit to a good idea into which I feel I want to invest, even if it is just at the idea stage. Obviously the person who is going to be running the company (or at least the entrepreneur with the idea) shouldn't be diluted from day one just because I have jumped on his idea. So, $1m is for the idea. Another $1m is added if any substantial or measurable work has been achieved towards proving the idea. This might be a prototype, development of a software, build-out of a portion of the website, studies that go in depth enough for me to believe that the idea has legs in the form of either audience reactions studies or something a little less formal. Something where I can see that we are beyond the idea stage and into the prototype stage, one way or the other. That's another $1m, making $2m.
>
> From there, I will add capital based on the quality of the management, the quality of any board already recruited and the further development and role out of any product or service. My value range is anywhere between $1m (which would be too low) and $60m. Typically the valuation model for me falls in a $4–5m range. So I invest early on in a deal, but not necessarily at the absolute germination of an idea.

Berkus method formula

Entrepreneur asset	*Value*
A sound idea	$1m
Prototype, website, market study	+$1m
Quality management team	+$1–2m
Quality board, further development	+$1m
Any roll-out, sales	+$1m
	Range $1m–$6m

CHAPTER 27

SPECIAL SECTIONS

1 ● WHAT NUMBERS ARE REASONABLE?

Here is what a few angels had to say about valuation and return expectations.

Mitch Kapor

❝ I have seen companies valued at anywhere from $1m to $10m… if it's a big bull market… even angel rounds are astoundingly high. ❞

John Hime

❝ Usually the first guy should pay $.5m to $2m. Over $2m is not interesting. At these valuations even with lots of dilution I can usually get a pretty good return. (He typically invests $100k for 5–10%.) ❞

Lucius Cary

❝ I like to end up with about 25%… this leaves the entrepreneur incentivized and allows for dilution later… my smallest stake was 3%. ❞

Betsy Atkins

❝ A 20% discount to the VC round is reasonable. ❞

Audrey MacLean

❝ $3m to $11m for early-stage… but don't obsess over it. ❞

Randy Komisar

❝ I never negotiate value. (Randy Komisar takes equity to get the company started, then, if he invests, he invests at a substantial discount to the venture capital round.) ❞

David Berkus

66 My value range is anywhere from $1m to $6m. Typically, the valuation falls in a $4m to $5m range. 99

Tarby Bryant

66 $1.5m to $20m is the range. Most are in the $3m to $7m range. 99

Andrew Filipowski

66 It comes down to what the buyer will pay and what the seller will sell for. 99

Angel investor, SG

66 The first round will usually cost the entrepreneur 40–60% of the company. 99

George Kline

66 I want to see a 10–12 multiple in three years... and I want a 35% annual return, overall (on all of his investments). 99

Dick Morley

66 A factor of 10 in five years. That's our target of success. Now, do we make that? Very seldom. But when we do, it pays for all the failures. Investment is a spuriously statistical project. In other words, we lose money in every deal and make it up in volume, once in a while we get the big hit. There are all kinds of theories on that... A typical angel makes between 20–45% compounded in real dollars. 99

Darryl Wash

66 There is somewhat of an accepted valuation range in early-stage non-infrastructure companies of $3m–10m pre-money in today's environment. Any companies that are within that range we feel relatively comfortable with, and anything beyond that range has to have met some significant milestones. 99

Craig Burr

‟ 30% IRR on an angel deal.”

Denis Payre

‟ If you look at the two and a half to three years' track record, I think I am on average (I've not done a formal calculation) at five to seven times, on average. So, already I am shooting for a 100 x or even more, but I know that is going to happen only, probably, once or twice, and that is already going to be great.”

2 ● WINNING DEALS: INITIAL VALUATIONS, AND THE INVESTOR RETURN

Apple Computer

In 1978 angel investor Richard Kramlich invested $22,500 of seed capital into Apple Computer at a pre-money valuation of around $10m. The investment grew in value to over $5m, which was 222 times his investment.

StarMedia Network

Darryl Wash, along with a group of co-investors, put approximately $500,000 into StarMedia Network in 1997 in three rounds. The pre-money valuation of the first round (January 1997) was $4.6m, which increased to more than $130m for the final private financing round, which took place 18 months later. The company went public with a valuation of $1bn. The market value was 30 times their original investment.

RealNetworks

Mitch Kapor invested in RealNetworks at a valuation of $12m. There was a venture round *"in the 40's."* When the company went public, its valuation increased to greater than $5bn. *"Today it looks like a pretty good investment,"* he says.

Bargaindog.com

David Solomont invested in Bargaindog.com at a valuation of $1.1m. Six months later the company sold for $35m, generating a return of 14x.

Amazon.com

Angel investor Tom Alberg invested $100,000 at a valuation of $4m. Unfortunately, the angel who referred the deal to him decided not to invest because he felt the valuation was too high. The value of Tom Alberg's stake at exit was $26m, 260 x original investment.

The Body Shop

Perhaps the greatest angel return ever, as estimated by *Sunday Times Rich List 2000*, is the investment made in 1977 by Ian McGlinn, then a Sussex garage owner, of less than £10,000 for half of the Body Shop. This essentially valued the company at £20,000 ($33,000). *Sunday Times Rich List* approximated the value of the Body shop at £53.3m, which means that McGlinn may have earned 2,665 x his investment.

3 ● VISUALIZING RISK AND REWARD

(Extract from *"How to Write a Great Business Plan,"* by Bill Sahlman)
When it comes to the matter of risk and reward in a new venture, a business plan benefits enormously from the inclusion of two graphs. Perhaps *graphs* is the wrong word; these are really just schematic pictures that illustrate the most likely relationship between the opportunity and its economics. High finance they are not, but I have found both of these pictures say more to investors than 100 pages of charts and prose.

The first picture (Figure 27.1) depicts the amount of money needed to launch the new venture, time to positive cash flow, and expected magnitude of the payoff.

This image helps the investor understand the depth and duration of negative cash flow, as well as the relationship between the investment and the possible return. The ideal, needless to say, is to have cash flow early and often. But most investors are intrigued by the picture even when the cash outflow is high and long – as long as the cash inflow is more so.

THE WORLD OF NEW VENTURES IS POPULATED BY WILD-EYED OPTIMISTS

Of course, since the world of new ventures is populated by wild-eyed optimists, you might expect the picture to display a shallower hole and a steeper reward slope than it should. It usually does. But to be honest, even that kind of picture belongs in the business plan because it is a fair warning to investors that the new venture's team is completely out of touch with reality and should be avoided at all costs.

The second picture (Figure 27.2) complements the first. It shows investors the range of possible returns and the likelihood of achieving them. The example shows investors that there is a 15% chance they would have been better off using their money as wallpaper. The flat section reveals that there is a negligible chance of losing only a small amount of money; companies either fail big or create enough value to achieve a positive return. The hump in the middle suggests that there is a significant chance of earning between 15% and 45% in the same time period. And finally, there is a small chance that the initial outlay of cash will spawn a 200% internal rate of return, which might have occurred if you had happened to invest in Microsoft when it was a private company.

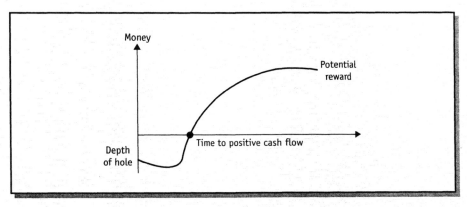

FIGURE 27.1

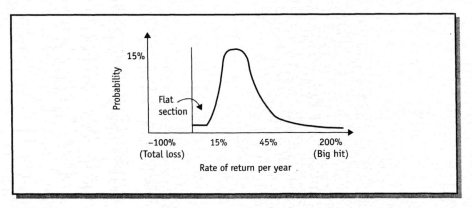

FIGURE 27.2

Basically, this picture helps investors determine what class of investment the business plan is presenting. Is the new venture drilling for North Sea oil – highly risky with potentially big payoffs – or is it digging development wells in Texas, which happens to be less of a geological gamble and probably less lucrative, too? This image answers that kind of question. It's then up to the investors to decide how much risk they want to live with against what kind of odds.

Again, the people who write business plans might be inclined to skew the picture to make it look as if the probability of loss is negligible.

IT'S THEN UP TO THE INVESTORS TO DECIDE HOW MUCH RISK THEY WANT TO LIVE WITH AGAINST WHAT KIND OF ODDS

And, again, I would say therein lies the picture's beauty. What it claims, checked against the investors' sense of reality and experience, should serve as a simple pictorial caveat emptor.

4 ● GREED

Not a lot has been written about this "dirty word". But it is out there and its green head has interfered with more than one promising deal. *"Greed is always a problem,"* say OH, *"Most failures I see come from greed or unrealistic evaluations."*

Greed, that ugly green word. In our interviews and experience in this area, this word represents a decision made by angel investors on how they approach deals.

Some angels look for every opportunity to better their position in a deal. They negotiate hard. They want very low valuations. They want the ability to fire the entrepreneur, even if they don't pay close attention to the business. Some won't like to think of themselves as greedy, they would probably say they are just being smart. They want long contracts and then, if the entrepreneur doesn't meet plan (which is what happens 99% of the time), they want even more equity and control. Although some of the winning angels interviewed for this book employ this style of investing, our experience is that a different strategy yields superior results in terms of fun, relationships, and ROI.

MOST WINNING ANGELS RECOGNIZE THAT THEIR RELATIONSHIP WITH THE ENTREPRENEUR IS ESSENTIAL

Most of the winning angels recognize that their relationship with the entrepreneur is essential, that the entrepreneur must be highly motivated not only to succeed but also to get a win for the investor. No contract in the world can force them to do this, and no contract, certainly, can inspire them to think creatively to reward their investor. One entrepreneur said:

❝ In my first deal, the angel spent all of his time trying to support me, even if he disagreed with a particular strategy, he would get behind the wheelbarrow and push, so to speak. Although he controlled the deal, he only interceded once on a strategic issue, the operations were left to me. I have not forgotten that guy and to this day, I offer to include him in every deal I do. ❞

Another entrepreneur describing an aggressive angel said:

❝ Those bastards forced me to take a contract that gave them 3% of the royalties aside from the equity and all the control issues. I had no choice since they were the only investor and we mutually owned the rights to the process. I'll be damned if I'm going to let them get one more ounce of value in this deal. ❞

Thus, many winning investors focus more on finding good people to work with, letting the more involved contracts and negotiations come later with additional rounds of capital. They believe that the first focus should be on their relationship with the entrepreneur, not what they can get out of him.

1 ● The simple and easy methods, such as the $2–5m angel standard, make the most sense.

2 ● Winners look for the potential to earn substantial returns in any deal (5 x or 50% ROI) or they don't do the deal.

3 ● Value is in the eye of the beholder.

4 ● The people in the deal are more important than the price.

Structuring

Every time I've been involved in a complicated deal structure I have lost all my money.

Bill Sahlman

28 ● Start section   181

29 ● Two camps   183
    Camp A: Structure is essential   183
    Camp B: Structure is irrelevant   183

30 ● Deal terms   185
    Dave and Ryan's menu of deal terms   185
    Appetizers   185
    Main courses   185
    Side dishes   187
    Desserts   188

31 ● The three fundamental structures   189
    Common stock   190
    Preferred convertible with various terms   191
    Convertible note with various terms   193

32 ● Future rounds   198

33 ● The VC perspective 202

Valuation 202

Efficient corporate action 202

Simplicity 203

Board of directors 203

Compensation 204

Founder stock 204

34 ● Winning angels 2000 205

What do most investors do? 205

What do the winners do? 205

Winning tools and tactics 207

35 ● Special sections 208

1 What kind of structure do you prefer? 208

2 CommonAngels standard term sheet 210

3 Interview with Bill Sahlman 213

4 Capitalyst™ – preferred deal terms 214

5 Draper Fisher Jurveston (DFJ) standard
   term sheet 214

4 TAKEAWAYS FROM STRUCTURING 222

CHAPTER 28

START SECTION

It has been said that the *what* and *who* of your investment are far more important than the terms. Deals change in subsequent rounds, and through unexpected events. No structure can foresee all the contingencies. Still, structure is important, and regardless of what principles you decide to follow, understanding the key elements could make or save you, say, $1m.[1]

Although winning angels agree on many of the tactics and strategies described in this book, in the case of deal structuring there are two distinct camps: structure matters; structure does not matter.

VCs, controlling angels, and previously burned angels think that structure matters. They want fine but strong ropes attached to the entrepreneurial team. They want to be able to: protect against downside, salvage the deal if necessary, claim more upside if it occurs, have a veto against certain kinds of activities, and protect themselves generally. They know that the moment of wiring the money is the moment when they have the greatest leverage and, that with the right contract, they can extend that power for a period of time.

Both enlightened and so-called virgin angels think that structure doesn't matter too much. They focus on trust with the entrepreneur or prefer to avoid hard negotiations, **VCS, CONTROLLING ANGELS, AND PREVIOUSLY BURNED ANGELS THINK THAT STRUCTURE MATTERS** which may sour the relationship. Additionally, they take the position that since the investment is a high-risk proposition anyway, downside protection is useless. If the deal succeeds, even common stock will deliver them a quality exit event.

It is not enough to just understand the various terms. Certain kinds of relationships are created based on the terms; relationships that include angel to entrepreneur, angel to angel, and angel to VC. In other words, you need to learn about the kinds of relationships that occur here and the impact that properly or improperly aligning your interests will have. Also, as we learned when we looked at negotiation, many angels think that negotiating to change the structure or the price is not a good start to their relationship with the entrepreneur.

Learning by doing is helpful here. But unlike the other fundamentals, a lot of what you need to know before doing deals you can learn by reading and thinking about the various terms, by reviewing term sheets that winning angels and VCs use (two are included in Chapter 34), and by discussing this with other angels and your attorney. After that, seeing the eventual outcomes of 100 deals is the only way to truly become an expert.

---

1 If the deal is a major winner, this is an underestimate as a poor deal structure might keep you from getting any liquidity.

Characteristics of sensible deals**

In my experience, sensible deals have the following characteristics:

- They are simple.
- They are fair.
- They reflect trust rather than legalese.
- They are robust – they do not blow apart if actual differs slightly from plan.
- They do not provide perverse incentives that will cause one or both parties to behave in destructive ways.
- They do not foreclose valuable options.
- The papers used to describe the deal are no greater than one-quarter inch.

** William A. Sahlman, Some Thoughts on Business Plans, Harvard Business School Case 897–101,
in William A. Sahlman, Howard H. Stevenson, Michael J. Roberts and Amar Bhidé,
The Entrepreneurial Venture 2/E. Boston: Harvard Business School Press, p. 165.
Copyright © 1996 by The President and Fellows of Harvard College.

CHAPTER 29

TWO CAMPS

While winning investors agree on many of the tactics and strategies in this book, this is one area that has bred real disagreement. From Jeff Parker who says, *"I will never do another common stock financing,"* to Dave Berkus who says, *"I want to have a trust built between the entrepreneur and me, so I almost always start my investment strategy with a common stock investment."* Winning angels have different strategies when it comes to structuring deals.

STRUCTURE IS ESSENTIAL

Many winning investors take a hands-on approach to negotiating structure, or they pay close attention – partly evaluating the deal based on the structure proposed. Tony Morris says, *"I have a rule, I will not invest in common stock, I will only invest in something that will be a preferred instrument."* He screens out common stock deals.

Controlling angels, coaching angels and lead angels are all likely to put their imprint on the deal structure as well as its price. One of the benefits of following an active lead is that the structure negotiation and review will have already taken place, at least usually.

> "I HAVE A RULE, I WILL NOT INVEST IN COMMON STOCK, I WILL ONLY INVEST IN SOMETHING THAT WILL BE A PREFERRED INSTRUMENT"

Silent angels, reserve force angels and others, might pay close attention to the structure, but never say anything about it. If their investment parameters are not met, they simply won't invest.

STRUCTURE IS IRRELEVANT

Many winning investors will take common stock, preferred stock, convertible notes, or whatever is offered. There are even investors who take common stock without a price attached to it!

Generally these silent or reserve force angels have made the judgment that the deal will either be wildly successful or it will fail. If it is a great success even the common stock investors without any protections will do fine. If it fails, the potential salvage operation (included in more involved contracts) will not be worth the time, energy or heartache.

Remember Doriot's *"A-quality"* maxim? It applies here as well. A-quality entrepreneurs are generally a better guarantee than any paper.

In some cases, angels arrive too late at the show to change the structure, and they simply decide based on the terms presented. *"If you're late in the process you have to accept the structure and terms that have been agreed to by others,"* says Darryl Wash.

A-QUALITY ENTREPRENEURS ARE GENERALLY A BETTER GUARANTEE THAN ANY PAPER

Regardless of the approach taken, investors should understand the fundamentals of early-stage deals, as they will certainly be confronted with them at some point in the near or distant future.

CHAPTER 30

DEAL TERMS[1]

DAVID AND RYAN'S MENU OF DEAL TERMS

Ich habe mein Mittagessen gegessen.

This opening quote is a German saying, which means, "I have eaten my lunch." It is used in deal making to communicate that the terms have been considered and accepted.

David teamed up with Ryan Schwarz at The Carlyle Group in Washington, DC, to bring you this special menu of early-stage and venture capital deal terms and structures. We hope you enjoy the selection!

APPETIZERS

Protection agreements (rarely eaten by angels, and indigestible to VCs)

● **Non-disclosure**

Investor will retain confidential information as confidential.

*[2]

● **Non-compete**

Investor will not compete for a certain period of time.

*

MAIN COURSES

Common shares (an old angel favorite)

● **Tag-along right**

Investor can sell shares when the entrepreneur, or anyone else, sells shares.

*****

● **Pre-emptive right**

Investor can invest in additional rounds to maintain percentage ownership.

****

1 For US investors. www.WinningAngels.com, will have terms for other countries.

2 Stars represent how beneficial this term is for investors taking into consideration not only financial aspects but the impact on the goodwill of the entrepreneurs and other investors.

- **Registration rights**

  Allows investors to register their stock in the event the company goes public, a must have.

  * * * * *

Preferred shares (the "preferred" choice of today's VCs)

- **Royalty rights**

  Investors earn a percentage of revenues (another porcupine fish dish).

- **Dividend rights**

  Investors get a preferential dividend, sometimes cumulative, sometimes deferred, sometimes not.

  * *

- **Registration rights**

  As above.

  * * * * *

- **Board rights**

  Investor(s) have the right to appoint one or more members of the board (or observation rights – earns an additional star).

  * *

- **Information rights**

  Investor has right to get certain internal information, sometimes in a structured report with deadlines.

  * * *

- **Liquidation rights**

  Investor gets additional superiority, other than sitting before common shares, in the event of a liquidation.

  * *

- **Conversion rights**

  Investor's shares can be converted into common (with any number of triggering events, such as a sale or the decision by the management or by the investor or both).

  * * * * *

- **Redemption rights**

  Investors can require the company to buy back the shares with a cumulative, annual dividend in a certain future year. This can be the investor's only protection against a profitable company that never creates an exit event (if set far out, e.g. five years).

  * * *

This decade's special

Convertible note (a new angel favorite).

- **Price conversion**

  Investor can convert into equity at a set price, such as $2/share.

  ****

- **Future price conversion**

  Investor can convert into equity at a price based on a future round, usually at a discount to that round (most popular = 10–50% discount to the VC round).

  *****

  (Note: Convertible notes have "triggers" which cause the conversion to happen. These are negotiable and include such options as: *"investor decides to"*; *"$1m+ is raised for the company"*; *"the company sells"*; or *"the company decides to".*)

- **Interest payments**

  Investor(s) get an annual interest payment, which is sometimes deferred. This can motivate the entrepreneur to create an exit event.

  **

SIDE DISHES

These terms or agreements can go with any of the courses.

- **Warranties and representations**

  Entrepreneur is held liable for making any false statements.

  ***

- **Anti-dilution**

  Investor is automatically given a new share price equivalent to any follow-on offering done at a lower price. Done either as a full ratchet (full re-pricing of investor's shares) or on a weighted-average basis (partial re-pricing).

  ***

- **Entrepreneur compensation limits**

  Not technically a term, it is often done through board or compensation agreements. It is a worthwhile addition to any deal since it motivates the entrepreneur to get an exit event through her shares, important when a lifestyle or empire builder entrepreneur may be present.[3]

  ****

- **Special voting or consent rights**

  Investor has a veto on major undertakings, such as a new share offer, debt,

---

3 See types of entrepreneurs on page 137.

insurance, sale of the company, acquisitions, etc. (more appropriate for VCs or controlling angels).

**

DESSERTS

● **Warrants**

In some cases, investors may take warrants as part of the deal to provide additional upside.

**

● **Follow-on financings**

In some cases, investors may have an option to provide the next round of financing. However, this often limits the company's ability to raise capital from outsiders.

● **Right of first refusal**

Investors get right to buy any shares sold by company founders/entrepreneur. Sometimes also if the entrepreneur leaves the company.

*

CHAPTER 31

THE THREE FUNDAMENTAL STRUCTURES

There are three structures which are common in angel investing. We list and describe them here, and with each structure, we comment on the following attributes:

- **Exit impact**

  Whether the structure promotes or reduces the likelihood of a timely and lucrative exit for investors.

- **Relationship impact**

  Whether there are no positive, or potentially negative ramifications.

- **Downside protection**

  The protection offered by the structure if the deal fails or "goes south."

- **Upside protection**

  The "protection" offered by the structure if the deal is highly successful. Protection might also be "upside opportunities." In any winning deal there is the potential to maintain a certain equity stake, usually by paying more, or to invest more in additional rounds.

- **Entrepreneur protection**

  Given the range of behaviors possible from the entrepreneur, are they constrained from causing damage to your investment in any way, aside from leading the company to failure?

- **Worst case scenarios**

  We list the potential outcomes that might make you cry.

- **Notes and suggestions**

  Anything else we can think of that you might want to consider.

You will notice that several of the significant attributes in this chapter have to do with negative scenarios. This is why some winning angels avoid dealing with structure or avoid negotiating at all costs. It is like starting off a marriage focused on the pre-nuptial.

TONY MORRIS: "THE RULE IS THAT YOU USE PREFERRED TO ATTRACT CAPITAL AND YOU USE COMMON TO ATTRACT STAFF"

COMMON STOCK

This is the *"complete faith"* option, which is used most often by family, friends, and fools, as well as winning angels who rely more on the integrity of the entrepreneur as well as their own ability to source and evaluate.

DICK MORLEY: "I LIKE JUST PLAIN OLD EQUITY, BECAUSE I DON'T HAVE TO THINK HARD. WHAT WE DON'T WANT TO DO IS SPEND A LOT OF TIME"

Angels who have been burned swear never to do it again, but the reality is that, unless they are going to control the deal, there is no structure that will keep them from losing money if the company fails or if the entrepreneur is dishonest.

This structure is the most simple, and simplicity has its advantages. A slightly more sophisticated and typical structure is to include pre-emptive and tag-along rights.[1] Either way, the offering agreements can be completed fast and there are no limits on the company in any way which would restrict raising further capital or its terms. VCs will be happy to see this structure as well, although they would never use it themselves.

ROB LOW: "INVESTORS WITH TIRE TREADS ON THEIR BACKS DON'T LIKE COMMON STOCK"

SUMMARY COMMON STOCK/UNITS

Exit impact
Common shares have no impact on exit.

Relationship impact
If the entrepreneur also has common, then your interests are nearly aligned.

Downside protection
None.

Upside protection
If the shareholder does not have registration or tag-along rights, they are at the mercy of the entrepreneur. However, with such rights and a cap on the entrepreneur's ability to take cash out of the company (i.e. through a large

---

1 Tag-along simply prevents a partial sale of the company, which could leave the investor with no exit opportunity. Alternatively, it may allow an entrepreneur to sell shares as long as the investor(s) can sell a similar percentage. Note that this does not mean a new investor is prevented from taking control, it simply means the entrepreneur cannot sell his shares without also offering the investor a similar exit.

salary, bonus or expense accounts), the shareholder does have reasonable upside protection.

Entrepreneur protection
None.

Worst case scenarios
1 You lose all your money.
2 The company is extremely successful and the entrepreneur sells her shares leaving you with a new partner.
3 The company fails immediately and the remaining capital is divided up according to shareholders' equity positions. The entrepreneur walks away with 60% of the remaining cash.

Best case scenario
You make a lot of money with limited time, involvement, and no additional risk.

Notes and suggestions
It is okay to use common with a quality person who is reasonably sophisticated, just get the pre-emptive and tag-along rights. If they didn't offer them, that is an indication of inexperience or bad faith on both the part of the entrepreneur and their attorney

PREFERRED CONVERTIBLE WITH VARIOUS TERMS $$$

This is the most common vehicle for VCs and many angels use it also. However, the VC agreement may have 40 terms and 100 pages while the angel's may have five terms and 10 pages.

TONY MORRIS: "I WON'T BUY COMMON STOCK, I WILL ONLY BUY PREFERRED"

Steve Walker, who has backed 35 early-stage companies, prefers preferred. He likes a liquidation preference, some dividend requirement, tag-along rights, registration rights, board representation, and the ability to put a market value on the company four to five years down the line to protect against a *"fiefdom."*

If the entrepreneur is proposing this, they are probably very experienced, or already have a lead investor. If this is not the case it is likely to take some negotiation to make the change. This is where a good lead investor can make a difference.

This structure is not that simple and will require some significant interaction with the entrepreneur in the hoped-for event that additional capital is raised or an exit obtained. Normal terms include: information rights, board rights, anti-dilution, redemption rights, pre-emptive rights, and tag-along rights. Investors have their own way of doing this and some entrepreneurs are sophisticated enough to already have their own desired terms.

Future required interaction with the entrepreneur depends on the general terms included in the preferred equity and the conversion terms. Likewise, any limits on the company will depend on those terms.

VCs will be less happy to see this structure as it may mean additional issues to resolve before they invest. However, they will respect it, since they usually pursue the same. The preferred share structure offers considerably more protection to the investor and this is why VCs require it and many angels come around to using it.

SUMMARY PREFERRED CONVERTIBLE WITH VARIOUS TERMS

Exit impact
Negative if any burdensome terms are included. Otherwise positive if the terms align interests of the entrepreneurs and investors.

Relationship impact
If offered by the entrepreneur, none. If negotiated, it's possible as the terms are reasonably complex.

Downside protection
The investor is ahead of the common shareholders, usually the entrepreneur and management, in the event of any liquidation. Additional terms, such as buy-out clauses or board seats, may provide added protection.

Upside protection
Yes, as long as you can convert into registerable stock with tag-along rights, which is normal.

Entrepreneur protection
To the extent it is possible. There is no fully protected situation short of control. Convertible preferred with aggressive terms can allow the investors to call votes, remove management, stop fund raisings, take future fund raisings, etc.

Worst case scenarios

1 You lose all of your investment.

2 The deal goes sideways and never generates significant returns but requires more time from you.

Best case scenario

You make a lot of money, including additional rounds, and you feel somewhat secure about it.

Notes

There are reasons why the VCs use preferred convertible. However, keep in mind that the nature of an angel deal and a VC deal are different.

Suggestions

Entrepreneurs who propose such structures should get more consideration. Negotiating with an inexperienced entrepreneur should be left to a serious lead or controlling angel.

CONVERTIBLE NOTE WITH VARIOUS TERMS $\boxed{\text{\$\$\$}}$

The convertible note is becoming a more common vehicle as financings are occurring in shorter time frames. Biotechnology, or more traditional businesses with long product development curves, would not be served by such a structure, unless the next capital round happens within 12 months. Some of the benefits of this structure include:

- Avoids a negotiation on price.

- Limits option pricing issues for the company (because it doesn't change the price of the common stock).

- Secures a liquidation preference in the event the company goes sideways.

John Hime, who has made 29 investments in early-stage technology companies, says:

> DAVID SOLOMONT: "WE'VE DONE A CONVERTIBLE NOTE, MAYBE TWO. I ALSO DON'T LIKE THOSE, BECAUSE ACTUALLY IT PUTS YOU ON THE WRONG SIDE OF THE TABLE FROM THE ENTREPRENEUR"

66 Since I am often the very first investor, and I prefer not to take common stock, I usually take a note that is convertible into preferred stock at some advantage (say 1/2 to 1/3) of the first preferred round. 99

Pricing by discounting to the VC round provides some complication. A 30% discount to the VC round, for example, means the price of the common shares is not set until a VC invests and then the conversion is based on a price 30% lower than that of the investor.

If the entrepreneur is proposing this, they are likely to be very experienced or they will already have a lead investor. If not, it will probably take some negotiation to make the change. Again, a good lead can make a difference. Some interaction with the entrepreneur will be required going forward although it may be as simple as, *"We raised our VC round and you are now an equity owner, per agreement."* The challenge of dilution is also removed, at least for the next round.

VCs will generally think this structure is okay, although they may not like the percentage discount if it is high. If they are far sighted, they will recognize that the angel capital played an important role, took more risk, and deserves a better valuation.

The 3-step note

This is a fairly new structure, which works as follows:

1 The investor "invests" $100k into a company as debt using a 10% note which can convert into equity based on the following formula:

   If venture capital is raised in 6 months, a 20% discount

   If venture capital is raised in 12 months, a 30% discount

   If venture capital is not raised in 12 months, the note becomes due

2 Although no one expects the company to pay the note, this provides real leverage to angel investors following disappointing performance of the entrepreneur. They can then use the notes to demand a sale of the company, to replace the entrepreneur, or to shut it down. In addition, in some cases a company will go sideways, generating small profits with no potential to get big. In this case, the entrepreneur may be able to pay back the notes, thus at least making the investors whole again.

3 If the business is successful, the angels will end up with equity on similar terms to the VC, except at a more angel-like price.

SUMMARY CONVERTIBLE NOTE WITH VARIOUS TERMS

Exit impact
To the extent it promotes a VC round, it has a very positive exit impact. Venture capitalists are the exit professionals.

Relationship impact
If offered by the entrepreneur, there is a positive impact, since most of the structure risk is removed from the deal. If negotiated, it can go either way depending on the people involved.

Downside protection
Having a loan note is just about the most powerful downside protection you can have, short of owning and leasing the assets.

Upside protection
The VC cannot negotiate a lower valuation than you since your pricing is tied to the VC's. Additional terms may include a right to participate in subsequent funding rounds with various stipulations.

Entrepreneur protection
Yes. You have a hammer if no institutional money shows up. If it shows up, you will be in the same boat as it is.

Worst case scenarios
1 You lose all of your investment.
2 The deal goes sideways and you spend some time negotiating a new outcome (generally a nice option to have).
3 The next round is valued at $30m and your 30% discount means you get a $20m valuation when you thought you were investing at $5m to $10m.

Best case scenario
You make a lot of money, including investing in additional rounds, and you spend almost no time negotiating or worrying about non-business risks.

Notes

If you put a cap on the valuation, say $8m, you solve #3 above.

Suggestions

Entrepreneurs who propose this are offering some significant leverage to the investors but are keeping the ability to increase the price significantly.

TABLE 31.1   THE APPROACHES AND HOW THEY WORK AT A GLANCE

	Impact on exit	*Downside protection*	*Upside potential*
Common stock/units no rights	None, except it gives the entrepreneur maximum freedom	None	Limited to initial shares/units ownership, no rights to invest additional capital
Common with pre-emptive and tag-along rights	None	None	1 Investor is given the chance to invest additional capital – to avoid dilution 2 Entrepreneur cannot sell his shares without also offering the investor a similar exit
Preferred convertible with various terms	Depends on additional terms. Complicated or irregular terms reduce the likelihood of second-round financings and some exit events	1 In the event of liquidation, the investor is ahead of the common shareholders 2 Additional terms may provide further protection, e.g. buy-out clauses or board seats	Depends on terms but is generally the best structure for capturing upside
Convertible note with various terms	Facilitates a VC round, and VCs are the exit pros	Loan note provides best leverage in the event of liquidation or work-out	Yes, if the conversion terms are favorable or if investors get the same terms as the VC

SUMMARY A FEW IDEAS ON FAILURE

"Don't invest with anyone who under any circumstances might do something that you wouldn't be proud of..." says Bill Sahlman.

Here are some ways to prepare for failure in a deal. Note that entrepreneurs should also think about failure and prepare for it. In Special section 4 of supporting (page 280), there is a letter, which you can give to your entrepreneurs about failing.

There are three ways you can get hurt:

- **Emotional**

It can be emotionally draining and unpleasant to participate in a failure, particularly if you have only done one or a few deals.

Best preparation:
Soul searching and acceptance up front that you can lose all of your capital. Recognition that a small percentage of early-stage companies succeed is also helpful. You are more likely to have failures than wins!

- **Financial**

If you have not planned accordingly, the financial loss can be significant.

Best preparation:
A financial review, as suggested in the "Know thyself" section Part I (page 5), is a must. Do not invest more than you can afford to lose!

- **Reputation**

Losing money in small amounts will not impact your reputation. However, if the entrepreneur misrepresents the opportunity to others, or your name is used to raise capital and anything funny happens (as in fraudulent funny not "hah-hah" funny), then there is reputational risk.

DO NOT INVEST MORE THAN YOU CAN AFFORD TO LOSE!

Best preparation:
Invest in "A quality" people and manage your perceived role with other investors so that it is consistent with reality. For example, if you are going to be a silent investor and are following other investors, be careful that you are not perceived as the lead.

Keep it very, very simple. You want to keep it very simple because the VCs get turned off by a complicated structure that they have to unwind or cannot do anything with.

Warren Adams, founder of PlanetAll and an active angel investor

Preparing for and thinking about future rounds is critical when choosing a structure and setting the terms. A bad deal structure can damage the company's ability to recruit additional investors, or even to sell at an attractive price. Winning angels are cognizant of the needs of venture capitalists, corporate investors, investment bankers, and other institutional investors that will provide the capital and support needed for the company to reach its best possible liquidity event. *"Typically the angel brings the deal to us – we invest together,"* says Tim Draper, of Draper Fisher Jurvetson.

Here are three examples of how high-potential start-ups progressed through multiple rounds.

EXAMPLE **INTERELATE FUNDING STEPS**

Interelate was described in the section on valuing (on page 157). It is headquartered in Eden Prairie, Minnesota, and is the first and leading Customer Intelligence ASP. The company launch took place in July 1999 and Wade Myers is the CEO and founder. He is a Harvard MBA, a seasoned entrepreneur, application outsourcing executive, and CRM subject matter expert.

Round 1
August 99–October 99
Raised $700,000

Deal structure and specific terms
• Common stock + pre-emptive rights
• $2m pre-money valuation

Round 2
November 99–January 00
Raised $4 million

Deal structure and specific terms
• Common stock + pre-emptive rights
• $10m pre-money valuation

Round 3
February 00–April 00
Raised $25 million

Deal structure and specific terms
• Preferred stock (pre-emptive preferential, + liquidation rights)
• $62m post-money valuation

EXAMPLE STARMEDIA FUNDING STEPS

StarMedia Network, Inc, ("StarMedia") is the leading online network targeting Latin America. StarMedia offers Latin Americans a large, pan-regional community experience, combined with a broad array of Spanish and Portuguese content tailored for regional dialects and local cultural norms. StarMedia consists of 17 interest-specific channels, extensive web-based community features, sophisticated search capabilities and access to online shopping in Spanish and Portuguese. StarMedia also provides internet access as well as Spanish and Portuguese language email, chat rooms, instant messaging and personal homepages.

INVESTMENT HIGHLIGHTS

- Significant first-mover advantage and faced little competition for the first year of its existence.
- Market share leader in rapidly growing segment of Latin American online users.
- Great penetration among users with very attractive demographics.
- Superb management team that has successfully created a large institution with offices in numerous cities in the US and in Latin America.

Current valuation
Publicly traded company with a market capitalization in excess of $1bn.

Round 1
January 1997

Deal structure and specific terms
- Common stock

Raised $506k
- $4.6m pre-money; $5.1m post

Round 2
April 1997

Deal structure and specific terms:
- Series A preferred stock

Raised $3.7m
- $5.2m pre-money; $8.9m post

Round 3
February 1998

Deal structure and specific terms
- Series B preferred stock

Raised $12m
- $23.6m pre-money; $35.6m post

Round 4
September 1998

Deal structure and specific terms
- Series C preferred stock

Raised $80m
- $130.0m pre-money; $210.0m post

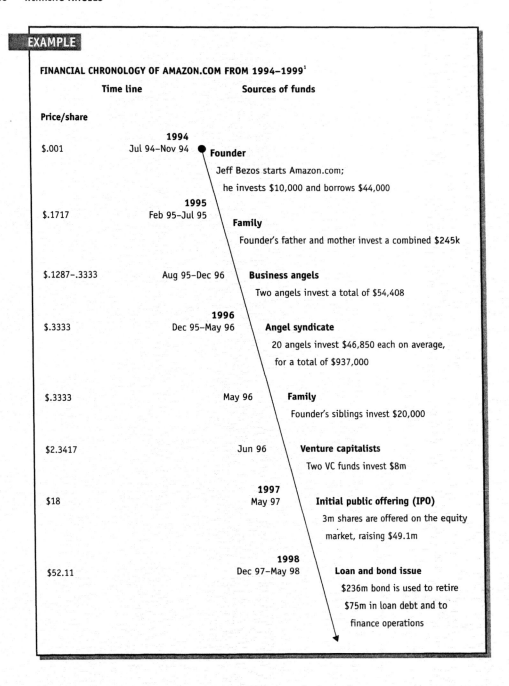

EXAMPLE

FINANCIAL CHRONOLOGY OF AMAZON.COM FROM 1994–1999[1]

| Time line | Sources of funds |

Price/share

1994
$.001   Jul 94–Nov 94   ● **Founder**
Jeff Bezos starts Amazon.com;
he invests $10,000 and borrows $44,000

1995
$.1717   Feb 95–Jul 95
Family
Founder's father and mother invest a combined $245k

$.1287–.3333   Aug 95–Dec 96   **Business angels**
Two angels invest a total of $54,408

1996
$.3333   Dec 95–May 96   **Angel syndicate**
20 angels invest $46,850 each on average,
for a total of $937,000

$.3333   May 96   **Family**
Founder's siblings invest $20,000

$2.3417   Jun 96   **Venture capitalists**
Two VC funds invest $8m

1997
$18   May 97   **Initial public offering (IPO)**
3m shares are offered on the equity
market, raising $49.1m

1998
$52.11   Dec 97–May 98   **Loan and bond issue**
$236m bond is used to retire
$75m in loan debt and to
finance operations

Source: Data partially adapted from Smith and Kiholm (forthcoming)

1 This figure is taken from *Angel Investing: Matching Start-up Funds With Start-up Companies*, by Mark van Osnabrugge and Robert J. Robinson, © 2000, Jossey-Bass, Inc. Reprinted by permission of Jossey-Bass, Inc, a subsidiary of John Wiley & Sons, Inc.

Here are three rules to follow in planning structure:

1 Keep it simple

Given that follow-on rounds will have different structures, it is imperative to keep the current round simple. This is to ensure that everyone can understand the first-round structure, and so as not to limit the ability of the management team or new investors to come to a new deal in a timely manner.

2 Don't restrict the company's ability to do future deals

Any restrictions on future dealing, except say, to protect against value discrimination or unreasonable dilution, should be avoided.

3 Make sure the valuation is reasonable

Many start-ups ran out of gas during take-off because the first valuation was so high that additional investors would not come in. Or, they came in at a better rate and everyone, including the old investors and employees with stock options were unhappy and demotivated.

CHAPTER 33

THE VC PERSPECTIVE

WHAT DO VCS WANT IN A DEAL ALREADY BACKED BY ANGELS?

Here is what Ryan Schwarz, a venture capitalist with The Carlyle Group, says about joining deals with angels.

Ryan Schwarz

> While the presence of experienced angel investors is undoubtedly positive in the eyes of venture capitalists, too often decisions made in structuring angel rounds get in the way of efficiently raising subsequent venture capital. Ideal angel-round terms are simple, clear, and not unduly restrictive. A few points are particularly important.

VALUATION

Valuation carries the greatest potential for havoc. Pricing benchmarks such as prior round valuation or company financial performance are usually absent in angel deals. In addition, pricing is often set by the entrepreneur rather than through a market-driven process. Angels with personal connections to the entrepreneur may not challenge proposed pricing. Resulting valuations can vary widely.

VALUATION CARRIES THE GREATEST POTENTIAL FOR HAVOC

In my experience, angel-round valuation can impede the first VC round, whether the angel price appears high or low in hindsight. If too high, the price inhibits serious VC interest. If too low, the entrepreneur feels "cheated" by his angel investors and seeks to recoup some of that value from the VCs.

To avoid such problems, price angel rounds at a fixed discount to the first institutional round price. Common discounts are 10–30%, or up to 50% if the angel round will fund a company for 6–12 months. Sophisticated entrepreneurs recognize that such a structure both speeds closing of the angel financing, and ensures that their angels will enthusiastically support the subsequent VC round. As noted elsewhere, this mechanism is most commonly effected through a convertible loan structure.

EFFICIENT CORPORATE ACTION

Poorly structured angel rounds can also paralyze subsequent corporate action, through ill-considered consent rights. Many experienced early-stage investors will negotiate VC-like voting provisions in which investor consent is required for major corporate decisions. Actions typically covered include subsequent financings, sale of the company, and amendments to existing corporate documents. Sophisticated entrepreneurs and angels will avoid an excessively democratic structure, in which such actions require the approval of a large number of individual investors.

Angels can try to structure their financings such that a few investors represent a super-majority of the round, or invest through an entity in which one person has voting authority. Alternatively, consider setting a sufficiently low threshold for investor approval that a small subset of all investors can bind the class. And avoid at all costs any major actions that require consent of 100% of existing investors, other than those mandated by applicable law.

In addition, investors' consent rights should be defined as shared by all preferred stockholders and convertible note holders, rather than separately held by each series of stock or notes. By setting this precedent in the angel round, subsequent investors can be added to the special voting rights class, rather than creating separate voting pools which further complicate corporate action.

SIMPLICITY

A simple angel round increases the likelihood of a simple VC round. The converse is also true: a complex angel round usually leads to complex amendment discussions with VCs. Early-stage investors should avoid, in particular, complex value apportioning mechanisms, such as ratchets, conditional warrants or participation features, that are expected to survive VC financing. If such features are included, the best that can happen will be an argument with VCs over removal. Worse, VCs may simply seek to mirror these features, and their much larger investment dollars will swamp the benefit early-stage investors could hope to gain from such structures.

BOARD OF DIRECTORS

The composition of a company's board of directors will change with each financing. Board seats properly are dependent, in part, on share ownership, which, of course, is a function of amount raised and valuation. Since the size and price of the next financing cannot be accurately predicted in advance, angels and entrepreneurs should not attempt to create a board composition mechanism that will *"accommodate the next round of investment."* In particular, avoid making legal or moral promises to specific investors of enduring board seats. Instead, offer observation rights to any early-stage board member who loses his seat post-VC financing.

COMPENSATION

This is one term that is most easily negotiated at angel-round stage, when the venture's financial resources are lowest. Consider reasonable limits on compensation for the entrepreneur and his

CASH COMPENSATION SHOULD NOT REQUIRE OR ENABLE THE ENTREPRENEUR TO CHANGE HIS LIFESTYLE POSITIVELY OR NEGATIVELY

team. A good rule of thumb is that cash compensation should not require or enable the entrepreneur to change his lifestyle positively or negatively. Only equity returns from an exit should do that. (Of course, this rule needs adjustment if the entrepreneur is leaving a large corporate employer or some other high-compensation environment.)

FOUNDER STOCK

Venture investors typically require protection in the event that the founders/entrepreneurs decide to leave the company. This is achieved either by applying a vesting schedule to founders' stock, or, less aggressively, obtaining a right to repurchase founders' stock upon their resignation/termination. Early-stage investors have the same interests as VCs in obtaining such protection. In addition, by negotiating these protections in the angel round, the entrepreneur won't feel that he is being asked to take a step backwards in a subsequent financing, by putting at risk of forfeiture share ownership which he had previously enjoyed without limitation. ▼▼

CHAPTER 34   WINNING ANGELS 2000

The following excerpts from *The Winning Angels Study* ©2000, by David Amis and Jocelyn Dinnin: "What do most investors do?", "What do the winners do?" and the selected winning tools and tactics, are reprinted with permission. Highlights of this study were published in *The Winning Angels Handbook*.

WHAT DO MOST INVESTORS DO?

- **Consider different perspectives and structure accordingly**

  To the best of their ability, most investors will try to do a deal that allows them to get their cash out with or before the entrepreneur and give the entrepreneur control of the venture.

- **Use debt to "lock in" the entrepreneur**

  Some investors will attempt to get the entrepreneur to mortgage their house or put up capital they don't have to make sure they are tied to the project.

- **Don't think about it too much**

  Many investors just accept the structure presented (and don't have much choice when they are one of several investors). Sometimes they are just relying on the entrepreneur to get a win and don't worry too much about the deal terms.

WHAT DO THE WINNERS DO?

- **Keep it simple**

  "It should be possible to get the entire agreement on one page," says Lucius Cary. Any investor who has worked with venture capitalists knows that complicated structures can turn them off a deal as easily as an untrustworthy entrepreneur. Perhaps more important, **COMPLICATED STRUCTURES CREATE MORE WORK AND LESS FLEXIBILITY DOWN THE ROAD** however, is that complicated structures create more work and less flexibility down the road. Simplicity is best to maximize the chances of entrepreneurial success. *"I prefer a simple structure,"* says George Kline, an angel who has made over 160 investments. *"Straight equity or a loan with warrants are both okay."*

- **Align interests**

  OH has suggested that one should identify the type of entrepreneur. Serial entrepreneurs are preferred to empire builders who are preferred to lifestyle entrepreneurs if your goal is an early and profitable exit. Structure can be used to bring this out by limiting the entrepreneur's salary potential, insuring that his exit does not occur until or after yours does. Winning investors make sure the entrepreneur is going in the right direction.

Bert Twaalfhoven says:

66 To make certain that you don't do it alone, that you have others who have more experience, that he sticks on his investments within 200 miles, and that you give top priority to your manager entrepreneurs who run the company. Tie them to the venture with stock options and make certain that they have complementary experience. 99

- **Get cash early whenever possible**

  "Investors should get their money back first," says Howard. A few of the winning investors prefer convertible debt plus equity, so they can get some cash early when the deal is successful. Others look for opportunities to structure preferred shares with dividends based on income.

- **Focus on the entrepreneur during evaluation**

  Smart, honest, and capable entrepreneurs with a strong desire to attain an exit will outperform any structure any time. Winning investors focus on the entrepreneur early in the process because they know how important it is at this stage (and how difficult to force performance or an exit through structure). *"Entrepreneur, entrepreneur, entrepreneur,"* says Heinrich von Liechtenstein.

- **Get pre-emptive rights**

  These rights, which give the investor the right to maintain their relative ownership in a company by investing more capital in subsequent rounds, are common to winning angel investors.

- **Leave it to the lead**

  John McCallion says that if the entrepreneur has his price set up and it feels about right, he would rather go with it and avoid the aggravation of spending huge amounts of time on such a small deal. If he was the lead investor and putting in large amounts of capital, then he would do it differently.

- **Limit the conflicts**

  Limit conflicts between themselves and the entrepreneur, and themselves and other investors. *"Exits occur faster when there are no conflicts,"* says OH, a European angel investor. OH advises to watch out for lifestyle entrepreneurs. He knows that only when an entrepreneur is highly motivated to achieve an exit is there likely to be one. Seeing that the entrepreneur cannot sell her stock without selling the entire company, and that their other upsides (such as salary, benefits, etc.) are not avenues for reaping substantial value, will help to ensure that the entrepreneur focuses gaining liquidity for herself and the investors.

WINNING TOOLS AND TACTICS

✕ Cary one-pager

Lucius Cary believes that any angel deal can and should be completed on one page before involving a lawyer.

---

1 Write out a one-pager describing the main elements of the deal between the entrepreneur and the investor.

2 Include the following key points:

- Capital structure (equity or debt, how much, special terms, etc.).
- Involvement of the investor (board, advisor, part-time manager, fundraiser, salesman, etc.).
- Expected minimum time entrepreneur will stay in the business.
- Salary level (and other benefits) for the entrepreneur until cash flow is positive.
- Reporting mechanism (if any).
- Other.

Use this to clarify the understanding between the two parties and as a basis for the legal document (this process alone will save you 1,000 times the cost of this book in legal fees (or perhaps it will save you your entire investment).

🐦 Building reporting into the deal

Carl Guerreri and other angels like to build reporting into the deal. A one-pager with bullet points of key events, cash position, head count, etc. will keep the investor updated and aware.

Make a monthly report from the entrepreneur part of the investment agreement.

CHAPTER 35

SPECIAL SECTIONS

1 ● WHAT KIND OF STRUCTURE DO YOU PREFER?

Here are the answers from some of our angels...

Andrew Blair

❝ The share structure always includes convertible shares. If an entrepreneur does not perform the equity structure can change to account for that – and the consortium can end up with 60% or more of the shares. ❞

Carl Guerreri

❝ I build access to a second round into the structure, if they use it, I get more equity. ❞

Peter Pichler

❝ Our structures are always with common shares. The way we structure the deal is, we value the company today at a reasonable amount, and we also put in additional debt financing – a loan, which if the company turns out to be really successful, then the debt financing is converted to equity at a later stage. This is the approach that we take because sometimes we have what's called a gap between the entrepreneur's and investor's valuations. We do not want to have discussions about the value of the company for three or four years. This is it now, we want to make it happen. We put in small amounts, and more as they need the money. We have a kind of stop-loss arrangement. If you realize, after half the money has gone in, that this is stupid or it doesn't make sense, we can always stop the loss. ❞

Audrey MacLean

❝ I typically invest in convertible preferred shares. In many instances I become part of the team at an advisory or board level. In addition to my preferred investment I typically have a common stock stake – I have a stake in the company the same way that employees do that vest. ❞

Brian Horey

❝ In some cases I have done common stock because the sums of money have been so small and it hasn't made sense to hire lawyers to do a complicated convertible preferred deal. In some cases the sums have been big enough for, typically, a convertible preferred deal. ❞

Howard Tullman

❝ With respect to structuring, our view has the basic test that if you worry about control, you are in the wrong place. Like the sign in the restaurant, if you came here for fast food, you are in the wrong place. Our view is that we have to have appropriate structural control so if it goes south, we can do what we need to do in order to preserve the investment and the business opportunity and change the management. ❞

David Berkus

❝ In my structures I have kept them clean because I want to have a trust built between the entrepreneur and me. So I almost always start my investment strategy with a common stock investment and usually try to form it with the founders at founder's value, if it can be, but often I am after the founders. So I come in at some arbitrary number determined by the valuation method that I have just talked about.[1] I invest basically in founders' stock or at least common stock. ❞

SG

❝ We try to make sure what we have is pretty standard convertible, participating preferred. It looks like a venture deal. I'm not interested in buying common stock frankly, except in the form of options or restricted purchase at founders' price, then common stock works fine. But if I'm putting up my money I want the kind of protection that a venture financing has. ❞

Tony Morris

❝ I am happy with a simple preferred. If things don't go right I get paid before the common stock holders. I've seen lots of term sheets, there are standard term sheets around that have lots of provisions, but I'm very comfortable with a simple preferred. ❞

---

1 See Berkus Method on page 150.

David Solomont

❝ I've done common. It tends to be a mistake. It screws up the option plan. You don't offer the investors the type of protection that the investors really should have, like liquidation preferences. And I've made that mistake before. And I don't intend to make it again. We've done a convertible note, maybe two. I also don't like those, because actually it puts you on the wrong side of the table from the entrepreneur. Then there's no incentive for the angel investors to want to maximize the valuation, or even increase the valuation along the way, because I'm not converting until the next round is set... it's not called CommonAngels because we take common stock. 99% of the time simple preferred: liquidation preferences, board seat, reporting. ❞

2 ● COMMONANGELS STANDARD TERM SHEET

David Solomont is the founder of CommonAngels, a Boston-based group of 50 private investors. Members have founded, co-founded, or run high-tech companies. They work closely with early-stage software, information technology and internet companies in the Northeast.

Here is an example of a standard term sheet used by CommonAngels.

David Solomont

SUMMARY TERMS FOR SERIES A PREFERRED STOCK
This term sheet summarizes the terms proposed for an investment by a group of investors (the "Investors") in _____, a _____ corporation (the "Company").

TYPES OF SECURITY: **Series A Convertible Redeemable Preferred Stock.**

AMOUNT OF
INVESTMENT AND
PRE-MONEY

Up to $_____ investment at a $_____million pre-money valuation, fully diluted, the total number of shares to include an unallocated employee pool of at least 20% of the total, in addition to founders' shares.

VALUATION:
DIVIDENDS:

Non-cumulative dividends as declared. Series A Preferred Stock to participate in all dividends declared on an "as converted" basis. No dividends payable on Common Stock or any other Class of Preferred without payment of similar and all accrued dividends to the Series A Preferred Stock.

LIQUIDATION PREFERENCE:	Liquidation preference equal to price paid per share plus accrued dividends. Any remaining proceeds to be shared pro rata among stockholders. Merger, consolidation or similar event treated as liquidation at option of investors.
CONVERSION:	Series A Preferred Stock converted on a one-for-one basis into Common Stock unless conversion rate is subject to anti-dilution adjustment. Mandatory conversion of Series A Preferred Stock on closing of underwritten public offering at an initial price to the public at a valuation of at least $50,000,000 and gross proceeds the Company of at least $15,000,000.
ANTI-DILUTION:	Full ratchet to any lower price in any subsequent round of financing.
VOTING RIGHTS:	Equal to common equivalent shares. Investors in Series A Preferred Stock, voting separately, to elect two (2) Directors of 5 person Board of Directors.
REDEMPTION:	Required offer of redemption between years 5 and 7 at an effective compound rate of return of 10% per annum plus accrued but unpaid dividends. Voting rights to elect majority of Directors and 18% cumulative dividend if failure to redeem.
INFORMATION RIGHTS:	1) Audited annual and unaudited monthly and quarterly financial information. Also annual budgets will be supplied at least 30 days prior to the beginning of each fiscal year.
	2) Quarterly unaudited financials within 30 days of end of quarter.
	3) Monthly unaudited financials within 30 days including cash flow report and report of capital expenditures proposed in excess of $10,000 in each case and new salaries payable in excess of $100,000 per annum. Also monthly summary technology update on progress and accomplishments since preceding update and anticipated progress against target in next period.
	4) Quarterly meetings with Investors to discuss information provided.
REGISTRATION RIGHTS:	1) Two demand registrations.
	2) Unlimited piggyback registration rights.
	3) Unlimited rights for investors to register on Form S-3 at Company.

4) All expenses of investors for registrations (other than underwriting discounts and commissions) to be at Company expense.

5) Registration rights will be transferable.

RIGHT OF FIRST REFUSAL ON SALES BY THE COMPANY:	Investors will have a right to maintain their pro rata interest in the Company on a fully diluted basis in any subsequent offering of securities other than a public offering.
FOLLOW-ALONG RIGHTS:	Investors will have the right to sell a proportional part of their holdings if management sells before initial public offering.
RIGHT OF FIRST REFUSAL ON SALES BY FOUNDERS AND CO-SALE RIGHTS:	Investors will have a 30 day right of first refusal to purchase a proportional part of shares offered for sale by founders and management of the Company ("Founders"), if management wishes to sell stock before an initial public offering, or if Investors so choose, have the right to sell a proportional part of their holdings along with Founders or management before an initial public offering.
NEGATIVE COVENANTS:	Consent of holders of two-thirds of Series A Preferred Stock required for merger, dissolution, sale of substantially all assets, dividends on common stock, amendments to certificate of incorporation and by-laws, etc.
NON-COMPETITION AND NON-SOLICITATION AGREEMENTS:	In addition to standard confidentiality/developments agreements, key employees to execute agreements not to compete with or solicit employees of the Company or its subsidiaries, directly or indirectly, for two years after termination of employment.
VESTING:	Stock and options issued to employees, directors and consultants would be subject to vesting/repurchase over 4 years. At least 75% of each Founder's shares would be subject to 3 years of vesting.
COST OF COUNSEL:	Fees of counsel to the investors, up to $25,000 and their reasonable expenses will be borne by the Company.
COMMONANGELS COSTS:	Administrative costs of $5,000 to be paid to Common Angels at closing.
PURCHASE AGREEMENT:	This investment will be made pursuant to a definitive purchase agreement and related documents which will contain customary representations, warranties, covenants and indemnities, which are mutually acceptable. Binding

obligations will be created only by the definitive purchase agreement.

CONDITIONS TO
INVESTMENT:
Satisfactory due diligence by Investors, and standard disclosure schedules, representations and warranties by the company.

3 ● INTERVIEW WITH BILL SAHLMAN

The following is an excerpt from an interview David had with HBS Professor and active angel, Bill Sahlman.

> With respect to the whole deal valuing, negotiation and structuring you have to have had a lot of experience of good and bad deals to know what's really important in the transaction.
>
> In fact there are two points. You have to know what the options are: so if you think about whether you should use convertible, preferred or common stock, it takes about 11 nanoseconds to sort out what kind of security you'd like to use...
>
> Would you like to have participating preferred stock instead of regular convertible stock? The answer is yes. There are a whole bunch of things you'd like. But what you also discover is that often the valuation negotiation and structuring is less important than making the right people / marketing choices.
>
> So what I try to do, or anyone I know in the business, is to find market opportunities that could be big, so that it's worth the investment to find first and foremost people who you think can execute credibly the opportunity and where it's not so capital intensive that it's in play at a different level.
>
> Then trying to sort out what a reasonable deal is isn't as critical – not if it's a $6m valuation instead of an $8m valuation. In deals that have long right-hand tails of distribution it doesn't matter. In Amazon, John Doerr was roundly criticized when he put money into Amazon at a $60m pre-money valuation. In the end the company achieved a $30bn market cap 2 years later. So whether he'd paid 60, 70, 55, or whether he'd used participating preferred, non-participating preferred – it didn't matter...
>
> If you look at the positive scenario it doesn't matter much what securities you use. If you look at the negative scenarios and my experience is that you lose 100% of your money in most of the companies you look at. Whether you have preferred stock or anything it doesn't matter because there's not much value left of the company anyway. So frankly I don't spend a lot of time on that part of the process.

4 • CAPITALYST™ – PREFERRED DEAL TERMS

TABLE 35.1

Common share structure	Preferred share structure	Convertible note
Must have	**Must have**	**Must have**
• Pre-emptive right	• Pre-emptive right	• Set conversion price or
• Tag-along right	• Tag-along right	discount
• Registration right	• Registration right	• Cumulative interest
• Reasonable price	• Reasonable price	(deferrable)
	• Anti-dilution	
Ought to have	**Ought to have**	**Ought to have**
• Entrepreneur compensation limit (not necessarily contractual)	• Visitation rights	• Convertible into preferred
• Anti-dilution	• Redemption rights	
	• Warranties and representations	
	• Cumulative dividend (although deferrable)	
	• Board representation (for all preferreds)	
Nice to have	**Nice to have**	**Nice to have**
• Warranties and representations	• Put	• Potential for payback with warrants to provide upside
• Put		
• Board representation (for all current-round investors)		
Must avoid	**Must avoid**	**Must avoid**
• A call	• Anything too complicated	• Forced conversion by entrepreneur without a trigger event related to significant progress
	• Anything that will turn off next investors	

5 ● DRAPER FISHER JURVETSON (DFJ) STANDARD TERM SHEET

Tim Draper

DFJ is one of the most well-known VC firms in the US, which has invested in over 150 internet start-ups and companies, including those funded by DFJ affiliates. In 1999, 10 DFJ portfolio companies went public, including GoTo.com and Digital Impact, among others.

Tim Draper, founder and Managing Director of DFJ, spoke with us about the terms he likes to see, and what follows is an example of a standard DFJ term sheet.

Sale of Series A Preferred Stock

of

XXXXXXXXXX

SUMMARY OF TERMS (XX/XX/XX)

THIS TERM SHEET SUMMARIZES THE PRINCIPAL TERMS OF A PROPOSED PRIVATE PLACEMENT OF EQUITY SECURITIES OF XXXXXXX (the "Company"). THIS TERM SHEET IS FOR DISCUSSION PURPOSES ONLY; THERE IS NO OBLIGATION ON THE PART OF ANY NEGOTIATING PARTY UNTIL A DEFINITIVE STOCK PURCHASE AGREEMENT IS SIGNED BY ALL PARTIES. THIS TERM SHEET IS SUBJECT TO SATISFACTORY COMPLETION OF DUE DILLIGENCE.

A. AMOUNT AND INVESTORS:	Draper Fisher Jurvetson Fund V, LP	$0,000,000
	Draper Fisher Jurvetson Partners V, LLC	$000,000
	SUB-TOTAL	$0,000,000

B. VALUATION: $0,000,000 post money.

C. PRICE PER SHARE: $0.00 ["Series A Original Purchase Price"].

D. CAPITALIZATION: 0,000,000 total pre-financing fully-diluted

Common shares and options issued, including:

Founder A	0,000,000
Founder B	0,000,000
Reserved for Employee Pool	0,000,000
SUB-TOTAL	00,000,000

This financing: 00,000,000 shares of Series A Preferred Stock issued as follows:

Draper Fisher Jurvetson Fund V, LP	0,000,000
Draper Fisher Jurvetson Partners V, LLC	000,000
SUB-TOTAL	00,000,000
GRAND-TOTAL	00,000,000

E. VESTING SCHEDULE: Unless the board determines otherwise, employees' Common Stock shall vest 25% at the end of the first year of full-time employment, and at a rate of 1/48th per month thereafter, with respect to stock granted prior to an IPO.

F. COMPENSATION: No Company employee shall receive annual compensation in excess of $100,000 (except those receiving commissions from approved comp plans) without consent of all of the directors until the company is merged, is sold, or completes an IPO. Any and all accruals shall be forgiven by the founders prior to this financing.

G. DIVIDENDS: The holders of Preferred shall be entitled to receive dividends at a rate of 8% per annum in preference to any dividend on Common Stock, whenever funds are legally available, when, if and as declared by the Board of Directors. Dividends shall be non-cumulative.

H. LIQUIDATION PREFERENCE: In the event of any liquidation or winding up of the Company, the holders of Preferred A will be entitled to receive in preference to the holders of Common Stock an amount equal to their Original Purchase Price plus all declared but unpaid dividends (if any).

Preferred A will be participating so that after payment of the Original Purchase Price to the holders of Preferred A, the remaining assets shall be distributed pro-rata to all share-holders on a common equivalent basis.

A merger, acquisition or sale of substantially all of the assets of the Company in which the share-holders of the Company do not own a majority of the outstanding shares of the surviving corporation shall be deemed a liquidation.

I. CONVERSION:
1. The holders of Preferred will have the right to convert Preferred shares at the option of the holder, at any time, into shares of Common Stock at an initial conversion rate of 1-to-1. The conversion rate shall be subject from time to time to anti-dilution adjustments as described below.
2. Automatic Conversion: All Preferred shares will be automatically converted into Common upon (i) the closing of an underwritten public offering of shares of Common Stock of the Company at a public offering price per share (prior to under-writing commissions and expenses) that values the Company at at least $50 million in an offering of not less than $10 million, before deduction of underwriting discounts and registration expenses or (ii) approval of 50% of the Series A Preferred.

J. ANTIDILUTION:
The holders of Preferred A will receive proportional antidilution protection for stock splits, stock dividends, combinations, recapitalizations, etc. The conversion price of the Preferred shall be subject to adjustment to prevent dilution, on a "weighted average" basis, in the event that the Company issues additional shares of Common or Common equivalents (other than reserved employee shares) at a purchase price less than the applicable conversion price.

K. VOTING RIGHTS:
The holders of a share of Preferred will have a right to that number of votes equal to the number of shares of Common Stock issuable upon conversion of Preferred.

L. REGISTRATION RIGHTS:
(1.) Demand Rights: If investors holding at least 40% of Preferred A (or Common issued upon conversion of the Preferred or a combination of such Common and Preferred) request that the Company file a Registration Statement for at least 20% of their shares (or any lesser percentage if the anticipated gross receipts from the offering exceed $2,000,000) the Company will use its best efforts to cause

such shares to be registered; provided, however, that the Company shall not be obligated to effect any such registration prior to the earlier of (i) XXX 00, XXXX, or (ii) within one year following the effective date of the company's initial public offering. The Company shall not be obligated to effect more than two registrations under these demand right provisions.

(2.) Company Registration: The Investors shall be entitled to "piggyback" registration rights on registrations of the company or on demand registrations of any later round investor subject to the right, however, of the Company and its under-writers to reduce the number of shares proposed to be registered pro-rata in view of market conditions. No shareholder of the Company shall be granted piggyback registration rights superior to those of the Preferred A without the consent of the holders of at least 50% of the Series A Preferred (or Common issued upon conversion of the Series A Preferred or a combination of such Common and Preferred).

(3.) S-3 Rights: Investors shall be entitled to an unlimited number of demand registrations on form S-3 (if available to the Company) so long as such registration offerings are in excess of $500,000; provided, however, that the Company shall only be required to file two Form S-3 Registration Statements on demand of the Preferred every 12 months.

(4.) Expenses: The Company shall bear registration expenses (exclusive of under-writing discounts and commissions and special counsel of the selling shareholders) of all demands, piggybacks, and S-3 registrations. The expenses in excess of $15,000 of any special audit required in connection with a demand registration shall be borne pro-rata by the selling shareholders.

(5.) Transfer of Rights: The registration rights may be transferred provided that the Company is given written notice thereof and provided that the transfer a) is in connection with a transfer of all securities of the transferor, b) involves a transfer of at least 100,000 shares, or c) is to constituent partners or shareholders who agree to act through a single representative.

(6.) Other Provisions: Other provisions shall be contained in the Purchase Agreement with respect to registration rights as are reasonable, including cross indemnification, the period of time in which the Registration Statement shall be kept effective, standard standoff provisions, underwriting arrangements and the ability of the Company to delay demand registrations for up to 90 days (S-3 Registrations for up to 60 days).

M. BOARD OF DIRECTORS:

The Board of Directors will consist of five seats. The Series A Investors shall be entitled to elect two members of the Company's Board of Directors. The third director shall be the Company's Chief Executive Officer. The fourth and fifth directors (and any additional directors) will be elected by the Preferred Stock and Common Stock voting together as a class; these directors are also expected to be outside directors. Draper Fisher Jurvetson will also have board visitation rights for its other partners. The Company shall reimburse Draper Fisher Jurvetson for all reasonable out of pocket expenses related to board meetings.

N. RIGHTS OF FIRST OFFER:

The Preferred A Investors shall have the right in the event the Company proposes an equity offering of any amount to any person or entity (other than for a strategic corporate partner, employee stock grant, equipment financing, acquisition of another company, shares offered to the public pursuant to an underwritten public offering, or other conventional exclusion) to purchase up to one half of such shares. If a Preferred A investor chooses not to exercise their right of first offer, the other Preferred A investors have the right to expand their investment to fill the gap.

The Company has an obligation to notify all Preferred Investors of any proposed equity offering of any amount.

If the affiliated groups of Preferred Investors do not respond within 15 days of being notified of such an offering, or decline to purchase all of such securities, then that portion which is not purchased may be offered to other parties on terms no less favorable to the Company for a period of 120 days. Such right of first offer will terminate upon an underwritten public offering of shares of the Company.

In addition, the Company will grant the Preferred shareholders any rights of first refusal or registration rights granted to subsequent purchasers of the Company's equity securities to the extent that such subsequent rights are superior, in good faith judgment of the Company's Board of Directors, to those granted in connection with this transaction.

O. CO-SALE	The Company, the Series A Investors and the Founders will enter into a co-sale agreement pursuant to which any Founder who proposes to sell all or a portion of his shares to a third party, will offer the Series A Investors the right to participate in such sale on a pro-rata basis or to exercise a right of first refusal on the same basis (subject to customary exclusions for up to 15% of the stock, gifts, pledges, etc.). The agreement will terminate on the earlier of an IPO or fifteen (15) years from the close of this financing.
P. RESTRICTIONS AND LIMITATIONS:	So long as Preferred A Stock remains outstanding, the Company shall not, without the vote or written consent of at least a majority of the Preferred A shareholders, authorize or issue any equity security senior to the Series A Preferred as to dividend rights or redemption rights or liquidation preferences. Furthermore, the Company shall not amend its Articles of Incorporation or By-laws in a manner that would alter or change the rights, preferences or privileges of any Preferred Stock without the approval of at least a majority of the Preferred shareholders. Written consent of a majority of the Series A shareholders shall be required for (a) any merger, consolidation, or other corporate reorganization, or (b) any transaction or series of transactions in which in excess of 50% of the Company's voting power is transferred or in which all or substantially all of the assets of the Company are sold.
Q. PROPRIETARY INFORMATION AND INVENTIONS AGREEMENT:	Each officer, director, and employee of the Company shall have entered into a proprietary information and inventions agreement in a form reasonably acceptable to the Company and the Investors. Each Founder and other key technical employees shall have executed an assignment of inventions acceptable to the Company and Investors.
R. PURCHASE AGREEMENT:	The investment shall be made pursuant to a Stock Purchase Agreement reasonably acceptable to the Company and the Investors, which agreement shall contain, among other things, appropriate representations and warranties of the Company, with respect to patents, litigation, previous employment, and outside activities, covenants of the Company reflecting the provisions set forth herein, and appropriate conditions of closing, including an opinion of

the counsel for the Company. The Company will obtain key person life insurance, payable to the Company, on XXX XXXX for $1 million.

S. LEGAL FEES
AND EXPENSES:

The Company shall pay the reasonable fees and expenses (not to exceed $5,000) of counsel to the investors and the Company.

The foregoing Summary of Terms sets forth the good faith agreement of the parties set forth below. By accepting this term sheet, the Company agrees to refrain from solicitation, consideration, or acceptance of alternative proposals to finance, recapitalize or sell the Company for a period of twenty-one (21) days from the date of the Company's signature below. This offer expires on XXXXXXXX at 5pm.

Draper Fisher Associates Fund V   XXXXXX

By:_____   By:_____

By: _____   By:_____

Date:_____   Date:_____

4 TAKEAWAYS FROM STRUCTURING

1 ● Make sure you understand the three structures: common, preferred, and convertible, as well as the most common terms.

2 ● Structure deals using preference shares when you can, only take common stock if the entrepreneur is AAA, and watch convertible for potential second rounds that are too high.

3 ● Keep it simple.

4 ● Spend more or less time depending on how much you are investing.

Negotiating

Part of angel investing is about having fun, and just getting a deal and signing a check is not fun. Negotiating the terms of the deal, making everybody happy to be working together – this is part of the excitement of early-stage investing.

David Solomont, CommonAngels

QUICK OVERVIEW

36 ● Start section   225

37 ● Angels who don't negotiate   226
Get someone else to do it   226
"Take a pass"   227

38 ● Angels who do negotiate   228

39 ● If you are going to negotiate   229
What are the objectives?   230
Negotiation issues   232
It's payback time   233

40 ● Winning angels 2000   235
What do most investors do?   235
What do the winners do?   235
Winning tools and tactics   237

41 ● Special sections 239

   1 Four investors talk about negotating 239

   2 Fundamentals of early stage negotiating 240

 4 TAKEAWAYS FROM NEGOTIATING 244

CHAPTER 36

START SECTION

Negotiating in angel deals depends on personal style, desired participation role, and the quality of the proposed terms. Investors new to early-stage deals may expect the negoti-

ation stage to be the longest of all of the stages. However, it is often the shortest because many winning investors simply do not negotiate. There are

NEGOTIATING IN ANGEL DEALS DEPENDS ON PERSONAL STYLE

two fundamental and valid approaches to negotiating early-stage deals:

- negotiate.
- do not negotiate.

The highly differentiated approaches mean that some angels accept or reject deals as they stand, while others become very involved in negotiating the terms to the benefit

of themselves and other investors. Some winners will say that the question is one of focusing on starting a relationship versus a one-time negotiation.

How you think about negotiation is important not only because it impacts the terms, price and overall structure of the deal, but also because it is a prelude to the highly interdependent relationship

NEGOTIATION IS IMPORTANT BECAUSE IT IS A PRELUDE TO THE HIGHLY INTERDEPENDENT RELATIONSHIP BETWEEN THE INVESTOR AND THE ENTREPRENEUR

formed between the investor and the entrepreneur. Many investors believe this relationship will impact their ROI more than the terms. For angels who do negotiate, there are generally four elements that concern them:

- structure (terms)
- price
- amount of capital that will be invested
- role.

Determining a negotiation strategy requires consideration of your preferred role, time availability, preferred relationship with the entrepreneur, whether you are the lead investor, and the amount of capital you intend to invest.

CHAPTER 37 ANGELS WHO DON'T NEGOTIATE $$$

It's always been a question of – do we have chemistry?...
will I add value?... if so, the negotiation seems to go away

George Kline

Angels who don't negotiate choose not to for three fundamental reasons:

1 They don't want to invest the time.

2 They are concerned about the efficacy of a relationship based on trust that starts with a fight for money and/or control.

3 Within certain limits, they don't think the terms or price are that significant.

Many of the same angels who do not care to focus on structure will also not want to spend time on negotiating, even to reduce the price. Many of these reserve force, part-time or silent angels[1] will expect someone else to assume a lead role and negotiate terms. Many of them also make the mistake of assuming someone has already negotiated.

SOME WINNING ANGELS WILL WAIT FOR AN ADDITIONAL CAPITAL ROUND WHERE MORE SIGNIFICANT CAPITAL IS NEEDED AND THEN NEGOTIATE ANY SPECIAL TERMS

However, sophisticated angels with a good understanding of the prices and terms that are available to them in early-stage deals, will screen deals based on certain requirements (such as $5m or less pricing or a preferred share structure). They want to maximize the likelihood of a positive relationship and so they do nothing to bring about conflict in the beginning. "*Let them have it your way,*" is Howard's favorite way to describe his approach. He lets entrepreneurs propose the terms, as this provides good information on what they want. Then he either accepts the deal as it stands or takes a pass. Bert Twaalfhoven says, "*In general, we follow the entrepreneur's proposal.*"

By giving the entrepreneur their own proposed terms, it should be hard for them to regret it later. Finally, some winning angels will simply wait for an additional capital round where more significant capital is needed and then negotiate any special terms.

GET SOMEONE ELSE TO DO IT $$$

One alternative to negotiating is to let someone else do it. OH, John Hime, and others, always require an attorney or someone else to be involved in the

---

1 For an explanation of angel participation roles, see pages 249–53.

negotiation. One major benefit is that it lets any ill feelings that may develop fall on their shoulders.

Some investors, such as Denis Payre and Mitch Kapor, like to see a VC or some other investor take the lead and do the negotiations. Denis describes his approach:

&& I am not getting involved in valuation negotiations, because these are very emotional negotiations, and I prefer to let the VCs play the bad guys and do the deals. And if the valuation is not right, I don't invest, but I am usually not leading the negotiation for the valuation. 99

"TAKE A PASS" $$$

Another alternative is to communicate to the entrepreneur that the project is good but just not interesting and, therefore, you will pass at this time. The focus should be on communicating positive feelings about the project (rejection is always a sensitive undertaking) along with whatever issues led you to your conclusion.

You might say, *"Thanks but I'm not interested at this price,"* refusing to give a number or get into a discussion. Later, the entrepreneur might come back with a better price or better terms, but let them do it on their own.

CHAPTER 38 ANGELS WHO DO NEGOTIATE

The Golden Rule: He who has the gold, makes the rules.

Angels who do negotiate are more likely to have an active role in their investment. Controlling angels, coaching angels, and some reserve force angels will negotiate. Lead investors who are cognizant of their role will negotiate on terms and price.

Their reasons for negotiating vary and go beyond gaining better terms. For example, Peter Pichler likes to negotiate in order to see how the entrepreneur thinks. Jeff Parker uses the negotiation as a test. He knows that the relationship with the entrepreneur will undergo some significant stress and he likes to see how they hold up under stress right away. *"If they get their back up... it's not going to work anyway,"* he says.

Approaches to negotiating vary but generally fall into one of three categories:

1 Negotiate directly and actively until the desired outcome is achieved or unlikely.

2 Quickly offer final terms in a one-shot offer.

3 Get someone else to negotiate (essentially a negotiating strategy used by a non-negotiator).

Direct negotiation in an early-stage deal is not much different than any other negotiation in business, except that it can be highly emotional with an entrepreneur and thus the policy of many angels to not negotiate.

ANGELS WHO DO NEGOTIATE ARE MORE LIKELY TO HAVE AN ACTIVE ROLE IN THEIR INVESTMENT

One-shot offers are a way to reduce the friction caused but may still result in some dissatisfaction in the relationship. John Hime doesn't spend a lot of time going back and forth, *"It's either my way or not at all. I see more fundable deals than I can afford."*

Carl Guerreri won't spend more than two weeks negotiating, after that time he thinks it doesn't make sense to invest.

Negotiation will almost certainly bring improved terms, but it is important to remember that this may be a highly interdependent relationship.

CHAPTER 39

IF YOU ARE GOING TO NEGOTIATE

> The only time I don't negotiate is when somebody brings me the deal and there is one piece of the deal left. Then, if I want to participate, it is a case of take it or leave it.
>
> **David Solomont**

First, realize that there are situations where you can negotiate and those where you cannot. Sometimes deals arrive at the end of the capital-raising process or the entrepreneur has real or high perceived leverage. In other situations, the project is early in the capital-raising process, the entrepreneur does not have high perceived leverage (although they may have it in fact), or the entrepreneur is looking for someone to negotiate and set the terms.

DO YOU NEGOTIATE WITH ENTREPRENEURS?

CRAIG BURR: "IF I'M THE LEAD, THEN YES"

FRANK LEVY: "ABSOLUTELY"

Second, there are a few principles that can be helpful to an early-stage negotiation:

- **Start from a position of perceived or real strength**

  Having "big wings" will make the negotiation go easier, because the entrepreneurs will believe that your involvement will directly impact their success. Characteristics of big wings include: strong reputation in the community, well-known success, and an entrepreneurial history. Most of our winning angels start from a position of strength. Mitch Kapor, Audrey MacLean, and Esther Dyson are so well known that they have entrepreneurs using every imaginable tactic to get face time. Other investors are known for industry leadership or connections.

- **Represent significant capital**

  If your own capital, or that of a syndicate that you lead, amounts to a significant percentage of the capital raise, such as 20% to 50%, it will generally facilitate good-intentioned negotiations. Angel investor CL often brings in several other $100k investors in addition to the $100–200k he may place in any deal. This makes it possible for him to require improvements in the terms.

- **Get to it**

  Lucius Cary makes an offer in the first meeting. He says, *"The quicker you are in the whole process the more likely you are to get the deal done – and get it done at a good price."* The offer he makes is informal at this stage, and he gauges the entrepreneur's reaction. Normally they are so delighted to have an offer there and then, that isn't going to be dragged out for months, that they informally agree.

- **Establish precedents**

  Angel investor CL likes to *"telegraph key punches early in negotiation."* In this way he sets expectations about what can happen and also shows that, as a negotiator, he has defined limits. CL is also good at sending entrepreneurs off to improve the deal before investing. *"This sets the right tone, allowing them to prove they can make things happen and beginning the hoped for habit of acting on his advice."*

- **Sell value-added**

  Winning angels position themselves as added-value participants and then add value. *"The entrepreneur needs to see more than just money,"* says Frans Kok, a DC-based angel. With support, the entrepreneur is more likely to win and to develop a positive relationship with the investor.

- **Don't gouge**

  Gouging will lead to a non-positive relationship. The worst thing you can do is pin the entrepreneur down for a low valuation and highly aggressive terms, and then do nothing to make the business go. Animosity will not help the entrepreneur build the business and so gouging will likely result in an overall lower ROI.

WHAT ARE THE OBJECTIVES?

Angels, if they do negotiate, focus the negotiations on four key areas:

1 The price.
2 The structure of the deal (e.g. the terms).
3 How much money they will invest.
4 What role they will play, if any.

Big wings $$$

Angels who arrive at the negotiating table with clout have significant advantages. Entrepreneurs will be willing to secede more favorable terms, or may show up with a better proposal just to increase the chance of winning them over. Angels with big wings have some of the following attributes:

ANGELS WHO ARRIVE AT THE NEGOTIATING TABLE WITH CLOUT HAVE SIGNIFICANT ADVANTAGES.

- **A history of successful angel investments**

  Even lucky fools who did one big deal are assumed to be masters. Multiple super-deal successes (such as Arthur Rock) are masters.

- **A history of successful business**

  Top corporate managers, such as Fred Smith, carry weight in any situation. Lesser but locally known successes, whether as a marketing VP or other are potentially high impact to an entrepreneur.

- **Name recognition**

  Even if it's not necessarily related to business (e.g. Samuel Jackson), it will be powerful if the association is positive.

- **A known style of doing business that is favorable**

  Honest, aggressive, fair-minded individuals have a competitive advantage.

- **Lots of capital** $$$

  Entrepreneurs need investors who can join in subsequent rounds and whose presence implies "money."

- **Are not afraid to pull the trigger**

  A reputation for doing deals in a timely manner has become more of a competitive advantage.

- **Excellent contacts**

  Rolodex or the number of bytes in one's contact database are instances where size matters.

NEGOTIATION ISSUES

Associate Professor Robert Robinson, who created the Entrepreneurial Negotiating course at Harvard Business School, says that the first objective in any negotiation is to openly get the issues on the table. Here are some likely interests of angels and entrepreneurs:

Angel investor wish list

If you are going to negotiate, it is best to start with a clear idea of what you want. Here are some suggestions:

- entrepreneur who treats the investor like a customer
- pre-emptive rights, tag-along rights, ratchet rights, etc.
- low price
- entrepreneur salary limit
- multiple exit opportunities
- pre-IPO investment opportunities
- no reputational risk
- additional warrants
- advisory or coaching salary
- part-time job?
- introductions to more deals
- introductions to winning angels
- board seat (usually with flexibility about withdrawing the VC round)
- anti-dilution rights
- first right of refusal on next capital round.

Likely entrepreneur issues

There are a few items which will almost certainly be on the entrepreneur's mind, and you would do well to consider how to address them ahead of time. They may include the following:

- control of the company
- valuation
- investor ability to affect management decisions
- reporting requirements
- potential follow-on funding from either the investor or the investor's network
- timing (when do they get the check)
- terms of the deal
- seriousness of the investor (they don't know until they get the check).

Depending on the age and experience of the entrepreneur (but the latter more so), he or she may be hesitant or fearful about doing a deal and may be facing a number of issues for the first time. Therefore, having a past relationship is helpful, but it is also beneficial if the entrepreneur has one or more advisors who can comment on the various terms and issues in the negotiation.

If you are going to negotiate, do so with an awareness of the unique factors in early-stage deals, particularly the sensitivity of the entrepreneur to his "baby" and the highly interdependent nature of the relationship.

IT'S PAYBACK TIME

Entrepreneurs in early-stage deals have a lot of power to give or withhold gifts. They are the kings and queens of their small enterprises. To the extent that the entrepreneur has gifts to give, your relationship will determine where you stand in line outside of any contracts. If you bet on someone because they are smart, creative, and a real problem solver who knows their company, then you are best not to gamble on their inability to get around at least some elements of your agreement.

In one of David Amis' first investments, an entrepreneur had developed a new kind of synthetic covering for digital disks. This patented invention would protect the disks from damage and, in fact, repair any previous imperfections from either the manufacturing process or from normal use! Substantial contracts were already in the works with major retailers and a distributor. In addition, a Chinese group was prepared to manufacture, a member of one of England's great families had signed on, and an off-shore investment bank was promising a venture round.

GIFTS OF THE KING

- First shot at follow-on rounds.
- Preferred opportunities such as in new developments.
- Referrals to other high-potential entrepreneurs.
- Networking to other key investors, venture capitalists, board members, etc.
- Information on company progress, plans or unique opportunities.

BEST CASE SCENARIO

What does a winning investor want when making an investment?

- Respect.
- The ability to share in the winnings.
- Information.
- Return of capital as soon as possible.
- A feeling of having contributed/made a difference.
- The ability to get out if circumstances change (e.g. death).
- Fun.

However, within a couple of months, relations soured when the entrepreneur failed to pay an outstanding liability guaranteed by one of the investors (and for which capital had been provided), no updates or board meetings had been held (one of the angels was a board member on paper and became concerned about the liability), and harsh words were exchanged.

Following this, the entrepreneur became unreachable, sending updates about once a year. He did raise the venture round but he also transferred the assets to an off-shore holding company, making all of the investors indirect shareholders through a company controlled by him. This meant that the new company, where the venture capitalists had placed their money, could go public or sell, and the original investors would be stuck with a minority interest in a privately held holding company completely dependent on the entrepreneur. At the time of writing, the company appears to be succeeding, but the entrepreneur has dropped any pretence of treating the investors with respect and will likely not allow them to share in any gain.

GENERALLY SPEAKING, THE ENTREPRENEUR WILL CONTROL INFORMATION, ADDITIONAL INVESTMENT OPPORTUNITIES, AND COMPANY SPECIFIC NETWORKING

Generally speaking, the entrepreneur will control information, additional investment opportunities, and company specific networking. The amount of information you have on the company is relevant both for your personal comfort and for making any additional financially related decisions.

Additional investment opportunities can include co-investment with the VC or other preferred opportunities. Finally, as early-stage investing becomes more and more competitive, having a successful entrepreneur who refers other entrepreneurs and industry people can be beneficial.

CHAPTER 40

WINNING ANGELS 2000

The following excerpts from *The Winning Angels Study* ©2000, by David Amis and Jocelyn Dinnin: "What do most investors do?", "What do the winners do?" and the selected winning tools and tactics, are reprinted with permission. Highlights of this study were published in *The Winning Angels Handbook*.

WHAT DO MOST INVESTORS DO?

- **Focus on the numbers**

  13% or 21%? Many investors consider their initial ownership stake to be the most important negotiating issue. They believe this will have the greatest impact on the future value of their stake and negotiate hard to increase it.

- **Spend a lot of time**

  Since the investor is not on the hook (as the entrepreneur may be, depending on their burn rate) they comfortably spend a lot of time negotiating and/or waiting for the entrepreneur to come around to their terms.

- **Focus on who gets what**

  Instead of looking for ways to align interests and get a good deal done, many investors go into their corner and come out fighting for more of the pie. Lots of investors and entrepreneurs come away from this process with bad feelings that do not bode well for their future relationship.

WHAT DO THE WINNERS DO?

- **Don't negotiate**

  Many winning investors do not negotiate personally. They know that many unneeded problems can be created from the negotiating process and prefer to leave those problems to another investor or to one of their representatives. Using a trusted attorney or a point man is a favored tactic of one investor who declined to be named. George Kline, who does not negotiate says, "*I never had to use legal power to remove an entrepreneur... they don't like it, but usually they go.*" This kind of productive relationship is only possible when the relationship starts off on a foundation of trust. Aggressive negotiating does not foster trust. "*We tend not to haggle a lot,*" says Steve Walker. "*We want a cooperative relationship.*"

- **Screen out "greedy" entrepreneurs in the evaluation stage**

  "Greed is one of the biggest problems," says one winning investor who will remain anonymous. *"I've dropped out of more deals because of it."* Winning investors look for unrealistic valuations right away when a deal lands on their desk. They know that they will either have to spend valuable time convincing the entrepreneur to change it or worry that after the negotiation the entrepreneur will resent them.

- **If they do negotiate, they do not leave the entrepreneur feeling short changed**

  Martin Rigby uses structure to compensate for entrepreneurial sensitivity over equity. Winning investors know that the entrepreneur's ego is closely tied up with the valuation and ownership of shares. If they do negotiate, they try to create a deal that leaves the entrepreneur feeling warm and fuzzy (or close!).

- **Focus on structure**

  By focusing on structure instead of price, winning investors can give entrepreneurs the deals they want. One angel described how he sometimes structured deals so that management gets a large percentage of the shares but will be diluted if they do not meet their targets. While many entrepreneurs may be *"greedy,"* as one investor put it, they also tend to be highly confident of their own abilities. Connecting ownership to performance is a productive way to let them have their pie if they can do a great job baking it!

  CONNECTING OWNERSHIP TO PERFORMANCE IS A PRODUCTIVE WAY TO LET THEM HAVE THEIR PIE IF THEY CAN DO A GREAT JOB BAKING IT!

- **Become the entrepreneur's advocate**

  Betsy Atkins believes her job is to support the entrepreneurs and she begins this process in the negotiation phase. She explains all the numbers in the deal and compares them to others she has seen. She also reviews the best and worst case scenarios with them so they can arrive at a valuation that makes sense.

- **Leave it to the lead**

  As mentioned earlier, John McCallion says that if the entrepreneur has his price set up and it feels about right, he would rather go with it and avoid the aggravation of spending huge amounts of time on such a small deal. If he was the lead investor and putting in large amounts of capital, then he would do it differently.

- **Make sure the entrepreneur is represented**

  John Hime says:

  "I insist they get one of four high-tech speciality law firms here in Austin, one of two accounting firms, and sign on as clients before I invest. This way they have representation in any discussions with me."

● Treat them well

"The VCs negotiate... I don't... I'm trusting and I think of them as partners," says George Kline. Betsy Atkins thinks of herself as the advocate for the entrepreneurs. *"You can take advantage,"* she says, *"but I'm on their side."*

● Negotiate aggressively

Jeff Parker actively negotiates before making an investment. *"You can beat them up but still have them feel you're on their side,"* he says. *"If the entrepreneur gets his back up, it's not going to work. If he's too rigid, it's not likely to work anyway."*

● Get it done and get on with the business

Lucius Cary makes an offer in the first meeting. He believes that the quicker you are in the whole process, the more likely you are to get the deal done, and at a good price. Carl Guererri says: *"If negotiations take more than two weeks, I am unlikely to invest."* He goes on to say, *"A lot of potential deals do not happen when the entrepreneur's and investor's perceived values are out of sync from the outset."* The same also applies to valuing. Winning investors adopt simple rules in order to quickly get to a reasonable deal. A small piece of a larger pie is preferred to no pie at all.

● Keep the lawyers from renegotiating or changing the deal

Using a one-pager will help with this. *"Remember that the lawyer works for you,"* is common advice from winning angels.

WINNING TOOLS AND TACTICS

🎯 Wait until the second round

"You can put the handcuffs on later," OH.

Some investors, knowing that the entrepreneur will need additional capital, wait until the second round to complete a more involved deal. In the second round they begin negotiating.

Another method would be to put a relatively small amount in the first round to begin the relationship and keep the project on your radar screen. Before the second round occurs, you will have more information and can decide not only how much you might invest but what type of negotiating strategy will generate the best results given the type of opportunity, the entrepreneurial team, your relationship with the entrepreneur, and the interests of the other investors.

> Put the negotiating off until the second round.

🎯 One shot offer $\boxed{\$\$\$}$

Some investors, who do not want to accept the entrepreneur's terms but likewise do not want an extended negotiation, will make one counter-offer, particularly if it is not much different from the terms offered. They will usually let the entrepreneur know it is a one-time counter.

Frans Kok says that, after discussions with them, he goes away and puts together a term sheet. He decides how much he wants to be involved and does not deviate much from it. He says, *"This is the way I'll part with my money."*

John Hime also has a similar approach, he determines what works for him, and then doesn't deviate much.

Errol Unikel is known for stating, *"I basically accept your terms and want to do the deal, but have a couple of minor points I would like to trade on."* This is a productive and positive way to make non-major changes.

> Set perimeters for the deal and don't deviate from them in a "one-time only"

🎤 Use a lightning rod $\boxed{\$\$\$}$

Get a front man to do the negotiating. Whether this is another angel investor, your lawyer, a consultant, or someone else, let them become the focus of any entrepreneur dissatisfaction with the negotiated result. They can become the lightning rod for emotional issues, not only of the entrepreneur, but sometimes of other people in the deal.

Denis Payre, OH, and William Weaver all get other people involved to handle the negotiation. OH often hires an attorney expressly for this purpose.

> Let another investor or one of your advisors negotiate with the entrepreneur.

🎤 Send them on a mission

Angel investor CL likes to give the entrepreneur(s) a target before investing. *"Set near term goals... (i.e. advisory board)... tell them to come back after they do it.*

SENDING ENTREPRENEURS AWAY TO GET SOME THINGS DONE WILL GIVE YOU INSIGHT INTO THEIR WORKING HABITS AND ABILITIES

They feel good, you know more about them," he says. This tactic starts the relationship in a positive manner and also allows the angel to see how the entrepreneur(s) make things happen. Sending entrepreneurs away to get some things done will give you insight into their working habits and abilities.

> Give the entrepreneur(s) an objective to meet before you will invest, thus starting the relationship right and getting improved value before you write a check.

CHAPTER 41

SPECIAL SECTIONS

1 ● FOUR INVESTORS TALK ABOUT NEGOTIATING

Darryl Wash

❝ We try to do a lot of negotiating, but as I mentioned, it depends on the stage. If you identify an opportunity when it is relatively late in the funding cycle, then you either invest based on the terms that others have agreed or you don't invest. If you identify it early and are able to go around to other angels for example and bring more capital to the table then you can try and get the best terms that you can. So with the StarMedia example while we didn't negotiate that much, we did to some degree because we were about one-third of the capital coming into that round. So what we say is we can bring this money but we need these terms. With the StarMedia example, the reason we did not negotiate that much is because it was in late 1996 and so at that time the valuations were not as lofty as they are today. So the pre-money valuation we invested at in StarMedia was about $5m which did not seem unreasonable. ❞

Angel investor SG

❝ Sure I negotiate. This is one of the reasons we put the angel group together. If you have 10 guys doing $100k each together, it is a different conversation to if you have got one guy doing $100k, and there are nine other separate guys doing $100k. Yes. We try to make sure what we have is pretty standard convertible, participating preferred. It looks like a venture deal. I'm not interested in buying common stock frankly, except in the form of options or restricted purchase at founders' price, then common stock works fine. But if I'm putting up my money I want the kind of protection that a venture financing has. ❞

Brian Horey

❝ If we are way far apart on valuation I don't try to talk them into something that they don't think they want to do. In NY it is probably a little less of a competitive market for angel-stage deals. The angel market is not quite as organized here, so it may be that it is just that there are not as many competing businesses as there might be in other places. But I have not encountered haggling often. Many of the companies are sufficiently cash strapped, and also the process itself is sufficiently inefficient, that they tend to want to get on with life. At least for the sums of money involved, there tends not to be enormous amounts of haggling. There are cases that I can think of where the prices in follow on rounds have gone way on up, to a point where I have decided not to participate. ❞

Mitch Kapor

❝ I am kind of a softie in terms of negotiating and so, to protect myself, I sometimes wound up structuring deals that anticipated subsequent VC rounds. I would essentially get a ride along on whatever they agreed to in the venture. So that saved having to work out lots of issues twice, since I knew various subsidiary terms would be thrashed out in a venture round.❞

2 ● FUNDAMENTALS OF EARLY-STAGE NEGOTIATING

This section was specially written by Robert J. Robinson, co-author of *Angel Investing*.[1] Rob created the Entrepreneurial Negotiating Course at Harvard Business School. Some of the concepts presented here are adapted from Lax and Sebenius (1986), and Sebenius (1997, in Lax and Sebenius, 1986).

Negotiation is consistently a deeply misunderstood, and poorly executed skill which is essential for entrepreneurs and angels alike. Here is a quick outline of some important concepts.

Rob Robinson

Interests, issues, and positions

Interests

There are three easily confused terms in negotiations which are critical to keep separate. These are interests, issues, and positions. Your *interests* in a negotiations are whatever you care about that is at stake. Put otherwise, your interests are a major part of the answer to, *"Why are you in this negotiation?"* Only a naïve entrepreneur limits interests to, *"How much money can I get?"* Some interests are *"hard,"* such as funding level, profit, timing, quality level, and specifications. Inexperienced negotiators often err by letting hard interests drive out *"soft"* considerations such as the relationship, the tone of the negotiating process, the precedent set, fairness to both parties, sustainability, the effect on reputation and self-image, whether trust is enhanced or eroded, etc. You should not automatically read selfish, short-term, and financial in front of interests. Of course, just as you seek to advance the full set of your interests, the other side(s) will be doing exactly the same thing. You should make assessing the full set of their interests a central part of your negotiation strategy.

NEGOTIATION IS CONSISTENTLY A DEEPLY MISUNDERSTOOD, AND POORLY EXECUTED SKILL

---

1 Adaptation of *Angel Investing: Matching Start-up Funds With Start-up Companies*, by Mark van Osnabrugge and Robert J. Robinson © 2000, Jossey-Bass, Inc. Adapted with permission by Jossey-Bass, Inc, a subsidiary of John Wiley & Sons, Inc.

Issues and positions

The *issues* in a negotiation are those items that are on the table for explicit agreement; such as amount to be invested, equity granted, terms of payback, etc. *Positions* are your stands on various issues. For example, in an equity negotiation an *issue* may be the amount to be invested, on which your *position* is a request for $150,000. Your underlying *interests* (as reflected in this request) obviously include gaining liquidity, but they may also involve internal organizational politics, external signals, and retention of control (Figure 41.1).

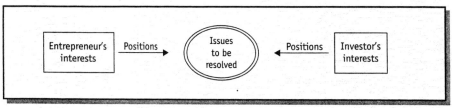

FIGURE 41.1

Positional versus interest-driven negotiations

The distinction between interests, issues, and positions has an important implication for the negotiation process. *Positional bargaining* sees the process as a "*dance*"– they come up a bit, you come down a bit, etc. – that if successful, ultimately converges on an agreement – or not, in the case of an impasse. *Interest-driven bargaining* sees the process try to balance conflicting interests. Although there is an important role for positional bargaining, a way to move stalled negotiations forward is to look behind conflicting positions to understand deeper interests. For example, an angel and an entrepreneur may squabble over the amount of equity the angel should receive, without realizing that the underlying interest is not really percentage of equity; for the entrepreneur it is a question of retaining control (which the angel may be happy to grant), and for the angel it is a question of ROI (which the entrepreneur is happy to grant as a legitimate interest). A classic solution in such a case would be non-participating – or non-voting – shares, which lock in the angel's equity and maximizes their ROI, but which allows the entrepreneur to retain control.

Alternatives and the bargaining range

An important factor in negotiations is the set of alternatives that each side has, relative to doing the deal in question. Your alternatives reflect what you will do if the proposed deal is not possible. Depending on the situation, it may involve simply walking away and doing without any agreement, or going to another potential investor or investment prospect. If asked whether you agree to a particular deal, you should be able to answer in your own mind the question by asking, "*As compared to what?*"

● **Alternatives determine the possible bargaining range.**

Your alternative sets the threshold that any acceptable agreement must exceed. The whole idea of negotiation is that both sides be better off after making the

THE WHOLE IDEA OF NEGOTIATION IS THAT BOTH SIDES BE BETTER OFF AFTER MAKING THE DEAL

deal than they otherwise would be, including their most likely alternatives. Alternatives can thus

determine the existence or absence of a possible bargaining range.

EXAMPLE

Imagine a simple situation in which the amount of equity to be invested has been decided (say, 25%). All that remains to be negotiated is the amount to be invested in exchange for this level of equity. In this case, the entrepreneur has another investor who has agreed to pay $125,000 for this 25% equity, which the entrepreneur finds a low but acceptable alternative. However, the investor has determined that he or she will not part with more than $175,000 for the 25% equity. A potentially profitable bargaining range exists – agreement can be better for each side than its alternative – and the negotiation process will determine where the parties end up within this range.

ENTREPRENEUR'S MINIMUM...   BARGAINING RANGE   ... INVESTOR'S MAXIMUM

$125,000 _____$175,000

In another case it is quite possible that no bargaining range exists: for example, the entrepreneur may have a more attractive offer than the investor can make. Sometimes the best deals are the ones you do *not* make.

● **Alternatives create negotiating leverage**

The ability and willingness to walk away from the table gives you power in the negotiation, and the better your alternative appears both to you and to the other party, the more credible your threat to walk away is – unless the deal is improved to your liking.

Negotiating strategies "at the table" versus those "away from the table"

Most people think of negotiation primarily as tactical and interpersonal actions at the table. Usually, however, the die is cast well before you ever sit down with the other guy.

Strategies *away from the table* make a huge difference. You can strengthen your position by looking around for other potential investors, cultivating other offers, creating publicity for your firm and product, generating favorable valuation models, finding out more about the other side's resources, etc. Contrariwise, if you face a tough negotiator and you have not taken the time to do any of these things (especially develop alternatives), you are in a very difficult position.

Properly done, negotiation need not be unpleasant. Get your interests straight, try and **NEGOTIATION NEED NOT BE UNPLEASANT** figure out those of the other side, develop the best possible alternatives, and structure a deal designed to meet everyone's needs. This is a process you will do again and again, whether you are an investor, or an entrepreneur, and you will improve with practice.

1 ● Many winners don't negotiate, or they leave it to someone else.

2 ● The entrepreneur has a lot of power to give or withhold gifts, and the relationship is highly interdependent.

3 ● There are many styles that work (including direct and tough negotiating).

4 ● "Big wings" can add to every element of negotiation.

Supporting

The role of the mentor was established right back at the start...

Andrew Blair

QUICK OVERVIEW

42 ● Start section   247

43 ● The five participation roles   249

Silent investor   249

Reserve force   249

Team member (full or part time)   250

Coach   250

Controlling investor   250

Lead investors   251

44 ● Value events   254

Examples   254

Interelate value events   256

45 ● The four types of start-ups   257

Product business   258

Service business   259

Retail business   261

E-business   262

46 ● Things to think about 264

Contributing 264

The best fit 265

Getting to the next round 266

Taking a board seat 269

47 ● Winning angels 271

What do most investors do? 271

What do the winners do? 271

Winning tools and tactics 273

48 ● Special sections 276

1 What role do you prefer? 276

2 How much time? 278

3 Resource bankruptcies 279

4 How to fail 280

5 A supporting story 281

6 Invest in three rounds, but never four 283

4 TAKEAWAYS FROM SUPPORTING 284

> There's building business models, hiring the right team,
> introducing the company to potential partners. Those are all
> things that need to happen for a company, an angel
> company to be successful...
>
> **Tim Draper**

You will be a better angel if you have been an entrepreneur, and a better entrepreneur if you have been an angel. This is particularly true when working together to make a business go. As Angel CL, who has invested in 20 start-ups, describes it:

❝ If there is a general judgment angle that I bring to everything I do, it's the fact that I have spent so much time building businesses and starting businesses. I look at the business idea from the point of view of someone who understands how you do those things, as opposed to a typical VC who has probably never run a business[1] ❞

Some investors specifically choose opportunities that need a lot of support. Jaap Blaak, who has been successful as an entrepreneur and as a venture capitalist, now prefers to get in early at the seed stage, and work with the entrepreneur through the entire process. Other investors prefer early-stage opportunities that already have teams and have made considerable progress.

Winning angels support start-ups by focusing on value events. A value event is any event which has a fundamental impact on the real or perceived value of the business, as well as its likelihood of success. Value events include: raising a VC round, signing up strategic partners, and achieving break-even. Many investors, such as CL and Richard Kramlich, like to get to know the entrepreneur better, sometimes by watching them make progress before investing. Some investors place conditions on writing a check, such as getting the first sale, finding a lead investor, or building a prototype.

YOU ARE INVESTING MONEY WITH SOMEONE WHO IS NOT RELATED TO YOU FOR A HIGHLY RISKY UNDERTAKING

---

1 CL would agree, however, that getting a VC in at the right moment makes sense. They are the pros at getting to liquidity events.

Behind many rapidly successful entrepreneurs are one or several experienced angels. In one of the initial studies at Capitalyst™, on identifying the predictors of success in early-stage deals, the involvement of an experienced angel came up time and time again. Depending on the partici-

BEHIND MANY RAPIDLY SUCCESSFUL ENTREPRENEURS ARE ONE OR SEVERAL EXPERIENCED ANGELS

pation strategies you employ as an angel, the entrepreneurial/angel relationship can be as complex as any other significant human relationship. After all, you are investing money with someone who is not related to you for a highly risky undertaking. This is why good self-assessment makes sense before getting started (see page 5). There are a variety of supporting roles that angels can take and many specific things they can do to help make a company go. That's what the sixth fundamental is all about.

CHAPTER 43

THE FIVE PARTICIPATION ROLES

You have many different roles, sometimes they change.

HS

Angel investors follow participation roles that are a combination of the needs and wants of the entrepreneur, the company, and themselves. Relevant experience and time availability factor in as well. For example, Cuno Pümpin had one investment that needed help getting off the ground quickly. The company had a new media concept with quality managers and a visionary, but they lacked the relationships to get strategic customers and partners quickly. Cuno *"helped them find customers and introduced them to well-known people in their industry."* This new media company leveraged Cuno's relationships to gain traction, and then went on to grow the company with other supporters and advisors.

Roles evolve and change, as in Cuno's case, where he subsequently became a silent investor. However, sometimes more involvement is required. If a company gets into trouble it may need a much more active angel. Or a new investor, such as a VC, may show up and prefer that the angels focus their energies elsewhere.

Let's take a look at the five fundamental roles.

SILENT INVESTOR

Pure financial investor, will take no active interest in the company, except to sign papers and hope for returns.

Howard often takes the silent investor role. But he can easily jump into a reserve force role when he sees an opportunity to have an impact and when he has the time. In other cases he has joined up with teams or acted as a coach. He is not interested in being a controlling angel.

RESERVE FORCE

Ready, willing, and capable to help as requested by the entrepreneur, impact depends on relevant skills and contacts and also on being called at the right time.

Andrew Blair and his partners often act as a reserve force. They maintain a 'hotline' for urgent access. For example, if an entrepreneur has a problem with the government bureaucrats and can't sleep, *"He can call through on the hotline and they will try to knock out the stressor for him."* David, through his company, Capitalyst,[1] also takes a reserve force role, providing upfront strategic advice and practical training on raising capital from high-impact investors.

TEAM MEMBER (FULL OR PART TIME)

Works in the company on particular projects or in a functional area. There is a risk of micro-managing the entrepreneur if the investor has a significant stake or represents a majority interest. Impact depends on relevant skills and contacts but also on the relationship with the entrepreneur which is likely tested in this scenario. An angel, who takes on the role of a team member, will have a high to negative impact.

As Jaap Blaak prefers true seed-stage deals he often gets actively involved. In one investment he had decided the scientist was *"definitely not a manager,"* and so he took on the CEO role until a full-time replacement could be found.

COACH

Perhaps the highest impact investor who does not control the company. Although in some cases they will have control that they do not exercise. Meets with the entre-

REMEMBER THAT COACHES STAY ON THE SIDELINES

preneur regularly and provides support, advice, and any assistance as needed and requested by the entrepreneur. Considerable experience in angel investing is a must. However, even a new angel could have impact if they remember to act as a coach. Remember that coaches stay on the sidelines.

Betsy Atkins sometimes plays a coaching role. She is available for monthly board meetings and weekly telephone calls. *"If there's something hot cooking, like an IPO, we will talk many times a day,"* she says. *"I'm there for them at all times as a supportive active investor."*

CONTROLLING INVESTOR

An investor who really becomes the entrepreneur by taking control (outright or through conventions) and manages the company. High impact.

Jeff Parker sometimes plays a controlling role where he invests the majority of the capital and gains voting control, control of the board, or control through the investment agreements.

---

1 See www.capitalyst.com.

LEAD INVESTORS

"My view is that if you can piggyback the professionals, for whom it is their daily job to help fix problems and monitor them, then that's a better way to approach it."

Bill Sahlman

Although controlling and coaching angels are almost certainly the lead investor in their deals, any angel can play this role. Craig Burr plays the lead role if he is the major capital provider or if he brings in other investors.

CL usually plays a reserve force role, unless the amounts get higher. "*My typical individual investment can be anywhere from $50–100k. If I am going up to $500k or approaching $1m, I'll be bringing in other guys,*" he says. Morton Goulder is often the first investor of the Nashua Breakfast Club to join in. Once Mort signs on, many of the others give it a serious look.

Aside from the entrepreneurial team and other attractive components of the start-up opportunity, the lead investor can be a significant reason for other investors to join in. They are the first to place their money, and perhaps their time and reputation, into the deal. Lead investors often have a significant impact on fund-raising. In some cases silent investors become leads without intending it, as they are so well known that their name attracts money. Thus it would be productive to have clear communication with the entrepreneur to understand who, if anyone, is the lead investor and why.

> **Who's on first?**
>
> Sometimes everyone thinks the other guy has done his homework or is paying attention. Make sure whoever you think is the lead is actually the lead!

There are different definitions and different expectations of lead investors. However, almost all include an expectation by other investors that the lead made an independent decision and is willing to actively participate in some manner. Although it is not widely practiced, it seems reasonable that lead investors should have some additional compensation for their role. A useful experiment might be to empower the entrepreneurial team to provide warrants worth up to 20% of the lead investor's stake, based on his contribution during the first 12 months. Angel CL plays the lead when he has organized the syndicate. He doesn't take additional compensation, "*Because it wouldn't be worth the hassle of setting up the limited partnership.*" Perhaps in our next edition there will be a proven method to better compensate leads.[2]

---

2 If you have any ideas on this, please send them to DavidandHoward@WinningAngels.com

> ### EXAMPLE EXPECTATIONS OF A LEAD INVESTOR
>
> At StartUpFund I,*** a Lead investor is highly preferred in each deal where the fund invests money. Some of the expectations of a lead investor include:
>
> - Acceptance and acknowledgment of the lead investor role until venture capital is raised, or another investor takes on a significant role.
> - Willingness to help the company raise additional capital through his or her personal network.
> - Willingness and ability to see that the investment terms are beneficial to the follow-on investors and productive for the company.
> - Five–ten hours per week availability and interest in supporting the start-up through its birthing and growing pains, probably until an institutional investor arrives.
> - Relevant functional and industry experience and relevant contacts.
> - Angel investing experience or a clear demonstration of a managed learning curve. The only way a new angel can be successful as a lead is to aggressively learn and develop the trade. The preferred lead will already have invested and actively supported more than one start-up.
>
> *** A diversified angel fund founded by David Amis and Jake Ben-Meir in 1999 and currently managed by Capitalyst Group, LLC in Boston, MA. StartUpFund I will invest in over 35 early-stage opportunities. See www.WinningAngels.com for more information.

Entrepreneurs quickly learn that despite their intelligence, experience, and good sense, many angels will act like sheep when it comes to early-stage investing, with everyone following each other. Therefore, clarify if there is a lead investor, who they are, and why. The lack of a lead does not a bad deal make, but just be sure you are investing for reasons that you understand.

What do start-up advisors and virtual CEOs do?

Here are the eight basic services that Tom Wharton, a start-up advisor, provides to start-ups. He says, *"Providing moral support and a sounding board is often just as important."*

1 **Strategic planning**

   Strategic planning includes an initial review of business strategy and injection of strategic adjustments where necessary, and ongoing review and adjustments of business strategy.

2 **Positioning and marketing**

   Early-stage positioning and marketing define the target customer base and a targeted marketing strategy.

3 **Business plan and revenue model development**

   Getting all the components of the business down on paper and defining the specific revenue and pricing models as well as future revenue extensions that we plan to develop. This is critical for the development of budgets and a focused business effort.

4 **Developing investor presentation materials**

   Managements ability to sell investors on this opportunity is critical. Presentation materials must deliver a logical and emotional reaction in the investor.

5 **Introducing the company to investors**

   Having a rolodex of potential angel investors and bringing an association to other successful opportunities will almost always get the company in the door!

6 **Implementation and operational practices**

   Young entrepreneurs don't always have experience managing or building an organization and tend to think they can do everything themselves. Helping them define business needs and someone to do them becomes critical to success.

7 **The development of the PPM, option plans, and other legal documents**

   Practical experience and a war chest of legal documents makes the development of legal documents more efficient and a big cost saver.

8 **Business negotiations and negotiation strategy**

   Negotiating strategic agreements is an art and an experienced business person can prevent a lot of missteps for a growing company.

CHAPTER 44 VALUE EVENTS

> A value event is essentially anything that brings a
> heightened level of excitement.
>
> **Tom Wharton**

The best way to think about managing your contribution to a start-up is to focus on supporting the attainment of value events. Value events are the key events needed for the company to succeed and for you to get a financial win. A value event represents a significant increase in the real or perceived value of the company. It usually also means the likelihood of success has increased significantly.

THE BEST WAY TO THINK ABOUT MANAGING YOUR CONTRIBUTION TO A START-UP IS TO FOCUS ON SUPPORTING THE ATTAINMENT OF VALUE EVENTS

For example, when Palm Pilot™ built its first working prototype, this was a major value event for the company. It meant they could build a personal information device that would fit in your hand. A lot of risk (although not all!) was removed. Equally important, it gave them something to show to investors.

Value events are often self-evident. But the best way to identify them is by asking the next potential round of investors, *"What would have to happen for you to invest in this company in the next round?"*

EXAMPLES

Following are several examples of value events by functional area of the business.

Marketing

- The first real sale or qualified letter of intent.
- Consummating one or more key strategic relationships.
- Repeated sales.
- Establishing a repetitive sales process.
- Market entry #2, product #2 launch.

Financial

- Discovering the size of the hole.
- Attaining positive cash flow.
- Attaining cumulative cash break-even.
- Raising an additional angel round.
- Raising a venture capital round.
- Securing debt financing.

Organizational

- Hiring professional managers.
- Setting up the executive board.
- Setting up an advisory board.
- Transitioning from a hustling entrepreneur to a delegating entrepreneur.

Operational

- Implementing the service/product/retail/e-business business.
- Attaining verifiable per-unit profit margins.

Production

- Building the first prototype.
- Completing the first production run.
- Building the first units at a cost that allows per-unit profitability.

Strategic

- Gaining a strategic investor.
- Gaining a strategic partner.
- Identifying potential buyers.

Other

- Proving the model.
- Proving the concept.
- Creating the foundation for growth.

INTERELATE VALUE EVENTS

Figure 44.1 shows the key value events for Interelate, the company which was described previously on page 157.

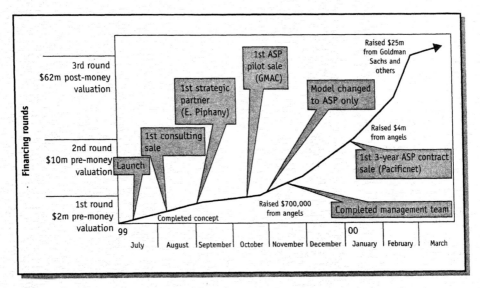

FIGURE 44.1

How one angel identifies value events

Angel investor SM, a British angel, was particularly good at identifying value events. He would complete the following process with each potential opportunity:

1 Meet the entrepreneurs and get a good understanding of the opportunity.

2 Meet with a few venture capitalists, angel investors or corporate investors and describe the opportunity to them, assessing their general interest.

3 If they are interested, ask them, *"What would have to happen for you to invest in this company?"*

4 Their answers include, "If they had a buyer, I would join in," or "As soon as the technology is proven, and at a manufacturable cost, then I would consider a second round of $3–5m," or "When they get their team together."

All of these answers are "value events" and angel SM lets the future investors or buyers state them clearly. Then he goes back to the entrepreneurs and says, *"I'm going to invest $300k in your company and here is what we are going to achieve over the next four months. When we do that, I know we will be able to raise our next round."*

Each business can be wholly different in its value events and the following questions will be helpful in determining the value events for a company:

● What is needed to raise more capital?

● Who is the most likely buyer and what do they want to see?

● What will allow us to create positive cash flow?

● How are our competitors valued?

CHAPTER 45

THE FOUR TYPES OF START-UPS

There are four fundamental types of businesses; three have been around for centuries and one is new and still defining itself. Although all four types are a productive way to think about the fundamental differences of start-ups, many businesses are a combination of two or more, such as Dell which makes computers but also provides a 1-800 service to help create the product just for you (product and retail business). Let's look at the four types and then we will examine the value events likely for each. Your job as a supportive angel is to help the company where you can make the biggest impact. First, you need to identify its potential value events.

1 Product business

Making and selling a product, such as the new Mach3 Gillette Razor™, or the PalmPilot™.[1] There are highly engineered products, such as houses and super-computers which have similar start-up issues given their inability to scale versus repetitive products, such as toy airplanes or cans of beans which have high throughput. Automobiles are highly engineered/high throughput which means outstanding amounts of capital are required.

2 Service business

Providing a service, such as Geico™ Auto Insurance, or Fidelity™ Mutual Funds. Personal services, such as consulting make for different start-up dynamics from generic services, such as insurance. The former can generate cash quickly but is more difficult to scale.

3 Retail business

Selling someone else's products to the public usually in a store setting, such as House of Blues™ restaurants (which sell both food and collectables) or the Body Shop™ which sells natural body care products.

4 E-business

Using the internet to create a business which can take many forms, such as Amazon™ selling books, Yahoo!™ providing web services, or eBay providing a marketplace for consumer auctions.[2]

Depending on the type of business, different value events will apply and many of the same events will have different meanings. When deciding where to focus your efforts, it is helpful to recognize where the key drivers of value lie.

---

1 Another example of a business which combines a product (the PalmPilot™ itself) and a variety of services (email, calendar, etc.)

2 Note that these companies have expanded beyond their original business model/offering. The internet is leading to drastic changes in some industries, minor changes in others, and wholly new industries in some cases.

PRODUCT BUSINESS

Making something you can see and touch is the traditional business. The value events unique to manufacturing and selling products (see Figure 45.1) include:

- **Defining the product** (*i.e. blueprints, market research leading to concept proposal*)

  Before the product can be built, it must be designed. This value event usually takes place before the angels show up, otherwise, there is not much for them to talk about.

- **Building the first prototype**

  The inventor entrepreneur is critical at this stage of the game. Until the prototype is completed, it is hard to get serious customer interest. The prototype can also prove the concept to potential investors.

- **1st sale** $\boxed{\textbf{\$\$\$}}$

  This demonstrates the value proposition! If someone will pay cash for the product, there may actually be a business.

- **Professional managers**

  It's not just about capital, management is the catalyst for a company to begin production and marketing in earnest. In some cases, angels will not invest until the arrival of professional managers.

- **Scale production**

  This demonstrates that the company can produce. The only other questions that remain are: Can they market the product? Can they produce and market without screwing it up too much?

EXAMPLE   A FEW EXAMPLES OF PRODUCT VALUE EVENTS

Apple Computer gains the interest of a venture capital firm (VenRock) which sends a signal to other VCs and industry pros.

Intel completes its business plan on a napkin (so the investors know what they are investing in and can write checks).

Aero Design and Engineering sells one of its planes to President Eisenhower.***

*** In the early 1950s, Aero Design and Engineering built the first twin-engine plane for private use in the US, the Aerocommander. When they sold one of their planes, with the approval of the US Secret Service, to President Eisenhower, it was a benchmark moment for the company and its credibility.

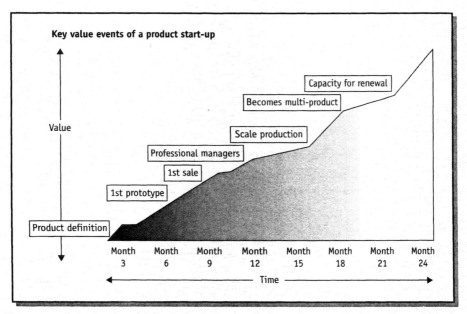

Key value events of a product start-up

FIGURE 45.1

SERVICE BUSINESS

Delivering any kind of a service to customers is unique in that it generally does not include a feel and touch product but rather an intangible benefit, such as insurance, or beauty, or health. The value events unique to service businesses (see Figure 45.2) include:

● **Service concept**

Completing the concept for the business is usually the first value event.

● **Raising first round of capital**

This gives the business some legs so it can build out its service offering or at least begin setting up the business.

● **Initiating operations**

Now comes the proof of the pudding. Initiating operations shows that the deal is real as far as the management team and concept are concerned. Next question: Will customers buy?

● **Demonstrable marketing event**

The business generates enough interest and sales through one or some combination of marketing events so that it demonstrates the value proposition and leaves the remaining question: can they do enough to get to positive cash flow or at least demonstrate profitable margins?

- **Raising value capital or attaining positive cash flow**

  Positive cash flow is a key moment since it not only proves the business is at a survival level and reduces the likelihood of bankruptcy, but it also improves the negotiating position. Alternatively, if the company has profitable margins and can raise additional capital based on some plan for attaining break-even, this is likewise a significant value event.

- **Hiring a professional management team**

  In a service business the management team may arrive after demonstration of the basic model in order to expand the business. Or, in an established industry, such as telecommunications, it may be desirable to have them in the beginning.

EXAMPLE **A FEW EXAMPLES OF SERVICE VALUE EVENTS**

Warren Buffet raises about $100k from Omaha investors to start his first fund.

Interelate begins repeat sales to Fortune 500 companies without the involvement of its founder.

Capitalyst recruits management from Lucent, BDM, and Merril Lynch.

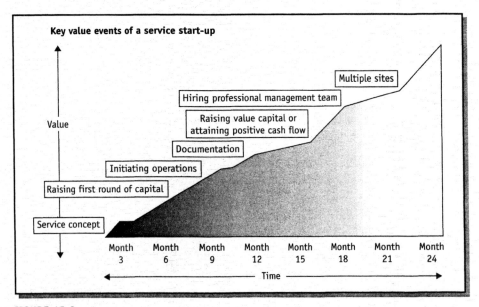

FIGURE 45.2

RETAIL BUSINESS

Retailers sell to the public. They will have stores or call centers in order to sell directly to the public. The value events unique to retail businesses (see Figure 45.3) include:

- **Retail concept**

  Formulating the retail concept, such as a clothing shop for pregnant women, allows the stakeholders to understand and question the proposal.

- **Management team**

  Retail, which include some non-business-oriented decision makers, is more dependent on a management team that understands its market. Many professional investors will not do retail, and they are even less inclined to do so without experienced management.

- **Raising first round of capital**

  Allows the company to get started. However, if the investors do not have industry experience, there is a still a question of validity of concept.

- **Identify property**

  Real estate, real estate, real estate. This is usually a major value event for location-oriented retail businesses.

- **Store launch**

  Another major value event as the concept can now be tested in the marketplace.

- **2nd store launch**

  The roll-out begins! And so does the test of whether management can expand the concept.

- **Expansion team**

  The arrival of an expansion team, particularly with experience in roll-outs, is an important indicator of likely success on a large scale.

EXAMPLE A FEW EXAMPLES OF RETAIL VALUE EVENTS

The Body Shop opens its second store marking the beginning of expansion.

Dell Computer delivers its first "made-to-order" computer demonstrating the entire sequence of marketing, production, and delivery.

Blockbuster completes its first acquisition of a local video chain.

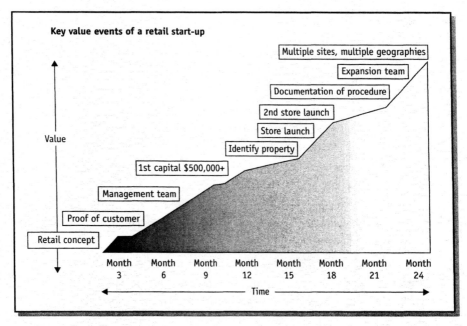

Key value events of a retail start-up

Value

- Multiple sites, multiple geographies
- Expansion team
- Documentation of procedure
- 2nd store launch
- Store launch
- Identify property
- 1st capital $500,000+
- Management team
- Proof of customer
- Retail concept

Month 3 | Month 6 | Month 9 | Month 12 | Month 15 | Month 18 | Month 21 | Month 24

Time

FIGURE 45.3

E-BUSINESS

The internet has created a renaissance of entrepreneurship and early-stage investing. There are several different e-business models and more developing. We will think of web browsers and new market creators (such as eBay) as e-businesses, because they exist solely on the internet as a business, while Cisco and others that provide equipment for the net are really product businesses. Others, such as ISPs can be thought of as service and e-businesses. The distinctions are not important. What is important is that you can identify the fundamental business and its value events. The value events unique to e-businesses (as of 2000) (see Figure 45.4) include:

● **E-business concept**

Completion of the concept, although likely to change, is particularly powerful if it is simple and already has a defined customer.

● **Build site**

Although building a quality site is do-able by most teams with some cash (some without), the site has a major impact on the perception of investors. After all, the "store" has been created.

● **Hire team**

The arrival of key team members, depending on the model (web developer, marketing manager, or alliance manager) positions the company to go fast, which is critical in e-businesses where the first-mover advantage can be powerful.

- **Strategic partners**

In many e-businesses, strategic partners are the name of the game and may represent a unique hold on the market or at least the credibility needed to reach critical mass.

- **Raise marketing capital**

Once the concept is basically proven and the management team has laid the foundation, it is time to go to market, usually in a big way. Raising $10m+ of marketing capital may be necessary for success.

- **Attain critical mass**

Particularly with market-making models, critical mass is required for the business to work. This is not like a dealership where you can sell one car at a time and four cars makes for a good day. It may be that thousands or hundreds of thousands of customers are needed for the business to work.

EXAMPLE   A FEW EXAMPLES OF E-BUSINESS VALUE EVENTS

Amazon gets orders from "as far away as New Hampshire" without any marketing.

StarMedia raises its first round of capital from investors with connections in the venture capital and investment banking communities.

FairAir completes an agreement with Northwest Airlines to support its secondary market in airline tickets.

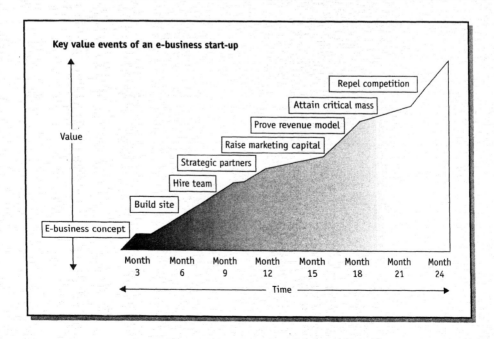

Key value events of an e-business start-up

CHAPTER 46

THINGS TO THINK ABOUT

CONTRIBUTING

> The risk that I can address is the early risk of establishing a business
> model and building a team, developing strategic relationships and
> securing financing. I know how to do that very well, and I can take an
> idea and an unproven team, and bring it to the next level.
>
> **Randy Komisar**

Given the five fundamental participation roles and the concept of value events, the
next question concerns the best way to contribute. There are a variety of ideas and
strategies for contributing to a start-up. Before we review them, let's consider the
five experiential assets that an angel can bring to a start-up. Most of the relevant
contributions any angel can make will be based on things they have done before.

Experiential assets

There are five kinds of experiential assets which an angel may bring to bear on a
start-up and they each come with a unique potential for contribution, as shown in
Table 46.1.

TABLE 46.1

	Experiential asset				
General contribution opportunities	*Industry*	*Functional*	*Network*	*Angel experience*	*Entrepreneur experience*
	Strategic advice Product development advice Introductions to industry players	Management advice Assistance in interviewing job candidates Hands-on assistance	Open doors: – New partners – New team members – New capital providers – Other professionals	Raise more angel capital Raise venture capital Allround advice on dealing with financial or growth issues	High-impact general advice and support on a variety of growth and management issues Hands-on assistance

Notes:
Entrepreneurs are good general supporters since they know what it's like to fight the start-up battle, and can advise on a
multitude of problems. Entrepreneurs are the best problem solvers around. Angels with harvesting experience are particularly
good advisors as they can help direct a start-up team towards the steps needed to achieve an exit.

THE BEST FIT

People who want to be angel investors had better understand that this is totally about some set of things other than hitting home runs. It's about wanting to be involved in new businesses, working with young people, trying to give something back to the community.

Howard Tullman

Having decided upon the angel participation roles that you prefer, and considering your experiential assets, perhaps as well as the unique needs of the start-up in question, you can think about how to create the best fit. There are no limits to how you can support a start-up or how you might structure a deal, but by making the right big decisions the little ones should flow. Table 46.2 shows the best fit for an angel and a start-up, considering the stage of development of the company and the capability of the entrepreneurs.

TABLE 46.2

<table>
<tr><td colspan="2"></td><td colspan="3" align="center">Company stage</td></tr>
<tr><td colspan="2"></td><td>Seed</td><td>Early stage</td><td>Pre-VC</td></tr>
<tr><td rowspan="6">Capability of entrepreneurial team</td><td rowspan="3">High</td><td>Reserve force</td><td>Reserce force</td><td>Reserve force</td></tr>
<tr><td>Coach</td><td>Coach</td><td>Silent investor</td></tr>
<tr><td></td><td>Silent investor</td><td></td></tr>
<tr><td rowspan="4">Medium</td><td>Controlling angel</td><td>Controlling angel</td><td>Team member</td></tr>
<tr><td>Team member</td><td>Team member</td><td>Coach</td></tr>
<tr><td></td><td>Coach</td><td>Reserve force</td></tr>
<tr><td></td><td>Reserve force</td><td></td></tr>
</table>

Notes:

1 Both medium-capability and high-capability teams may prefer silent investors as they do not interfere. Silent investors should be clear about the bets they are making and are best suited to deals where less outside influence is needed or there is a good active presence from other angels.

2 Some medium-capability teams actually need control taken away from them to succeed. Higher capability teams could be de-motivated by a controlling angel.

3 Coaches and reserve force angels are suited to any kind of start-up but are best for the high-capability teams. The best coaches only work with superior individuals.

Summary of best fit

- A high-capability team includes three to four team members with relevant experience, proper motivation, track records, etc. These are the people you can invest in with relatively little worry.

- A medium-capability team is made up of one to two team members, lacking in some basic functional or industry experience. They can do it, they just need another member or two with appropriate experience or some very active angels.

- A low-capability team is not included in Table 47.2 because you don't have time to deal with them. The classic case is an inventor who may be ignorant of business practices but makes up for it with his stubbornness.

- Seed stage refers to deals that are very young, whether they have management or not, there is not a lot more than a concept or a business plan, or at most, a prototype.

- Early stage refers to the typical angel investment period where the company is on the brink of its first sale or has already demonstrated something of the value proposition. A chunk of the risk is gone but some still remains.

- Pre-VC refers to an opportunity that is already working on raising VC, and, in fact, has a good likelihood of doing so. It has significant sales but not positive cash flow. In other words, the business is going forward and is successful by most standards. It needs that final push to achieve enough sales to reach break-even.

GETTING TO THE NEXT ROUND

Angels put in their own money as a way of getting the company started, not as a way to finance the business. It's a big difference. Then we pass it along to intermediate VCs, the funds here in New England tend to be $25m to $100m, and then they pass it along to the big professional guys who are very custodial, and then most of the time the company sells out. The IPO thing in history is very unusual, so most of the time you sell out to your biggest customer. We go from angel to small VC to large VC and finally to liquidation.

Dick Morley

Perhaps the most important contribution an angel can make is to help the company get to its next round of financing. Although some winning angels invest in every round of their companies, most consider their role to end when an institutional investor arrives or the company attains an exit event. *"The role I play is that I facilitate, as a catalyst, to get the company to a liquidity event such as an acquisition or an IPO,"* says Betsy Atkins. Many venture capitalists look for angel involvement. 3i (a UK VC) has a special unit assigned to creating angel relationships. *"We love having venture angels attached to our companies,"* says VC Tim Draper of Draper, Fisher and Jurvetson. Winning angels contribute in many roles, but recognize that a hand-off to some larger investor is a common and preferred occurrence.

"The highest return was where I could contribute," says Cuno Pümpin.

Here are specific contributions that angels can make, organized according to the general participation strategy where they normally fit. How they are organized isn't important. What is important is making a difference and getting your money out.

Silent investor

- Invest.
- Lend use of name (by investing).
- Make three referrals.

Reserve force

- Raise additional capital.
- Sell a customer.
- Sell a strategic partner.
- Advise on a project.
- Closing supporter.
- General advisor.
- Functional advisor.
- Introducer.

Two questions

All of this may be good thinking, but remember that the best two ways to figure out how to contribute are to:

- Ask the entrepreneur what they want.
- Do a lot of deals so you know what they need.

These two questions should be taped to your mirror since their 17 words are as important as the 1,240 that preceded them.

Team member (full or part time)

- Take on any operational role.
- Take part on a short-term full-time basis.
- Take part on a medium- to long-term part-time basis.
- Consult to the company.
- Raise venture capital.
- Sign up strategic partners.

Coach

- Take on the role of mentor.
- Take on the role of daily advisor.
- Provide "name" support.

Controlling investor

- Take on the role of CEO.
- Be chairman of the board (high activity and power).

Monitoring

Originally the title of this fundamental was monitoring, based on the VC perspective. However, as we interviewed winning angels, time and time again, they replaced this word with "supporting". Most angels think of themselves as members of the team, or at least as cheerleaders. However, most do actively monitor their investments in some manner. For example, angel investor Carl Guerreri requires monthly financial statements and yearly externally audited accounts.

Bert Twaalfhoven does the following

❝ I communicate with them a couple of times a week, usually starting on Monday... sometimes my secretary got on the phone... to get the information... we had annual budgets by month, adjusted budgets by quarter, and a five year plan. Then we have the negative plan, the survival plan. I say, let's go for a worse case, and see how long we can survive... we do all kinds of scenarios. ❞

Many angels such as Betsy Atkins, Dave Berkus, and Lucius Cary will monitor the company through their role on the board. Steve Walker likes to build a reporting mechanism into the deal. Many winning angels monitor in some structured way.

Then there are angels like Dick Morley, who have a pretty different perspective: "I am almost always not on the board. And then I never see them again... I'm just as surprised as they are when they make it."

TAKING A BOARD SEAT

"The question is what is the role of a board member? It's trying to anticipate what the financing needs of the company will be and making sure you're positioned to do that. And that means making sure you have a plan that makes sense, and making sure you anticipate far enough in advance when you need money."

SG

Angel investors take varying views on board seats, which depend mostly on the role they intend to adopt. Hands-on angels, like Bert Twaalfhoven, often sit on boards to facilitate the control they think is necessary. Coaching and controlling angels and anyone taking a lead role is probably better off with the proximity the board seat will allow. David Berkus often takes the *"lead director role"* as he describes it, assuming chairmanship of the board and helping to recruit other directors. Carl Guerreri often takes an option to sit on the board, even though he is usually a silent investor.

HANDS-ON ANGELS OFTEN SIT ON BOARDS TO FACILITATE THE CONTROL THEY THINK IS NECESSARY

However, there is risk involved in a board seat and an angel should only join if the entrepreneurs are trustworthy and if he has time to pay attention. Lucius Cary does not mind sitting on boards, *"if all of the right insurance is there."*

Many investors, such as Dick Morley and OH avoid board seats. *"I try to avoid board seats because of the time commitment, but am always available for specific projects or problems,"* says John Hime. One European investor said he could not sit on an American board because, *"The IRS is worse than the devil! If they think you have income in the US, they try to tax you on everything!"*

THERE IS RISK INVOLVED IN A BOARD SEAT

Raising capital, giving strategic advice, counseling management, and ensuring that the company fulfils its duties to shareholders are all normal roles for board members. In early-stage companies, planning for additional financing rounds and helping management to focus on critical value events are especially important.

David Solomont says, *"I sit on boards. I get off them also... I usually get on when I help organize a round, and I usually get off when we bring in the VC money."*

Most angels who do join boards exit when any company-changing event occurs, such as a VC round, a strategic sale, or if a particularly large investor joins in. However, some will continue to serve throughout the lifecycle of the business.

Most angels serve on no more than four boards at one time, and these tend to be semi-professional angels who spend all of their time on angel investing. Other angels may take only one or two board seats but they always think seriously about the liability and ensure they are able to give enough time and focus to this important role. For example, Tony Morris limits the number of boards he sits on:

66 I am on three boards and three boards of advisors... but I am reluctant to go on the board of directors for more than four companies at a time. That's because on the board of directors you have a fiduciary obligation that really limits your freedom. So I don't go on boards without a certain amount of compensation. 99

WINNING ANGELS 2000

The following excerpts from *The Winning Angels Study* ©2000, by David Amis and Jocelyn Dinnin: "What do most investors do?", "What do the winners do?" and the selected winning tools and tactics, are reprinted with permission. Highlights of this study were published in *The Winning Angels Handbook*.

WHAT DO MOST INVESTORS DO?

- **Nothing**

  Many investors take a "wait and see" position, not necessarily helping and not asking for information (which is often not sent).

- **Demand changes**

  Some investors play armchair quarterback and attempt to redirect the entrepreneur in one of many directions, asking, advising, or demanding changes to the operating plan.

- **Monitor and support as they can**

  Especially if they put a reporting mechanism into the deal structure they will have regular updates. Many investors do take action when asked or when they identify some area in which they may be of help.

WHAT DO THE WINNERS DO?

- **Give active support often at the strategic level**

  OH chooses carefully the entrepreneurs he invests in and also when he is willing to take a lead investor role. But when he does, he arranges monthly day-long meetings to get an assessment from the entrepreneur and to help him think through and solve the company's challenges. *"I see helping as my primary role,"* says Lucius Cary. *"Concentrate on promoting management process rather than on trying to double guess management,"* says Martin Rigby. Winning investors actively support their entrepreneurs.

  WINNING INVESTORS ACTIVELY SUPPORT THEIR ENTREPRENEURS

- **Emphasize the entrepreneur during evaluation**

  We have said it so many times it has got to hurt your ears. But the winning investors choose their entrepreneurs carefully so that when things do not go as planned, they have a solid businessperson to rely on. Who said, *"Entrepreneur, entrepreneur, entrepreneur"*?

● **Expect the 2x rule**

Having raised $500,000 from an angel investor to buy a company, David once returned with a plan to double the size of the company, requesting an additional $200,000. *"Okay,"* the investor said. *"Let's do that and I'll expect it to cost $400,000."* Winning investors know that if there is any rule of thumb in this game, it is that everything costs twice as much and takes twice as long. They are prepared for this eventuality.

● **Take care of the entrepreneur during structuring**

Now is the time when those investors who like to "mortgage" the entrepreneur to the business pay. Developing a good relationship (warm and fuzzy, if possible) with the entrepreneur will make this part of the process go better.

● **Build a team around the start-up**

"Bring the right players to the start-up," says Andrew Filipowski, who has led dozens of early-stage investments, including StarMedia. This will provide the support the company needs as it grows. Essentially, Filipowski prepares for the troubleshooting before it happens by recognizing that the need for such activity will be apparent soon enough.

● **"Own" the start-up**

Some angel investors only do deals that they control. *"If you invest and leave it alone, you will have a very different rate of return,"* says Andrew Filipowski. He believes you need to, *"Start with the right team, have plenty of capital, and never give up."* Carl Guerreri (three stars, two living dead, two failures) always takes a minority stake, *"usually less than 25%."* He and other investors prefer to leave a majority of shares in the hands of the entrepreneurs.

● **Prepare for later stages**

Carl Guerreri writes the second round into the first-round deal. If entrepreneurs need it, he gets more equity. These angel investors know from experience that additional rounds are not only highly likely, but usually necessary.

● **Build monitoring into the deal**

One angel described how he usually holds back some of the investment, requiring the entrepreneur to provide a one-page report at the beginning of each month to get a check. Carl Guerreri requires monthly financial statements and yearly externally audited accounts.

● **Require a monthly one-pager**

"They must communicate monthly, put down on one side of one piece of paper, cash balance, what did you do this month?," says Jeff Parker. *"The best deals are when the entrepreneur enjoys communicating with the investors,"* says Parker. *"The minimum involvement I have is quarterly meetings and monthly updates of the accounts,"* says Lucius Cary.

- **Monthly meetings**

  OH shows up monthly for one eight-hour day solely focused on the entrepreneur and the business. Jeff Parker has *"issue weekends"* where they meet with the entrepreneur to work on whatever issues are occurring. *"Monthly board meetings"* says Betsy Atkins. *"weekly telephone calls... unless there is something hot cooking."* *"First bi-weekly, then every month, and then quarterly,"* says Andrew Blair.

- **Cheerleader**

  "I'm a cheerleader," says George Kline. *"I walk in, see how things feel... I like constant monitoring."* One heightened fear of entrepreneurs is when they lose a key employee. *"The largest single thing that I find myself reassuring the management over is that we will replace whoever is leaving and the business will not burn down,"* says Howard Tullman.

- **Help the entrepreneurs to find and use advisors**

  "Learning how to use advisors is one of the key skills of an entrepreneur," says OH.

- **Bring VC relationships**

  "I'm in the side funds of eight major VC funds," says Audrey MacLean. *"I talk to several VCs on a regular basis,"* says Betsy Atkins. Randy Komisar says:

  "There's a symbiotic relationship between me and the VCs that helps in the screening and filtering process. When I have a deal that I think is ready for financing, I will vet it against a set of VCs and use them as my screen. When they need a mentor to guide a team or someone with pertinent experience to review a deal, they often call me. So, it is symbiotic: I'm a source and screen to them and they are a source and screen to me."

WINNING TOOLS AND TACTICS

🎤 Lead investor monthly meeting

Schedule a meeting each month with the entrepreneurs, usually for a half-day or so. At this meeting, all aspects of the company are examined, plans are re-assessed and modified, and opportunities to support the entrepreneur are identified. You are demonstrating to the entrepreneur that you are there to help, and by devoting a set period of time each month you will be able to make a real difference.

When David was the Managing Director of VCR in Oxford, England, his primary angel would come meet him in London for one day a month. At this meeting, an update of the business was presented, along with issues and questions to resolve. At the end of the meeting, based on mutual decision making, an action plan was completed for some issues while others remained open for later discussion.

> Schedule a monthly, day-long meeting and use it to support the entrepreneur in thinking, planning, and taking action to make the business go.

✷ Three hurdles management

There are three key hurdles that an entrepreneurial company must overcome and if you focus on helping them do these things, their success is much more likely (most of the other problems will be self-made or due to lack of professional management which can be solved).

> Focus on helping the company achieve these three major hurdles:
> 1 The first prototype.
> 2 The first sale.
> 3 First outside capital.

✷ Investor update $$$

Give this form to the entrepreneur and have him/her commit to complete it monthly:

- Sales activities and results
- Capital-raising activities and results
- Organizational events/issues
- Other wins/setbacks
- Number of team members
- Sales this month
- Cash in the bank
- Burn rate and expenses this month
- Accomplishments
- Risks avoided

- Opportunities ahead
- Risks ahead
- Decisions needed
- Questions on which input would be desired.

Get a strategic investor

"You need to be able to articulate the market model and how it relates to your strategic investor," says Steven McGeady, angel investor and venture fund manager, and Vice President of Intel's Internet Technology until June 2000.

Many corporations now have business development or strategic equity groups which invest in companies where they can provide unique value or gain unique benefits. Having such a partner can make a major impact not only on the operations of the business but also on its ability to gain recognition in the marketplace and raise more capital.

Get a substantial strategic partner.

1 ● WHAT ROLE DO YOU PREFER?

We asked our winning angels what role they prefer to take in their start-ups, here is what they said.

Tony Morris

❝ The role I prefer to have changes over the time. The younger the company the broader my role. I am a strategy consultant and I'm eager to be involved.❞

Darryl Wash

❝ It is a question of mind share... that is the type of supporting role I can play, really trying to be non-intrusive, non-invasive. There are enough tasks to perform and challenges that entrepreneurs have to face in building a business and they don't need angels showing up asking them questions. They really need angels to be value added. So we will maybe fire off an email saying, hey, did you think about offering this, hey, I know this person, would you like an introduction and quite honestly to accept that if they don't respond it's because they are doing something that is hopefully more important for the company.❞

Audrey MacLean

❝ I see myself as a guardian angel. That is someone who is going to invest and really become part of the team, by helping you raise money, recruiting people, fleshing out the business model, refining the strategy, helping formulate strategic alliances, and so on. I do this from the advisory or board level. Lots of times I end up recruiting a CEO or core members of the team. It is very different from angel investing as an investing only proposition.❞

Brian Horey

❝ Generally speaking, I try not to be involved in things where I am completely passive, but on the other hand I do not have enough time to be serving a highly active role, so I am somewhere in the middle.❞

Dave Berkus

66 I will often take the lead director role and sometimes the chairmanship in a corporate board that in many cases has not been formed... So I will help in the recruiting of the board. So I will become the CEO coach spending an average of, depending on the kind of investment, a half up to two days a month in the actual investment company itself. 99

Steve McGeady

66 For my personal or angel investing, I always like to add some value other than simply money. I try to get involved in things where I can help out personally, and in the riskier companies I naturally expect to spend more time. My time might be management help, technology counseling, or help raising funds, but the time spent is an important part of my investment. 99

OH

66 I want to invest where there is a Lucius Cary (he is known for being hands-on) because I don't want to be involved with the entrepreneur. I don't have the time. 99

Lucius Cary

66 I don't so much monitor as actively participate. My rule of investing in a business within a one-hour drive makes it much easier to be close to what they are doing. Early on my role is supportive and I contribute practical, useful involvement, for example one entrepreneur rang me every day for three years asking for advice and support – which I was more than happy to give. When the business was sold to a Californian company, I made four to five times my original investment. It is always hard to know in advance what will be needed of an investor, but I will take on any contribution that I feel will help. I have carried out tasks from transatlantic negotiations to looking at marketing material. 99

2 ● HOW MUCH TIME?

We asked a few winning angels how much time they spend in supporting a start-up. Here is what they said.

David Berkus

❝ I will become the CEO coach spending... a half up to two days a month. ❞

Tony Morris

❝ Far more than I anticipate. My business model has been half-time consulting, quarter-time new business, quarter-time working on portfolio companies. In actual fact the time spent consulting has gone down, and the time spent on new business has gone up. ❞

John Hime

❝ About four hours per company per month, with notable exceptions. ❞

Andrew Blair

❝ Regular meetings are held between the management team and the angels: initially every two weeks, then every month, and then quarterly. The whole time a "hotline" is maintained for urgent access. ❞

Betsy Atkins

❝ Usually supporting involves monthly board meetings and weekly telephone calls but, if there's something hot cooking... we will talk many times in a day. ❞

Brian Horey

❝ In some cases I have had very little involvement, and in others... I am almost completely passive. Maybe one or two times a year we have a conversation about what is going on in the business, beyond that I am not at all involved. In another case I went on the board and was pretty active in terms of helping form the strategy and helping introduce the company to sources of money. In other cases, where I am not on the board, probably once a month or more frequently I have a conversation with the CEO. ❞

3 • RESOURCE BANKRUPTCIES

In his book, *Better Than Money!*,[1] David Berkus describes what he calls "resource bankruptcies." This concept will prove useful to angels and entrepreneurs alike.

> It's kind of like hearing the engine sputter when you're flying 1,000 feet over one of the Great Lakes. Is the problem real? Can it be fixed in the air? Is there someone at the other end of the radio who can give some quick and very effective advice? Or is it time to think more of staying upright in your survival raft than worrying about whether you remembered to drain any water from the bottom of your fuel tanks before taking off?
>
> Resource bankruptcy, which can and does include financial bankruptcy, is the recognition that you've just become unable to continue "flying your plane." You've run out of runway ahead (while landing), or altitude below (while flying), and it's time to plan to terminate your flight prematurely. Now this unhappy circumstance may face you either because of pilot error or equipment failure. But the net effect is the same. The only thing to remember then is that any landing you can walk away from is a good landing "'cause you'll live to fly again tomorrow"...
>
> All forms of resource bankruptcy usually happen so slowly that the pilot and crew don't fully realize that they're losing control and running out of options – until it becomes very costly. You've heard the example about a frog being placed into a luke warm kettle over the stovetop flame. The slow increase in temperature is imperceptible to the frog, who initially could have jumped right out of the kettle, but instead slowly heats until he becomes someone's dinner.
>
> Or, as Mark Twain said over a century ago, when talking about bankruptcy: "You go out of business slowly, and then suddenly!" It's just like a plane crash. It's not the loss of altitude that's the biggest problem; it's the sudden stop when you arrive at the ground.
>
> Companies seldom "suddenly go out of business." Few regulatory, competitive or management driven events could make a company bankrupt overnight. Barring acts of God, it usually takes more than one bad decision or bad break to bring down a business. We learn that in flying too. Identify and fix the problems early and they won't combine with other small problems to become one big one, capable of bringing down the plane.
>
> Experience alone is a powerful but very inefficient teacher. She tends to give the test first, then teach the lessons later...
>
> Few of us have enough time or money to make a lot of mistakes and still stay in the small business game...

---

1 *Better than Money*, by David Berkus and Bob Kelley. Copyright 1994, D. Berkus and R. Kelley. Reprinted with permission. (To order your copy call (001) 626.355.5375.)

So experience, used as a resource at just the right time, can be, and often is, "Better than Money." And someone else's experience can sometimes provide a much better lesson (before you are tested) than your own inexperience (after failing first).

The five resource demons identified, in flying terms, are: "running out of runway," "running out of fuel," "the navigation nightmare," "help me! I'm lost up here!," and "Lindbergh flew it alone, too." We also label them, respectively: "time bankruptcy," "fiscal bankruptcy", "process bankruptcy," "context bankruptcy," and "relationship bankruptcy." 🙵🙵

4 ● HOW TO FAIL

There really is such a thing as failing right and we thought you would like to know about it so you can tell any entrepreneur when you make your investment. Failing right saves the entrepreneur's reputation.

The rules for failing right include:

- Be honest, even when it hurts.
- Observe all the laws.
- Save all the value that you can.
- Shut down early if possible.
- Do not leave a legal mess.

Entrepreneurs should handle their potential failure as they would any other potentiality in their business, that is professionally and with contingency plans. Handling failure right will maintain their reputations and many of the investor relationships.

Copy the letter that follows as is or re-type it on your own stationery and hand it to any entrepreneur when you give them a check.

🙵🙵   Dear Entrepreneur

We have every belief that you will succeed and hope for it. Starting a new business is a Herculean task and you have our admiration just for trying.

Many successful entrepreneurs failed once or many times before they finally hit it. This may be your big win, or it may be one event on a path leading you to that win.

In the highly unlikely, but possible, event that you will fail you should make sure you fail right. Here is what failing right means:

1 Provide honest and regular updates to your investors. If failure comes, don't let it come unexpectedly.
2 Give your investors every opportunity to help you make it work. Suggestion number one will go a long way towards accomplishing this.

3 Don't leave a mess. Announce failure before you have no cash, so you can complete the necessary arrangements, legal and otherwise. Do not, in any case, leave your investors with financial or time obligations to clean up after you.

4 Recognize that failure is part of the game. Be frank, positive and do your best, it's the only thing any angel investor can expect.

Sincerely

David Amis and Howard Stevenson ""

5 ● A SUPPORTING STORY

Tom Wharton, a founder of DoubleClick.com, and an active start-up advisor, worked with Winfreestuff.com, beginning in 1999.

I met the husband and wife team of Stephanie (CEO) and Mark (President) Healy in 1999. Stephanie had uncovered a market demand for email addresses for marketing purposes, partly through her work at Omaha Steaks in the online group. The premise was that if you could get people to agree to be marketed to on the internet and if people would show a preference to what they wanted to have, you would have a marketing list that advertisers would be willing to pay for.

With my experience in marketing, it was not hard to see the correlation between this same demand in the off-line world, and the added cost savings and efficiencies in the online world. Additionally, Stephanie's insights were that creating an ongoing affinity relationship with these consumers would allow her to continue to evaluate and adjust the demographic characteristics of the customer in addition to a direct revenue stream attached to the direct communication from the company.

Stephanie then tested the idea of finding out what would entice a consumer to give up their email address. This began the concept of allowing a consumer the chance to "winfreestuff" and in doing so created the opportunity for the consumer to OPT-IN to receive information from numerous companies and from "winfreestuff.com." The strategy worked! Consumers gave their email address and advertisers wanted to buy them. After this initial feedback, Mark Healy quit his job as a medical professional and joined full time.

After struggling to raise $400k Stephanie and Mark realized that they needed more help to really make the company go. That is when I met them. They decided that my past experience in growing companies and raising capital was worth paying for.

My first focus was to assess the opportunity and make sure I wanted to join them. I came to several positive conclusions: The management team was exceptional and connected in the direct marketing industry. The business model was simple. Even the math was simple! Winfreestuff had multiple long-term revenue streams and it was scalable on a global basis. The margins would increase over time. It looked like a good business opportunity.

My second focus was to improve the opportunity and make it more sell-able to investors. We determined that an opt-in strategy would go way beyond the proprietary winfreestuff.com website and take it to thousands of other sites on the web. I like to call it a "Pan Web" strategy. We leverage the traffic generated at thousands of other websites to build the winfreestuff.com database.

The next job ahead was to build the business plan, business plan summary and an investor presentation. My credentials as a founder of DoubleClick were added to the board. This also gave us leverage in getting additional funding.

There were also some missteps the company had taken in raising their first $400k and we needed to correct them first. The company had taken minimum investments of $5,000 per investor and had thus raised little money but had over 60 investors. It was critical that we raised more capital without increasing the pool of investors. Also, there were some founders that needed to become full-time employees and who needed employment agreements, etc., the usual stuff.

Once all of this was done, we set out to raise more capital. Within 30 days we raised another $600k from the same investors, and another $1.5 million from John Bacus and Jim Lynch of Draper Atlantic. What made the sale with Draper was a combination of efforts, contacts, presentation, good strategy, good management, and good association. Stephanie Healy was a passionate presenter and also an excellent direct marketer. Draper loved the Pan Web business strategy and we walked out of the first meeting with a term sheet!!

My continued role as an advisor takes many twists and turns. I felt that exceptional web developers were needed and I introduce them to a team of local guys; Tom Margrave and Louis Carlson. This was based on my recommendations to start building an organization and structure to support the growth that was sure to come. I offered insights into their option plan strategy, their budgets, their hiring plans, and the speed of their expansion. All of which is adjusted in accordance with changes in market conditions and cash burn rate.

I continue to offer my insights in strategy meetings, ops meetings, etc. Part of the business planning effort defined the business strategy changes and revenue model changes that we expected to make as the market evolved. The technology evolution of the internet requires a constant and aggressive review of the business strategy. The company as grown from a database of 35k email addresses in January of 2000 to over 1.5 million as of July 27th, 2000, my 39th birthday. The company has built a Pan Web network of over 6,000 websites and has moved up in PCData's sight rankings to 155th on the web, beating out some much larger competitors. The company is projecting break-even by the end of 2000 and is well positioned for their next round of financing.

There are a lot more details to the winfreestuff experience but that is enough for now. It's exciting to see it on paper and to know where it can go!

For every opportunity I get involved with:

1 I never assume management has the answer, instead I assume they don't know what questions to ask.

2 I always tell them what I think they are doing wrong and how I believe to do it right, and I offer business insights like never burn bridges or throw away relationships that appear of no value.

3 I introduce them to anyone I know that could potentially bring value or know someone that could.

4 I complement them to death on their successes. They need to feel good about their hard work! 〞

6 ● INVEST IN THREE ROUNDS BUT NEVER FOUR

Dick Morley has several rules of thumb that he sticks to when angel investing. He is a co-founder of the long-established Nashua Breakfast Club and has made 70+ investments, predominately as a silent angel. Here is what he says about drawing the line at three rounds.

〝 In the venture capital business, we generally finance a project for three rounds. Why three rounds? Don't really know! We just know that from our experience and that empirical evidence indicates, no one ever meets his budget on the first go-round. By the time you get to the fourth round, something is significantly wrong with the project. A typical scenario might be: we as angels will invest $200,000 but initially only finance the company for one-third of the value. By the time we get to three rounds, we will terminate any further funding independent of how well the project is going or how badly it needs money. This is a key element. If the project is going badly, clearly do not fund. If the project is going well, get funds from someone else. The purpose of research and development, particularly the creation of wealth, and front-end R&D is to establish and turn on the lights, not to bring the entire project to fruition.

Conclusion of the projects, i.e., subsequent funding, must be done in separate stages and called new projects. This allows one to go back to the base of the tree and grow new buds and sprouts depending upon what has been learned in the initial subproject. Since these projects are by definition seven people for optimum size, and typically three years, one can state that a given project will run between one to five million dollars. Normally, we do not tell the researcher, the entre-preneur, or the young company president what we have in mind for the total. As it turns out, independent of what the budget constraints are, almost everyone overruns projects consistently and thoroughly. 〞

1 ● There are five fundamental roles: silent investor, reserver force, team member (full or part time), coach, controlling investor.

2 ● The key to supporting is helping to achieve value events, which vary by industry, business and stage of development.

3 ● There are good and bad ways to fail.

4 ● Ask the entrepreneur what she wants you to do.

Harvesting

You got to know when to hold 'em, know when to fold 'em
know when to walk away and know when to run.

A line from Gambler famously sung by Kenny Rogers

QUICK OVERVIEW

49 ● Start section   287

50 ● The seven harvesting methods   289
Walking harvest   289
Partial sale   293
Initial public offering   294
Financial sale   296
Strategic sale   297

51 ● Negative harvests and other exits   299
Chapter 11   299
Chapter 7   300
The living dead   301

52 ● Harvesting value events   303

53 ● Things to think about   306
Why VCs are the pros   306

54 ● Winning angels 2000   309
  What do most investors do?   309
  What do the winners do?   309
  Winning tools and tactics   311

55 ● Special sections   313
   1 Winning angels talk about exits   313
   2 A successful harvest story – PlanetAll   315
   3 Planning for the ultimate exit   317
   4 A failed harvest story   319
   5 A successful harvest story – LifeMinders   320
   6 Interview with Steve McGeady   321
   4 TAKEAWAYS FROM HARVESTING   323

CHAPTER 49

START SECTION

As for farmers, the likelihood of a good harvest is determined long before the harvesting equipment is brought out of the barn. Unlike farmers, however, you will probably leave money on the table, since at least half of all companies keep going up after you sell. In one investment that Howard made in Telemex, the Mexican telephone company, he bought in at $6 per share and later sold at $70. The shares dropped subsequently to $50. However, in an investment in Amazon.com, he sold too early, and missed gaining another 3x on his money. *"Selling is always wrong,"* Howard states without reservation.

Darryl Wash believes that, *"Angels rarely have enough control to meaningfully influence an exit."* Aside from issues, such as the goals of the entrepreneur, the structure of the deal and the very nature of the opportunity, your relationship to date has the largest impact on whether you can effect a harvest. Otherwise, you are pretty much dependent on the entrepreneur or the new CEO, and any controlling or major share-holders. This is why having a positive relationship and aligning interests is so critical (see Figure 49.1).

THE LIKELIHOOD OF A GOOD HARVEST IS DETERMINED LONG BEFORE THE HARVESTING EQUIPMENT IS BROUGHT OUT OF THE BARN

Perhaps the best impact an angel can have here is to facilitate the interaction between potential buyers, bankers and others that could provide an exit event for the angel and entrepreneur.

There are five fundamental types of positive harvests: IPO, strategic sale, walking harvest, partial sale, and financial sale. And there are two types of negative harvests: Chapter 11 and Chapter 7. You can think of the last two as, *"harvesting whatever time or cash savings remain."* Strategic sale is the most common form of exit, and it is estimated that tens of thousands occur each year, compared to several hundred IPOs.[1]

Harvesting is the endgame of early-stage investments, the financial score by which you will measure your success. It is not as controllable as the decision to write the first check, but with advanced thinking and strategic action by both you and the entre-preneur, the likelihood of success can be increased dramatically.

---

1 544 companies went public in the US in 1999. (*Source:* Venture Economics & National Venture Capital Association).

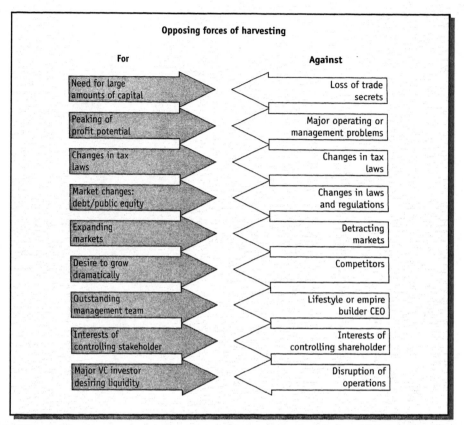

FIGURE 49.1

CHAPTER 50

THE SEVEN HARVESTING METHODS

There are five positive harvest methods and two negative ones. Each method has its advantages, and contrary to all of the stories in the press applauding grand IPOs, strategic sales are the most common and often the most lucrative. In addition, they offer other advantages over IPOs and other forms of harvest. Winning investors understand the various options and are constantly assessing the prospects of their investments.

In some cases the entrepreneurial team will effect the harvest, in other cases, new management or major shareholders might effect it, and in a few cases, you can effect it. Figure 50.1 gives you an overview of the five positive harvest methods and the two negative methods, together with their various advantages and disadvantages. Review this, look at the summary in Table 50.1, then read the more thorough explanation of each on the following pages.

1 ● WALKING HARVEST

"The exit has to be engineered as carefully as the deal itself"

Andrew Blair

The walking harvest is used in two situations:

1 When the multiple of cash flows, on any sale, is so low, say two to four times cash flow, that the owners would rather just take the cash out as it is earned.

2 When the controlling investors, hopefully in agreement with all of the investors, decide they would rather have a positive cash flow stream and/or continue to own the business for other reasons.

Primary benefits

Once decided upon, this harvest strategy is unlikely to fail, as long as management is willing to agree to it and continues to perform competently. There is none of the distraction that will occur when selling the business and no information can get to competitors or anyone else.

Walking harvest
The company distributes cash directly to
investors on a regular basis

Partial sale
The investor's stake is sold to management, to
another shareholder, or to an outsider

Initial public offering
The company sells a percentage of its shares which
are listed on NASDAQ, NYSE or another exchange,
creating a market for investors' shares

Financial sale
The company is sold to an financial buyers who
purchases it for its cash flows

Strategic sale
The company is sold to an industry buyer who buys
it for strategic reasons, such as marketing synergies

Chapter 11
The company is reorganized and the investors
typically lose most of their upside

Chapter 7
The company is liquidated and investors, depending
on their place in line, get little or nothing

FIGURE 50.1

Primary drawbacks

There is no potential to get an outstanding valuation based on someone else's
perceived value of the business, such as in the case of an IPO or strategic sale. If
active involvement from the angel is required for ongoing operations, this may not
change despite the revised expectations.

TABLE 50.1 Summary of harvesting methods

	Timing of cash payment to investors	Total amount of cash payment	Sale price multiple	Certainty of pulling it off	Reps and warranties	Disruption of current business operation	Ongoing role of founder	Ongoing role of investors	Costs	Leakage to competitors	Future financial liability	Complexity of structure
Walking harvest	Slow	Depends on future performance	n/a	Reasonably high control	None	None	Yes/ unchanged	Unchanged	None	None	Unchanged	Simple
Partial sale	Fast	Low, depends on buyer	Med-low	Narrow market	Some	Depends on who sells	High/ unchanged	Removed? New partner?	Low $30-50k	Fair amount	None &/or by contract	Moderate, depends on contract
Initial public offering	6-12 months	Low, depends on buyer	Depends on after market performance	Depends on market conditions	High	High	Changes, public company	Subject to terms, except controlling shareholders	$250k or less	Total (see Edgar)	Depends on lawyers	Med-high
Financial sale	Fast	Med-high	Med-high	Market conditions - you control it	Med	Med-high	Likely to continue with drastic changes	Out	Moderate $30-50k + success fee + broker	High	Low	Low
Strategic sale	Fast	Med-high	Highest	Depends on industry and market - you control it	Low (cash buyers)	Very high	Generally short	Out	$30-50k	Extremely high	Low	Low
Reorganize: Chapter 11	Very long	Low	Very low	Low and decreasing	None	High	Yes	Washed out, or they buy in again	High $50k-250k	High	None	High
Bankruptcy: Chapter 7	Slow– nothing	0	Negative	110%	None	Total	End	Done	+$20k –$100k (lawyers)	High and employees leave	None, except fraud	High

Returns

Over a long period of time, the returns are essentially a cash flow stream, like an annuity, which can be attractive if income is desirable. Otherwise, since there is no sale event, the potential to get a multiple of cash flows today is not part of the picture. Therefore, returns are a direct function of what you paid into the deal and the cash you will now receive per annum.

Risks

Business risk, economic risk, and internal risk are influenced by the relationships between any owners and managers.

EXAMPLE

In one investment by Howard's son-in-law[1] in a cosmetic mail order business, they could not find a buyer who would pay more than a 5 x multiple. With positive cash flow of about $400k, this meant the best offer was about $2m. Although the growth prospects were not significant, they felt the future success of the business was fairly predictable.

The general manager was earning $150k in salary and also owned a significant stake in the business. They decided to execute a walking harvest by splitting the $400k according to each shareholder's equity interest. After that, the shareholders had a nice annual cash flow stream for many years.

The Mars family with candy bars or the Macmillan family with their publishing business are similar but larger examples of walking harvests. Both of these closely held businesses throw off cash to their owners on a regular basis.

Special notes

This is generally a back-up option or a method appropriate to closely held businesses.

2 • PARTIAL SALE

"You can lead a horse to water but you can't make him drink."

Old cowboy saying

The partial sale normally occurs in one of two situations, both of which include the investor wanting to exit a moderately successful company that does not have good exit prospects. There are two typical methods:[2]

1 The investors sell their shares to management through a cash or, more likely, a buy-out agreement.

2 The investors sell to one of the few investment companies that specialize in buying minority positions in small and medium sized companies.

Primary benefits

The investor gets to exit an otherwise non-liquid investment.

Primary drawbacks

There are very few buyers of minority positions so the investor is unlikely to get an outstanding valuation.

Returns

Three to five times profits if there are any, otherwise, the sale price is purely negotiated based on perceived fairness or other intangible factors. Finally, if a shotgun or other contractual arrangement is in place, the price may have already been set.

---

1 Howard has lots of family members in business. We have slightly disguised this information but the basic story is accurate.

2 Sometimes sales occur to other shareholders, but this is uncommon and usually not wise since it lacks the potential upside of a strategic sale or IPO. In one Amis Family investment, a co-angel invested $200k in a young communications company but then sold out to another incoming angel for $400k two years later. Everything happening in the company suggested it was on its way and the angel may have had personal reasons for leaving early. But the major value moment always comes in a major sale or offering. In this case, the company went public eight years later and the investor missed a $20m gain. These are real numbers.

EXAMPLE

Back in the 1960s, the partners in Missouri Valley Machinery Company, a Nebraska-based Caterpillar dealership, decided they wanted to take their money out. R.T. Amis,[3] the President and majority shareholder, offered them a combination walking harvest and partial sale. Every time they took a share of the profits directly, he kept his in and the ownership percentages were changed accordingly. After a few years of this, RT owned all of the company; his two partners had taken their money out.

Risks

Once the sale occurs, there is no risk (unlike a walking harvest where the business risk remains). The only real risk is that management becomes cemented to its position that you should not leave and you never will, or it takes advantage of the situation forcing a very low price.

Special notes

If the investor perceives that a sale to management is in the future, there are investment terms that can facilitate this eventuality. For example, the mutual buy/sell agreement allows either the entrepreneurial team or the investor(s) to state a price in writing for the company. The other party then purchases the remaining part of the company or sells its shares at the offered price.

3 • INITIAL PUBLIC OFFERING $$$

"Initial public offerings are not the end of the road, they are a financing event along the way. If you believe in management, and you believe in the business... then as a public company the investment should still continue to perform. You aren't waiting for the public offering, you are waiting for the point at which the company has created the most value."

Darryl Wash

There were 544 IPOs in the US in 1999.[4] VCs and other sophisticated investors like to see IPOs when the markets are hot and/or when the company is going to need a lot more cash to maximize its market penetration, execute a roll-up, or develop follow-on businesses. IPOs allow the management team to continue to run the

---

3 R.T. Amis is David's grandfather who was an active midwestern angel and entrepreneur throughout his 60-year career, which started when he bought his own wagon team and hauled goods in the 1930s (yes, that is wagon team as in horses).

4 *Source:* Venture Economics & National Venture Capital Association.

company, although with significant scrutiny, while also providing liquidity to investors and creating a major new channel for raising capital.

Historically, IPOs are losers for investors, meaning that they do not retain their post-IPO valuation for long. Since most early-stage investors are "locked up" for six months, they often do not get the original IPO price. Still, any public price is usually several times better than their paid-in price. And in some cases, the post-IPO price does increase dramatically.

Primary benefits

Liquidity for investors and the potential to capture outstanding multiples, particularly in a bull market; from the company's perspective, having a publicly traded stock generally makes it easier to raise more capital.

Primary drawbacks

Investors will have restricted stock that cannot be sold for six months, partly dependent on the requirements of the investment bankers. Therefore, their first possible exit price depends on the market, which is not particularly dependable. In addition, the company will go through significant disruption and *all* of its information will now be available to competitors. Finally, the company cannot control this exit strategy and will be dependent upon investment bankers who, of course, get paid either way.

Returns

High variability depending on when you sell. It is nearly certain that you will sell too soon or too late.

Risks

The markets become the primary risk.

EXAMPLE

Howard invested in etoys.com at $0.30 per share in its angel round. It went through additional financings and finally went public during the internet craze in the late 1990s. Its share price climbed to $60 (a 200x multiple!). It would be great to say Howard sold at this point. But as Mark Twain once said, *"The only people who buy at the lowest price and sell at the highest... are liars."* As of June 2000, etoys was on its way back to $0.30 per share. Howard sold somewhere in the middle, or so he says.

Some more well-known IPOs by angel-backed companies which are described in this book include: StarMedia, Apple Computer, and Amazon.com.

Special notes

Although a company does not need a VC to execute on a public offering, it is the preferred exit strategy of most VCs. Many have outstanding experience and contacts for achieving exits via IPO.

4 ● FINANCIAL SALE

"As the company creates value, the exit will become apparent. There is always a market for good companies."

Frans Kok

In a financial sale, the buyers are typically purchasing the company based on its current and expected cash flows, so the multiples are somewhat predictable. Financial buyers are not industry pros and will have their own opinions about the quality of management, which may or may not result in drastic changes.

Primary benefits

Financial buyers are usually purchasing the entire company with cash. If you have cash flow, your likelihood of executing a sale is good.

Primary drawbacks

The multiples one might find in a strategic sale are not possible. Management cannot count on continued employment.

Returns

Returns are consistent with whatever the buyer thinks they can make out of the purchase. In some cases, a financial buyer intends to break up the company or merge it with something else. Multiples of 5–20 times profits are normal.

Risks

Since financial buyers often pay with cash there is no risk after the sale. Initially, there is some risk of leaking information but the risk can be mitigated by avoiding strategic buyers who are often competitors or industry players.

EXAMPLE

In 1998, an affiliate of Kidd, Kamm & Company, along with Oaktree Capital Management, bought the Berwind Railway Service Company in a financial purchase. Berwind refurbishes, repairs, cleans and lines railcars with facilities in Pennsylvania, Kansas, Iowa and Texas. *"This was a consolidation play in the railcar repair and maintenance industry,"* said Steve Dollinger, one of the lead principals in the transaction.

The investors went on to combine Berwind with another company, bring in a new CEO and CFO, and arrange additional financing. Berwind was purchased for $34.25m in cash in an asset purchase. It had $6m in EBITDA[5] and thus was bought at a 5.8x multiple. The transaction took 150 days to complete.

Special notes

Almost any size of a business can attract a financial buyer, whether positive cash flow is $200k or $200m.

5 ● STRATEGIC SALE $$$

"The best returns generally come from strategic sales."

Bert Twaalfhoven

Perhaps the best and most likely harvest method for a successful company. The buyer is typically an industry player that will pay value beyond what the cash flows might suggest. Marketing, operational, financial, and other kinds of synergies means that the buyer will reap more benefit from the purchase than almost any other kind of buyer.

Primary benefits

Price, relatively less due diligence and faster negotiating time – they know the business. There is a higher likelihood that management is encouraged to stay around (if they are good). In addition, if there are several industry players, an auction environment can be created.

---

[5] For people who were not in financial services in their previous lives, EBITDA is earnings before interest, taxes, depreciation and amortization.

Primary drawbacks

It may be necessary to share all of the company's information directly with potential competitors.

Returns

Multiples of profits range from 10x to 40x. A lot of this information is held tightly, but there are many instances where strategic purchases were made of companies that lacked any profits.

Risks

The entrepreneur(s) may get a side deal, including a consulting contract or options in the new company which affects their judgment on the deal.

EXAMPLE

PlanetAll was purchased by Amazon.com in 1999 in a strategic purchase for $100m. PlanetAll provides a calendar and personal planning system that had over 1.5m users.

Amazon was willing to pay for this service and its customers. With negligible revenues and no income, the company was valued without regard to sales or profits, which shows the difference between a strategic and a financial sale. If this were the latter, its actual price would have been nominal since there were no positive cash flows.

Special notes

This is one of the harvest methods that can be planned from the beginning. Discussions with potential buyers can occur long before it is time to effect a transaction. In addition, the strategic purchaser is often a partner of the company.

CHAPTER 51 NEGATIVE HARVESTS AND OTHER EXITS

> What strikes me as peculiar is that there are people who
> believe that their businesses will only last for 24 months and
> in that time pray to God that they will attract the attention
> of one of the big fish buyers.
>
> **Howard Tullman**

When a company goes south, the only chance to recoup any of the investment depends on the steps you took during the structuring phase.

What are the items of value in this deal? Machinery? Strategic contracts? Name brand?

If you want to prepare for a potential negative harvest, then the following steps should be taken:

1 Write the contracts so that you and/or a group of investors can take control if the business begins to fail.

2 Own the value items so you can assume possession immediately if needed. (For example, own the machinery and lease it to the company, or own the rights to the name but license it to the company as long as certain payments are made.)

3 Prepare for one or a group of investors to have the time necessary to execute a negative harvest, which could well mean a major commitment of time.

6 ● CHAPTER 11

"How did you go bankrupt? At first gradually then precipitously."

George Bernard Shaw

A reorganization bankruptcy generally means that all equity holders are washed out significantly, or reduced in their ownership share. The likelihood of earning a return is significantly reduced but it is better than with Chapter 7.

Primary benefits

Saves the company from Chapter 7 and gives it another chance to make it.

Primary drawbacks

Aside from the money being lost? It is a complex process that will distract the management as well as the investors. It will also cost someone a lot of money in lawyers' fees and reorganization expenses. In addition, the beneficial tax loss is postponed.

Returns

Minimal, if any.

Risks

The primary risk at this point is time. However, a Chapter 11 can also be a way to unload the company onto the shoulders of another group of investors and managers.

Special notes

In such a situation, an investor should think about how to save their time and emotional energy – perhaps a Chapter 7 will make more sense from this standpoint.

7 ● CHAPTER 7

"Only those who dare to fail greatly will ever succeed greatly."

John F Kennedy

Chapter 7 represents total annihilation. Everything is lost and only the lawyers and a few debtors get paid.

Primary benefits

No more wasted time! No more outstanding liabilities as long as there was no fraud involved. One judge makes the final determinations, so there are time and energy savings on negotiations and decisions that would normally require more than one party.

Primary drawbacks

Aside from being totally annihilated? There are strict and complex rules which must be followed.

Returns

None, even negative if there is no money in the company to pay for the filing expenses.

Risks

There is always the potential of investor lawsuits, if you are a director or major participant. However, in most cases the story ends with the judge's orders.

Special notes

A clear-cut end is more welcome than one might suppose in angel investing.

THE LIVING DEAD

"My experience is that companies either get traction and escape velocity or they don't. You tend to know early on if a company is struggling, and most of the companies that struggle fail. And what's happened in the most recent short period of time is companies that are struggling don't fail because they still can get access to money. So only in the most recent period have we seen companies live on and on, which has been interesting, so if you're in a hot sector of the market and you have pretty smart people you can capture some value even if the thing isn't working out."

Bill Sahlman

Unfortunately, early-stage opportunities often result in something other than a fantastic failure or a mesmerizing success. Given the proliferation of angels with money who do not know what they are doing, many companies that should not have received their first or second rounds of capital continue to press forward. They make little money, just enough to keep the dream alive. The entrepreneurs can't give up because they have invested so much emotionally, financially and otherwise, but the business lacks any disastrous moment of failure. These situations are known as the "living dead."

How does one evade the living dead?

1 Decide to mentally write off the investment and accept a failure (whether it is certain or not).

2 Recommunicate with the entrepreneur any agreement or expectation on active participation. Discontinue any more investment of time.

3 Sell, offer to sell, or transfer the ownership of shares to a third party.[1]

Sometimes offering to sell can be a productive exercise because it allows one to let go of the investment in a healthy way, to see if there are any potential buyers and to motivate a discussion about what is going to happen next. Sometimes, such an offer, if met with excitement from management or other investors, can be very telling.

The most important thing to do with a company going sideways is to not give it any more money or energy.

Factors that contribute to a successful harvest

- A long line of sophisticated and experienced investors.
- A management team focused on creating value and then exiting.
- A-Quality event all around.
- Cooperative markets.
- Hungry and wealthy strategic buyers or hungry investment bankers with institutional investors.

---

1 Only do this if you are absolutely sure the investment will go nowhere. Winning investors tend to leave their money in on the assumption that they will earn a big win or lose it all. Trying to second guess any particular investment is not a good use of time or risk management effort unless one is very close to the project.

CHAPTER 52

HARVESTING VALUE EVENTS™

> "When a defining moment comes along, you define the
> moment, or the moment defines you."
>
> **Kevin Costner** in *Tin Cup*, 1996

While many angels are focused on achieving an IPO or company sale, the next important value event for an angel investor is often the venture capital round. Nearly 50% of IPOs in 1999 had VC backing.[1] Still, strategic sales are much more likely exit events for angels. In addition, as **STRATEGIC SALES ARE MUCH MORE LIKELY EXIT EVENTS FOR ANGELS** angels increase in numbers and become more competitive with venture capitalists, there are increasing numbers of financial sales, walking harvests, and even IPOs that are completed without VC involvement.

We reviewed value events in the supporting section as they vary by type of business and functional area. There are six fundamental value events (see Figure 52.1), which, once attained, signal a good likelihood of a near or eventual harvest.

1 Profitability or cash flow break-even

Once a company can pay for itself or begin making profits, the likelihood of failure decreases substantially. In addition, the company has increased leverage with VCs, since they cannot wait until the company is on fumes to make their final offer. During the internet craze of 1998 to 2000, it was unattractive to have profits as this seemed to indicate a lack of growth potential. A company that can make money can create a harvest event.

2 Acquisition of certain strategic partnerships

In some industries there are a limited number of potential strategic partners. "Locking up" these relationships can have significant value. In one early-stage company that David evaluated in 1999, Changemyaddress.com, several major real estate companies had agreed to exclusive relationships. One of the industry competitors wanted to own these agreements and the company sold for $4m within six months of its start-up, even though the company had few customers and no profits.

---

1 *Source*: Venture Economics & National Venture Capital Association.

3 Development of a brand name

In some cases, a company will develop a strong following which is attractive to an industry competitor or a strategic partner. The brand name and customer base will have value in and of themselves.

What does it really take to get a VC in the deal?

- A four- or five-star team.
- Simple structure.
- Compatible and value-added investors.
- 60–80% returns.
- The perception that there is a short fuse.
- A hot area.
- Good benchmark against competition.
- "dot.com" in your name (only good in 1999 – what's next?).

---

4 A VC investment

VCs are the pros at harvesting. Using other people's money to make investments, it is essential for their livelihood to generate strong returns as quickly as they can. "*I would always get, circumstances permitting, a VC in there at the right time, because they just – they are machines. They know the right guys... and once a VC invests, you know there will be a driving force to get to a liquidity event,*" says angel investor CL.

5 Demonstration of a new product or service offering in the marketplace

In one French start-up, a company which provided software for self-help desks was bought by Hewlett-Packard only months after start-up. Hewlett-Packard was trying to build a service that required the use of such software. This is how fast a company's value can increase after it demonstrates its product in the marketplace. In addition, proving the capability to develop follow-on products and services can also be a powerful value event.

6 The creation of a great team

As much as financial capital is essential to success, human capital is what drives the business forward every day. Winning angels know that the team, as well as its capability to attract new team members, is a major contributor to the value of a company and to its likelihood of success.

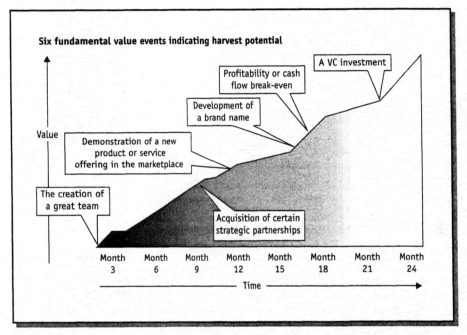

FIGURE 52.1

CHAPTER 53

THINGS TO THINK ABOUT

> We can introduce them to later stages of funding and then
> we can introduce them to the right investment bankers, and
> then they can go public.
>
> **Tim Draper**

WHY VCs ARE THE PROS

VCs spend 75% of their time on harvesting. Given that one or two out of 10 VC deals are significant winners, an angel has a 10–20% likelihood of success when a

AN ANGEL HAS A 10–20% LIKELIHOOD OF SUCCESS WHEN A VC STEPS UP

VC steps up. VCs, of which there are now thousands in the US, represent more than $50bn in capital and have been around since the 1940s. The 271 venture-backed companies that went public in 1999 raised $23.6 bn. The total valuation of those companies on the IPO date was $136.2bn.[1]

VCs have their own association, the National Venture Capital Association (www.nvca.com), which has training programs. There is even a major non-profit, the Kaufman Foundation, which provides free training to selected aspiring VCs.

More important, as a group, VCs have a long track record of generating high and liquid returns on capital. If a VC with experience and a solid rolodex is behind your deal, you can usually expect the following:

1 Significant deal structure demands which give them power over the entrepreneur or management team.

2 Board positioning through original seats, the ability to impact additional seats, and, in some cases, the option to take over the board if certain conditions are not met.

3 An active and immediate focus on harvesting.

4 Professionalism: A VC is unlikely to have ever started or managed a company of significance, but has valuable experience of sitting on boards and influencing management.

5 Preferential terms whenever VCs can obtain them, even in relation to the initial angels in the deal.

---

1 *Source:* Venture Economics & National Venture Capital Association.

6 No interest in allowing the angels to exit early. We think the entire market would work better if VCs adapted the habit of allowing angels to exit, at least partly, in the VC round, as this would free up more sophisticated capital to do angel deals. But most VCs are not so far sighted about their own industry.

7 A presumption of being the "big gun" and smarter than everyone else. This has been true for many years and may remain so for some time. However, as more VCs enter the fray, the competition may make for some kinder, friendlier attitudes towards entrepreneurs and other investors.

8 A substantially higher likelihood of deal success and historically better performance after the IPO as well.

9 A sharp focus on obtaining an IPO. VCs are less interested in selling the company or obtaining other kinds of harvest events.

EXAMPLE HOW CAN A MINORITY SHAREHOLDER IMPACT HARVEST?

From a minority investor's perspective, 95% of the harvest potential is based on steps taken before the investment is made. In other words, invest in the right deals, with the right management, the right structure, and the right co-investors, and you are likely to achieve a quality harvest. If you do not do those things, there are major limits to what you can do. Here are the actions you can take to maximize the likelihood of a harvest event somewhere in the future of your investment:

1 Make sure your deal is made up of the core components attributed to significant winners:
   - Sophisticated and hungry management team.
   - Large and growing market opportunity.
   - Fundamental business model that will allow the company to make money.

2 Promote the inclusion of first- or second-round investors who have done early-stage deals before and exited from them. They will be assessing the deal from an exit standpoint themselves and their involvement both suggests the likelihood of an exit as well as the influence of another pro-exit group.

   By the way, if you doubt the existence of investors who do not want early and lucrative exits, you need only look so far as a lifestyle entrepreneur, lifestyle board director, or rich family member/friend who does not care but likes the annual company ski trip.

3 Ensure a structure, to the extent that it is possible, that promotes the entrepreneur or CEO to effect such an outcome. Professional CEOs will always make the sale or IPO decision much easier than a founder CEO. The founder has all the child-rearing and personal issues that go with years of investment in a loved one. Salary limits or tag-along rights are examples of structural incentives to achieve an exit for investors.

4 Promote venture capitalists as second-round investors. They are the pros of achieving liquidity events. Given that they answer to the institutional investors who back them, they are focused on delivering a return on investment in real time. Check out the background of the firm and see what deals they have taken to market. If they know what they are doing, and they invest a significant amount, which is the norm, then your investment increases in value and likelihood of achieving liquidity on the day they join.

WINNING ANGELS 2000

The following excerpts from *The Winning Angels Study* ©2000, by David Amis and Jocelyn Dinnin: "What do most investors do?", "What do the winners do?" and the selected winning tools and tactics, are reprinted with permission. Highlights of this study were published in *The Winning Angels Handbook*.

WHAT DO MOST INVESTORS DO?

- **Nothing, but keep their fingers crossed**

  Many investors are frankly so inept at the whole process of early-stage investing that when they reach this point, without having done any preparation, they quite rightly can only sit and hope for the best.

- **Bother the entrepreneur**

  Some investors will regularly harass the entrepreneur to exit.

- **Support by calling on buyers or later stage investors**

  Some investors take action to facilitate an exit by talking to approaching buyers or identifying next-round investors.

WHAT DO THE WINNERS DO?

- **Get a VC involved**

  Mitch Kapor, angel investor in winning deals such as RealNetworks, and currently a venture capitalist with Accel, believes, *"bringing in a venture investor always struck me – if it was the right one – as the right thing to do for a lot of projects."* Given their focus on ROI and their speciality of investing in private companies, a venture capital investment is usually a strong sign that an exit is viable and certainly that someone is focusing on it very hard.

  Winning investors invite VCs to the party whenever possible.

- **Hear the entrepreneur say "exit" several times**

  We have mentioned exit many times in this book because it is so crucial. If you have chosen the entrepreneur well, he or she will be geared towards the harvest event throughout the project.

- **Aligned interests during structuring**

  "Be sure you're not in competition with the various power groups: entrepreneur, lead investor, etc," says OH, an active European angel. *"Make sure as many people as possible have the same incentives."* At this stage in the game, if

everyone's interests are aligned, there will be minimal friction in harvesting everyone's investments.

- **Do not upset the entrepreneur during negotiation**

  "Try hard to respect and support the entrepreneur's wishes," one angel said. Winning investors know that a good relationship with the entrepreneur(s) is key to maximizing the chances of a successful harvest.

- **Develop relationships with VCs**

  "I have a symbiotic relationship with VCs," explains Randy Komisar, who screens deals and refers appropriate ones to the VCs and sometimes they refer deals to him.

- **They choose the company well in the evaluation stage**

  William Weaver, an angel and leading technology lawyer in Chicago, says:

  "What happens eventually in a niche is that two or three companies rise to the top and the others fall off... part of the trick therefore is to ask yourself the question, 'Is this one of the companies that is going to be a player?'"

  Some angels believe that if you choose right, the exit will happen.

- **Wait**

  Winning angels with minority positions know they are limited in impacting the harvest event. Sometimes they just have to wait and see, as Darryl Wash describes:

  ❝ Because you don't have any control as an angel and even sometimes as a VC it's a much more passive process where you wait until the company has either gone public, and the lock-up has expired, or the company is sold and you are given shares or cash. You really don't have a great ability to do anything as you are not in a control position. You have to just believe that the managers are looking out for the best interest of the shareholders to achieve the maximum liquidity in the minimum time. ❞

WINNING TOOLS AND TACTICS

📢 Listen for the magic word

Frans Kok says if an entrepreneur says something like, *"I want to pass this on to my son,"* he would be really worried. He talks with them about their aspirations, he wants to be sure that everybody is heading in the right direction before investing.

Winning angels make sure that the entrepreneur is thinking about how to get them out, which means an "exit" event.

> The magic word was said when you met the entrepreneur, when you read his plan, and in subsequent meetings before you invested. It is likely that the entrepreneur has continued to focus on the *exit* and is already doing it without much persuasion from you.

📢 Scaling out

"Sell absolutely as soon as you can," says angel investor CL. Since the ride is often not over at the IPO, it is important to have the discipline to take the win and run, or to scale out. Scaling out means selling some, perhaps 50%, as soon as possible, then selling the remaining 25% in a few months or after a reasonable time to get a further increase. Finally, the last 25% might be left for some time to see if the company continues to grow successfully.

> Sell 50% as soon as possible to recoup the investment and secure some winnings. Follow with the remaining 25% in a few months and leave the final 25% long enough to see if an even greater win develops.

📢 Create a structural incentive

During the structuring phase of the investment process, create incentives to motivate the entrepreneur to get an exit. For example, cap the salary to cover living costs and push all or most of his upside to the day you get an exit.

> Build an incentive into the structure to motivate the entrepreneur to reach an exit sooner rather than later.

●< Show him the future

Many entrepreneurs become used to the lifestyle of running a company or have trouble letting go of their "baby." Help the entrepreneur to see the greater and grander things he can do after selling the company. Perhaps introduce them to angel investing!

> Help the entrepreneur to begin identifying opportunities for life after their company.

●< Take it public then sell it

William Weaver says:

❝The best thing is to take the company public, and then sell it... If you sell it before, the negotiations are based on intrinsic value... after the IPO, it's based on the public price... generally there is a premium... So if you can go public, even if you want to sell the company, it's better to do that first.❞

> Sell 50% as soon as possible to recoup the investment and secure some winnings. Follow with the remaining 25% in a few months and leave the final 25% long enough to see if an even greater win develops.

1 ● WINNING ANGELS TALK ABOUT EXITS

Audrey MacLean

❝I usually invest in the seed round so it is typically a dollar or less when I put my money in on a preferred basis. If we do our job right, we have an additional one or two rounds of venture capital and corporate partners investing in the company and we go public. If we handle that properly, by the time we go public we are priced appropriately in the $17–18 share range. If we have done that right, that is not the end of the story by a long shot, it should climb significantly from there. I would say that my expectations are that if I invest a dollar in a company it is because I believe the potential exists for that company to be a $50–$100 per share opportunity.❞

Brian Horey

❝ I have generally taken my money off the table pretty soon after the IPO because I feel like I have had the money at work in those situations for a long enough period of time, and have other things I want to put back into. I want to keep some powder dry for new deals that come along.❞

Darryl Wash

❝ In StarMedia's case the company filed to go public in early 1999. We had shareholdings from several different rounds. What needs to happen in that case is that shares need to be put in some sort of brokerage account so that they can actually be traded and then there was lock-up agreement that was requested by the underwriters for six months which was signed with respect to the large portion of our shares. There were some shares that were not subject to that. When the company then goes public it becomes a question of at what point does one actually truly harvest and sell the shares. Now I still have not sold the majority of shares in StarMedia. Initial public offerings are not the end of the road, they are a financing event along the way... StarMedia, for example, is still a very young company; it is only four years old and it has a phenomenally talented management team that we believe will continue to drive the business forward and increase the value.❞

Angel investor SG on a 70x winner

❝ I spent hardly any time on that deal. The ones you spend a lot of time on are the ones that aren't quite working. ❞

John Hime

❝ Best deal to date: After I invested, company exceeded goals in both product functionality and timing; company was sold to a public company for freely tradable stock. Net-net – I made back 40 times my original investment in 15 months. The bad news: I was so delighted that I sold the stock as soon as possible, and it then almost immediately doubled. I could have made 80 times my original investment had I been more patient... I used to cash out shortly after the IPO, not wanting to put my 20 to 1 return at risk. Now I still cash out shortly after the IPO, not wanting to put my 50 to 1 return at risk. But, in the last four deals where I have done this, I have missed out on an additional 4 to 10 times on my return... I haven't figured out, yet, whether this is good or bad. ❞

Dick Morley

❝ Most angels put in their own money as a way of getting the company started, not as a way to finance the business. Its a big difference. Then we pass it along to intermediate VCs, the funds here in New England tend to be $25m to $100m, and then they pass it along to the big professional guys who are very custodial, and then most of the time the company sells out to its best company. The IPO thing in history is very unusual, so most of the time you sell out to your biggest customer. We go from angel to small VC to large VC and finally to liquidation. ❞

2 ● A SUCCESSFUL HARVEST STORY – PLANETALL

In August 1996 Warren Adams started PlanetAll to provide a simple web-based service, enabling members to keep up with all-important personal and professional contacts using a self-updating address book. Members were also provided with a web-enabled calendar and access to real-world groups.

Initially he financed the start-up using his own credit card and modest savings. With the help of Josh Lerner and Bill Sahlman of the Harvard Business School, Warren crafted a convertible note offering that would convert into preferred stock once a venture capital firm invested in PlanetAll. The share price for the note holders would be discounted below the price paid by the VC. In order to create an incentive for angels to invest as soon as possible, the discount amount was based on how soon the angels invested. Three investment tranches were created, each with its own investment deadline and discount. As protection for angels, the note set a ceiling of $1m as the maximum amount that could be raised under the

The early PlanetAll team: Seated, left to right: Michelle Toth (Acting Director of Marketing), Warren Adams (Co-founder and CEO), Sam Maggio (Marketing Communications), Rachel Burger (Director of Community) Standing, left to right: Frank Levy, Brian Robertson (Co-founder and CTO), Diana Hu (Administrative), Steve Carbone (Systems administration), Tim Huckaby (Acting Director of Finance)

terms of the note. It also provided for conversion at a pre-defined price per share if no venture capital firm invested by a certain date or if the company was sold before it received a VC investment.

Warren raised about $150,000 under the convertible note right away from friends and family, but then there was a lull and fund raising became difficult. Frank Levy, an early employee who assisted Warren in the fundraising process, recalls this time:

❝ By January of 1997, we had already launched the site but our accounts payable were about $200,000 more than what we had in the bank. We were beginning to think about cost-cutting measures that would have been very traumatic to the business. We developed a backup plan that we called "viral mode": the company would shrink down to just the co-founders and one additional engineer. Like a virus that can hibernate until it finds its next host, the company would hibernate until it found a source of funding. But we didn't give up hope quite yet. Warren's best lead for fund raising was a business school classmate based in London. A call was scheduled for early the next morning, London time. When we all left the office that night, Warren just crawled into a ball under his desk and set an alarm for 2am. By the next morning, he had closed on enough money to keep things going.❞

This angel investor was Uday Kempka. They had been in the same class at HBS, and sometime later they bumped into each other in London. Warren wouldn't tell Uday what he was doing, just that it was hot. Uday always thought Warren would do something big. Some months later, Warren called and asked if he wanted to invest. Uday didn't know they were out of money. He made the decision in a few days, because: 1) *"Warren is a great guy"*; 2) the concept was easy to understand; 3) it was *"sticky,"* so if it worked it would probably be big.

Ultimately, Warren was able to raise the full $1m allowable under the terms of the convertible note by March 1997. While the angel fundraising process was still underway, Warren had begun to make his pitch to venture capital firms in parallel. CMGI@ventures became pretty interested in March. They gave PlanetAll a term sheet for $4m in May and the money was in the bank by June. PlanetAll went on to raise a second round of $7m from CMGI@ventures and Lycos in April 1998.

Two years after the company was started, in July 1998, PlanetAll was acquired by Amazon for $100m. Warren Adams talked to us about the harvest event:

❝ On July 9, 1998 we had our first contact with Amazon. We received an email into our directory of business development in our customer service queue. It said that they were interested in talking to us. The deal happened very quickly, within three weeks of receiving this email. So this was followed by a telephone call, which led to Jeff Bezos, and some others, coming to visit us in Cambridge. Four days later we were at Seattle visiting their offices, and within a week we had a handshake on a deal. ❞

At the time of Amazon's approach, PlanetAll had 45 people on the team, $7m in the bank, and had just raised the second VC round. It had over one million members, which was growing at a rate of 1,000 per day. It was the board rather than the angels that participated in the decisions relating to the harvest event.

In the space of two years, the angels who backed PlanetAll earned between 10 and 20 times their money, depending on which tranche they invested in.

The stock performance post-acquisition was something that Warren was mindful of:

❝ Of course, it is important to note that when you sell a company, instead of going down the IPO route, you are betting on the stock of that other company being healthy. We chose Amazon because we really liked Bezos, the team and the vision. Ultimately we went with Amazon because the stock would appreciate. The stock went up six times what it was bought for. So for those that held on, they did even better. ❞

After the acquisition the company moved to Seattle, with 85% of the team moving out. PlanetAll was all about community, so when it became part of Amazon it was put in charge of the community applications, such as friends and favorites, member pages, discussion boards and reviews, and all interaction.

3 ● PLANNING FOR THE ULTIMATE EXIT

"Whoever dies with the most toys wins."

Anonymous

"Whoever dies with the most outstanding early-stage investments, causes the greatest headache for his spouse and surviving family members."

Anonymous estate trustee in Omaha, Nebraska

There are four personal events, which could affect your angel investing activity significantly:

1 Death (yours).

2 Major family event (baby, divorce, sickness, visit by aliens).

3 Bankruptcy/financial trouble.

4 Personal move/career change.

For both your family members and the entrepreneurs who may be relying on you, it is productive to have contingency plans for any of these events. As you consider the potential implications of this list, you will see why looking at your exposure capability (page 5) is worthwhile. Also, the decision you make regarding your angel strategy (page 12) is relevant, as a high-control or an active coach strategy means there is an entrepreneur depending on you.

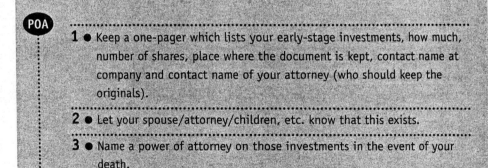

POA

1 ● Keep a one-pager which lists your early-stage investments, how much, number of shares, place where the document is kept, contact name at company and contact name of your attorney (who should keep the originals).

2 ● Let your spouse/attorney/children, etc. know that this exists.

3 ● Name a power of attorney on those investments in the event of your death.

The following solutions can/should be implemented:

1 Death (yours)

The trustee of your estate will hand the one-pager and the power of attorney to whomever you have chosen. If you are really organized, there will also be a folder with all of the agreements, notes, and share certificates/options. Now any issues relating to these investments can be handled promptly.

2 Major family event (baby, divorce, sickness, visit by aliens)

ENTREPRENEURS ARE BEST WHEN THEY HAVE THE FACTS AND KNOW WHAT AND WHO THEY CAN RELY ON

Get out your one-pager and consider the expectations and needs of the entrepreneurs on your list. Decide if you can still meet them while you face your current personal challenge. If not, let them know right now. Entrepreneurs are best when they have the facts and know what and who they can rely on. Find a replacement if possible, take care of yourself and your family, then come back to the project later.

3 Bankruptcy/financial trouble

Same as above, except you may be tempted to try to liquidate. This is unlikely to be an option, however it is sometimes possible. In the early days at Amis Ventures, one of the partners ran out of cash and needed to sell some of his shares. David managed to do this and at the same time benefited the company by selling the shares to a new board member, who was looking to increase his stake and invest more time. So the partner got some cash (albeit at less than the market rate), the company got to keep the partner working, and a board member became involved and motivated.

4 Personal move/career change

Get out your one-pager and consider the expectations and needs of the entrepreneurs on your list. Can you still meet them after you move or change careers? If not, let them know. Alternatively, find a way to continue supporting them, even if you have less time or will be farther away.

In some cases, the founders and other investors may have already considered future shareholder issues. For example, when David started Amis Ventures, the three founders (Dale Pederson, Danny Tomeh, and David Amis) all agreed that in the event of the death of one of them, the voting rights of their shares would pass back to the company. This avoided the potential situation of two partners being forced to go into business with a family member of the lost partner.

4 ● A FAILED HARVEST STORY

Our appreciation to Dave Berkus for sharing a failure story with us. All angels have 'em, they just don't talk about 'em! Dave Berkus, an active angel investor who has made 19 early-stage investments, and author of *Better than Money*, talked to us about one of his non-successful investments.

> I had created a front office reservation system for the hotel industry which was the second successful national system that came into the marketplace back in 1975. In that field I had developed some very deep relationships with chain executives around the world so it was natural for me to try and lead another company in the hotel industry and the technology sector and take advantage of those relationships. And I did.
>
> The company was formed in 1993 to take advantage of new wireless technologies that could be applied to the hotel industry. And you may remember back to 1993 from some of the other companies that pen-based computing wasn't really a dominant type of computing nor was it a separate type of computing.
>
> So we developed a pen-based, remote check-in for hotels and we developed a kiosk system of which we sold two. We developed a cell phone that connected to the room phone so that you could roam anywhere in the city and whenever your hotel room phone would ring, your cell phone would ring. You could also dial out through the hotel and the hotel would route through landlines. (This was before cell phones had taken off.)
>
> The company was composed of two former sales executives from my previous company and myself. I located it in Boston, which was a mistake, only because it violated my rule that I wanted to be near the CEO and organization to help coach it.
>
> The two executives had never run companies before – that was my second mistake.
>
> My third mistake was that we under-funded it. Although I put $1.5m into the company, it took three years to do it. I leaked the money in over time so we never really had a dramatic show at the early stage, which we should have done.
>
> Mistake number four was that we formed the company around a premise which I now think to be flawed. And the premise was brand-new, gee-whiz technology, which will, of itself, create demand.
>
> It was an excellent idea until digital phones became ubiquitous and people carried a phone in their pocket everywhere, even the phones in the rooms were no longer of value.
>
> So the company still has leases for those cell phones outstanding and I am harvesting by letting the leases play out. In the end the value I'll receive from this, my worst investment, is probably one-half or two-thirds of what I invested.

5 ● A SUCCESSFUL HARVEST STORY – LIFEMINDERS

Frans Kok talks about the successful harvest event of LifeMinders, which generated a 30 x return on his investment.

❝ My first thought as an early-stage investor is about harvesting. Not in the sense that I determine in advance how to get liquid, but rather I try to figure how to help make the company in which I am planning to invest attractive enough so that someone in the near future will offer more for my position than I paid. For example, in the case of LifeMinders I paid about 80 cents per share of common stock for a position in the low six figures. At the same time I brought in a bevy of local venture capitalists who paid the equivalent amount per share of preferred stock. This took place toward the end of 1997 and gave the company $1.25m of expansion capital with a soft commitment to add another $1m later in 1998.

Frans Kok

The key to harvesting in LifeMinders was to sign up as many users of the service in as short a time and at as little cost as possible. LifeMinders' business plan called for the company to sign up large consumer products companies and retailers as "sponsor" companies. The names of companies contacted were impressive and included Toys Я Us, Home Depot, Jiffy Lube, Procter & Gamble, Blockbusters, etc. The sponsor companies, which at that time had very little web presence, would promote LifeMinders with their clients and LifeMinders would remind those clients once or twice a week of important events that affect the customers. It sounded simple and became very complicated. The major corporations were very slow in signing up, demanded concessions and in some cases, such as Blockbusters and Loewes, when they finally signed up the store managers had no incentive to promote LifeMinders with their customers.

One year later, toward the end of 1998, LifeMinders had less than 10,000 users and scant interest from the "sponsors." It had spent about $1.8m and had only about $400,000 left. At that point two things happened. First, I was able to raise another $4m for the company. Second, the board of directors, including me, asked management to devise and experiment with ways to bring users in without aid from sponsor companies. Our view was that the sponsor companies would sign up once we had the users.

Management executed this brilliantly. By May 1999 the company had almost a million users and raised another $10m without major problems at a valuation of about $40m. On November 19, 1999 the company went public. It had about 4m users and was valued at $275m or $14 per share. The company is now trading at about $30 per share (July 2000) and has been as high as $90+ per share. It has about 16m users. I still own the stock because I have a great deal of faith in the management team, but I have also liquidated a significant portion of my holding.

I resigned from the board of directors in May 1999 since the company was on track and I could not contribute significantly to its further success. It makes it easier to liquidate my position without running into conflict of interest problems. My impression is that both the venture capitalists and angels stay on the boards of successful companies too long. They tend to want to share the limelight of success. Once the company is tracking those directors should be replaced for the benefit of the company and for the benefit of the venture capital partners. 🙶🙶 ....

6 • INTERVIEW WITH STEVE MCGEADY

Steven McGeady, angel investor and now venture capitalist, was the VP of Intel's Internet Technology until June 2000. While he was still at Intel we spoke to him about his two distinct investment activities in early-stage companies.

Steve McGeady

🙶🙶 One is my personal investing. The other direction is the portfolio my group has built as part of Intel Corporation's Business Development operation [now called Intel Capital]. The Intel investments have somewhat different parameters and goals than my personal investments, which are made at an earlier stage.

We told a joke about Intel's criteria for investing: imagine a two-by-two matrix, on one axis are the legends "good financial prospects" and "poor financial prospects," and on the other axis are the legends "strategically aligned" [with Intel's interests] and "not strategic." The argument was that if a company was not strategically aligned with us we shouldn't invest, and of course, if they had poor financial prospects we shouldn't invest. However, if they were strategically aligned, and they also had good financial prospects, then they wouldn't have any trouble getting money from venture capitalists, so we shouldn't invest there either! Of course we didn't really implement this policy, but the joke illustrates the frustrations we had getting deals through the review process.

The truth was that companies that were more aligned with Intel were more likely to get investments: we were more likely to take a business or financial risk, and we were more likely to see whether we could provide some additional value to the company in question. This aligns with my personal investing style as well. In Intel's case, the more strategically aligned the company was, the more willing we were to invest or put in their assets like technology licenses, management assistance, etc.

In approaching either Intel or myself, one of the key things for a company seeking an investment is to clearly articulate a market mode (including the size, structure, and existing players) and how that market model relates to a higher level strategy. It is important that the company has a strongly held worldview about the market into which it intends to deliver goods or services. The one can have a dialogue about how that market model impacts the investor's strategy and direction. Identifying and articulating that strategic interest is very important when the investor interest is more than financial. Another thing that is very important is to identify something the strategic investor can provide other than, or in addition to, money. This may be access to markets or channels, technology, or executive management experience. There are companies that don't require this strategic fit, and for those one can simply pitch financial return, but that is not the domain of most tech investors, such as Intel or Microsoft.

With Intel, it is often the case that people just want the halo of Intel as an investor. Intel tends to look somewhat cynically on that, although Intel Capital did a study which showed that companies in which Intel was an investor commanded a 30% premium after Intel became an investor. But Intel tends to look for things that are more tangible than its name, things such as a technology license, or some additional market insight or access, or other areas where they have something specific to offer to the company.

So, on a "Gives and Gets" foil, which is always part of an investment review, Intel likes to see something in addition to cash as the investment. It may be a technology agreement, or marketing help, or any number of other things, but something other than money is really important. 〞 ·······················

4 TAKEAWAYS FROM HARVESTING

1 ● Harvesting should be engineered from the beginning.

2 ● Sometimes a negative harvest is the best harvest.

3 ● Strategic sales are the most common harvest method, followed by financial sales, and IPOs which are rare.

4 ● VCs are the pros of harvesting.

PART III

Angels
and other
investors

QUICK OVERVIEW

56 ● Biographies of the angels in this book 327

Contributing angels 327

In-depth profiles of 15 angels 335

BIOGRAPHIES OF THE ANGELS INTERVIEWED IN THIS BOOK

CONTRIBUTING ANGELS

Any angel investor who sends a suggestion, quotation, tactic or tool that we use in the next edition, will receive a reference or acknowledgment in the book and a free copy.

If you are interested in being interviewed for the second edition, please contact us at davidandhoward@WinningAngels.com.

If you know of an entrepreneur who should be interviewed for our next book, *Winning Entrepreneurs*, then please direct them to www.WinningEntrepreneurs.com.

We would like to thank the following angel investors for giving some of their precious time to help us in creating these materials. A few of these angels have provided further information about themselves and their investment history on the following pages.

Tom Alberg – Madrona Investment Group (Seattle, Washington)

A former lawyer turned angel, who was an early investor in Amazon.com and has done over 50 deals. He is the founder of Madrona Investment Group, which focuses on software, internet and telecommunications start-ups.

Betsy Atkins – Net Angels (Coral Gables, Florida)

A hands-on, coach angel who has made 30 investments to date and is an advocate for the entrepreneurs. Betsy Atkins, age 45, Director of Lucent Technologies, recently appointed; founder of Ascend Corporation; general partner Net Angels (venture capital fund); Director Paradyne Networks, Inc; Polycom, Inc; Olympic Steel, Inc; Selectica, Inc. Retired CEO of Nci Corporation (1991–1993). Chairman of the board of Amplitude Software, now a critical path company.

Dave Berkus – Berkus Technology Ventures (Arcadia, California)

The founder of BTV, he represents three angel funds that have invested in 18 companies. He often takes a lead director role, preferring internet and software deals. He was referred to by *Inc* as a "professionalized angel."
Email: dberkus@berkus.com

Jaap Blaak – Tailwind BV (Netherlands)

Entrepreneur and VC who invests in high-tech and biotechnology early-stage companies, taking on a variety of roles from coach angel to lead investor.

Andrew Blair – Business Angels International (London, England)

Co-founder of Business Angels International, he has made 18 investments. He likes to invest as part of a syndicate and targets specific industries, according to the group of investors that will be involved in the deal.

Tarby Bryant – The Gathering of Angels (Sante Fe, New Mexico)

An angel who organizes The Gathering of Angels in Santa Fe. They screen 40–50 plans per month, and tend to invest in companies with $3–4m valuations.

Craig Burr – Burr Egan Deleage & Corporation (Boston, Massachusetts)

Craig Burr has invested in over 30 start-ups as an angel, and has also invested as a VC in over 200 companies.

Lucius Cary – Seed Capital Ltd (Oxford, England)

A well-known, supportive coach angel in the UK, who has made over 50 investments. He has experience of raising and investing early-stage capital, as well as matching angels with entrepreneurs. He focuses particularly on high-tech businesses within one hour's drive of Oxford.

Esther Dyson – EDventure Holdings (New York City, New York)

President of EDventure Holdings. She has invested in over 40 angel deals, and gets involved on an as-needed basis to varying degrees. Her focus is on high-tech companies in US, UK, Sweden and emerging markets, such as Eastern Europe.
    Email: edyson@edventure.com

Andrew Filipowski – divine interVentures (Chicago, Illinois)

Founder of PLATINUM technology, inc, which was sold to Computer Associates for over $3.6 bn. In 1999, he founded divine interVentures, inc, an internet holding company actively engaged in e-commerce infrastructure through a coalition of associated companies. divine has acquired significant interests in more than 70 companies in the US and internationally. Filipowski has invested as an angel in dozens of early-stage companies.
    Tel: (001) 630.799.7500, Fax: (001) 630.799.7501.

SG (Boston, Massachusetts)

Has been an investor for over 20 years, and a full time angel for the last three. He has invested in 50–60 companies, 60% as an angel and 40% as a VC. His focus is on software and data telecommunications equipment. He is a member of a Boston-based angel investor group.

Josh Green – Venture Law Group (Menlo Park, California)

He has been a lawyer in Silicon Valley, working with start-ups for 20 years. He has worked on 500–600 early-stage deals, with 150-200 IPOs and 200 acquisitions.
  Email: jgreen@vlg.com

Carl Guerreri – Elecontronic Warfare Associates (Herndon, Virginia)

He was given a break by an angel himself 20 years ago, and has himself made four early-stage investments. He takes on the role of a silent investor, but is always available to help the entrepreneur.
  Email: cguerrer@ewa.com

John Hime – Curly H Ventures (Austin, Texas)

A supportive coach angel, who is often the lead investor, has backed 18 deals. His typical deal has an internet focus, and he generally invests $100k for a 5–10% stake.

O.H. (Oslo, Norway)

A Norwegian active angel investor who takes on various roles, ranging from silent to coach angel.

Brian Horey – Equity Growth Management (New York City, New York)

Founder of New York New Media Association, which runs an angel investor network. He has made 10 investments, and while not completely passive, does not have enough time for a highly active role.
  Email: bhorey@compuserve.com

Mitch Kapor – Accel Partners (Palo Alto, California)

A partner at VC firm, Accel Partners. Mitch Kapor is the founder of Lotus, and has been working with entrepreneurs and investing in start-ups for over 15 years. As an angel he has backed around 25 companies, including RealNetworks and UUNET.

George Kline – Brightstone Capital Ltd (Edina, Minnesota)

Has made over 160 investments, 90% of which are in the Minnesota region. His focus is on technology and medical deals. Two of his deals have returned over 100 times the original investment. He has served on the board of 55 public companies.

Frans Kok (Washington, DC)

An investment banker (contributing to his deal flow) who has made three investments, two of which successfully went to IPO, with his trophy being Lifeminders.com.
   Email: fkok@hekelaar.com
   Tel: 301.656.7870 (Johan Hekelaar, Inc, MD).

Randy Komisar – WebTV Networks, Inc (Mountain View, California)

Usually invests time, or "sweat equity" rather than cash, and gets involved in companies as a virtual CEO, for example with WebTV.

Richard Kramlich – New Enterprise Associates (Menlo Park, California)

Co-founder and general partner of VC firm NEA. Invested $22,500 in Apple back in 1978, which, by the time he exited, had grown in value to $5m.
   Email: dkramlich@nea.com

CL (New York City, New York)

A coach angel, who often acts as part of a syndicate and has made 20 deals with a media-related focus, two of which have IPO'd.

Frank Levy (San Francisco, California)

He is the founder and CEO of FairAir.com and the managing partner of Wasabi Fund, which made 18 investments into early-stage companies. He joined PlanetAll as one of its first employees prior to its sale to Amazon and he is an HBS alumnus.
   Email: franklevy@wasabifund.com

Nigel Lovet-Turner (Hampshire, England)

A serial entrepreneur turned angel, who has made one deal as a lead investor. He likes to work with the company before investing, and takes an active coach role.

Audrey MacLean (Saratoga, California)

Describes her role as a "mentor capitalist." She has made 24 early-stage investments, of which five have IPO'd and five have been acquired. She focuses on high-tech deals.

John McCallion – Merlin Investments (Buckinghamshire, England)

With a blue-chip commercial marketing career, John created and shared in a £100m capital profit in three years on an MBO. Founded Merlin Investments in 1998, which has invested in 10 companies. John is founding investor and chairman of three companies and non-executive director of two others. John takes an active role in each business advising on strategy, marketing and raises seed and VC funding.

Email: john.mccallion@btinternet.com

Steven McGeady – Drumlin Ventures (Oregon)

Steven McGeady, now a venture fund manager, was Vice President of Intel's multimedia, internet and e-health operations during his 15 year service at Intel Corporation. He is an angel, focusing on net businesses. He sits on the board of his investee companies, including Webcriteria and Sidetalk.com.

Email: mcg@drumlin-holdings.com

Dick Morley – R Morley, Inc (New Hampshire, US)

Co-founder of Nashua Breakfast Club, he has invested in over 70 high-tech start-ups to date. He is mainly a silent investor, and often has no involvement in a deal once the investment is made.

Anthony Morris – Morris & Associates (Boston, Massachusetts)

A member of Walnut Venture Associates and a member of CommonAngels. He is a consultant as well as an investor, and focuses mainly on internet companies. He has backed 19 deals, one of which was idealab! generating a return of several hundred times.

Jim Newton – TriState Investment Group (Chapel Hill, North Carolina)

Administrator for TriState Investment Group, which has over 100 angel members, each of which puts up at least $50k. It has been operating since 1989, and in total 35 companies have received investment of $20m. They focus in the most part on technology and biotech companies.

Website: www.tignc.com

Jeff Parker – CCBN (Boston, Massachusetts)

An active speaker and writer in the investor relations arena, has an extensive history of success in both entrepreneurship and angel investing. Currently, Jeff is the CEO and founder of CCBN (Corporate Communications Broadcast Network) in Boston, Massachusetts. Prior to CCBN, Jeff was the creator and CEO of several successful financial service companies.

Denis Payre – European Technology Ventures (Brussels, Belgium)

Entrepreneur turned angel. Co-founded Business Objects in Paris, which was the first European software company to go public on NASDAQ. He is a coach angel who has made 10 investments in Europe.

Peter Pichler – Berndorf AG (Austria)

An angel who has made two private investments and eight through his company, Berndorf AG (an industrial finance holding company). They try to be the sole or lead investors and offer support to the entrepreneurs.
　　Email: pp@berndorf.co.at

Cuno Pümpin – IPA Services (Switzerland)

A Swiss coach angel who has made more than 10 investments, mainly in Europe. He likes to contribute advice and takes on the role of strategist.
　　Email: puempin@puempin.com

Bill Sahlman – Harvard Business School (Boston, Massachusetts)

Professor of Entrepreneurship at Harvard Business School, and active angel investor. He has made over 50 deals in a 20-year period and tends to take a passive role.

David Solomont – CommonAngels (Boston, Massachusetts)

Founder of CommonAngels, the Boston-based angel network which has a closed membership of 50 angels and a focus on software, IT, internet-related deals. In the last 18 months he has made over 30 investments.
　　Email: david@commonangels.com
　　Web: www.commonangels.com
　　Tel: (001) 617.566.0212.
　　PO Box 67385, Chestnut Hill, MA 02467.

Cliff Stanford – Redbus (London, England)

A successful entrepreneur, having founded Demon Internet in 1992 which he sold in 1998 for £66m. He then set up Redbus Investments to provide financial, operational and management support to British companies and individuals with new and innovative ideas. A directory of Redbus-invested companies can be found at http://www.redbus.co.uk.

Howard Tullman (Chicago, Illinois)

Successful serial entrepreneur turned angel. He teaches an MBA class called Start-ups: Start to Finish.
  Email: tullman@aol.com
  Tel: (001) 312.642.7560.
  640 N. LaSalle Street, Suite 590, Chicago, IL 60610.

Bert Twaalfhoven – Indivers BV (Netherlands)

A leading advocate for the entrepreneur, he is founder of the European Foundation for Entrepreneurial Research and Europe's 500. He has made 23 personal angel deals and 50 through his company, Indivers, which he tends to control though the use of business development managers.

Reg Valin (London, England)

A successful entrepreneur turned coach angel, who normally takes an advisory role. He has made seven investments to date with a leisure and retail focus.
  Tel: (44) 020.7371.1872.

Manny Villafana – ATS Medical Inc (Minneapolis, Minnesota)

Entrepreneur turned investor who has backed over 50 angel deals in the medi-tech sector. A highly influential investor in the Minneapolis region, he sticks religiously to his area of expertise and is regarded as the "make or break" ingredient of medi-tech start-up companies.

Prince Heinrich von Liechtenstein (Vienna, Austria)

"Henry," as he is known to friends, is an active angel and entrepreneur, based in Vienna, Austria. Currently on leave from Boston Consulting Group to start another company, he is widely active in developing entrepreneurship in Europe and is a co-founder of Growth Plus, the association of high-growth entrepreneurs.

Steve Walker – Steve Walker & Associates (Glenwood, Maryland)

As a member of Capital Investors, the Washington network of angels, he has made 35 deals to date, focusing on emerging technologies. He likes to take an active role in his investments.

Email: steve@stevewalker.com

Darryl Wash – Ascend Venture Group (New York City, New York)

Investment banker turned angel, Darryl Wash, is a co-founder of the Ascend Venture Group. He has backed 20 early-stage companies and his focus is on technology investments.

Email: dwash@ascendventures.com
Tel: (001) 212.324.2225.

William Weaver – Sachnoff & Weaver Ltd (Chicago, Illinois)

A leading technology lawyer in Chicago, who has become an angel investor. He has invested in numerous start-ups, mostly in high-tech and software-based companies, where he will often sit on the board.

Email: wweaver@sachnoff.com (please only contact if based in metropolitan area, Chicago)

Tom Wharton – Wharton Consulting (Omaha, Nebraska)

Tom Wharton is the President of Wharton Consulting. Previously he was the co-founder of DoubleClick and Poppe Tyson Interactive.

We'll take a closer look at a few of our angels now.

IN-DEPTH PROFILES

Audrey MacLean

Professor Audrey MacLean, who often takes the role of a "mentor capitalist" has made 24 early-stage investments, of which five have gone public.

Audrey MacLean has a track record for entrepreneurial success as a founder, CEO, seed investor and board member in a variety of high-tech and consumer industries. She has been listed by *Business Week* as one of the 50 most influential business women in America and in 1999 was featured by *Forbes* in a cover article on angel investing. They described her as the *"Angel investor who seeds the next super-stars of technology."* She jokes about the article they ran, saying:

Audrey MacLean

❝ For a long time I referred to myself as the stealth angel, because I tried to be very inconspicuous. I am afraid I blew that last year. They put it on the cover and now every entrepreneur in Sri Lanka, Ukraine and South America thinks they must have me. It is unbelievable. ❞

In 1993 she made the decision to become an angel investor. This would enable her to cut back on the long hours that being an entrepreneur requires, and allow more time for bringing up a young family. Since that time she has made 24 investments, with her focus on the tech industry. She comments about these: *"Most of my high-tech deals have returned roughly 50 times my initial investment."*

The companies she has seed funded which have gone public include: Pure Software, Pete's Brewing Company, AdForce, dsl.net, Selectica. Companies that have been acquired include: Avidia by PairGain, Firefly by Microsoft, Internet-Middleware by NetworkAppliance, Amplitude by CriticalPath, specialtyMD by Chemdex. Some of her other deals include: Schoolpop, Achieva, eVoice, Informed-Diagnostics, WorkExchange, AutoDaq, Napa Style, Gigabeat, CaseCentral, and Coulera.

MacLean is a hands-on investor, providing active support to the entrepreneur.

❝ I am kind of a guardian angel – someone who is going to invest and really become part of the team: helping raise money, recruit people, flesh out the business model, refine the strategy, and help formulate strategic alliances. I do that stuff from board level. Lots of times I end up recruiting a CEO or core members of the team. It is very different from angel investing as an investing-only proposition. ❞

Before making the transition from entrepreneur to angel, Audrey MacLean gained over two decades of combined experience in the computer and communications industry. She co-founded, and was Vice President of, Network Equipment Technologies (NET) which went public in 1987. She later co-founded and was CEO of Adaptive, which merged with NET in 1993.

In 1997, MacLean joined the faculty at Stanford in the Graduate School of Engineering where she is the Lead Professor on the Stanford Technology Venture Program's flagship course entitled Technology Venture Formation. She is also a contributor to the annual STVP roundtable of university leaders from top technical institutions nationwide which examines issues surrounding the imperative for entrepreneurship education for 21st century engineers.

MacLean actively works to support the development of entrepreneurial studies nationwide through her role as a board member of the Kaufman Foundation's Center for Entrepreneurial Leadership. She holds a Bachelor of Science Degree from the University of Redlands and is an alumnus of the Stanford Graduate School of Business.

Dave Berkus

Dave Berkus, who takes on the role of a "professional angel," focuses full time on angel investing. He has backed over 20 early stage businesses, and his investment preferences are that the companies be in the internet and software sector and based in southern California.

Dave Berkus

Dave Berkus talked to us about his role as a "professional angel." He has been actively angel investing since 1993 and has made over 20 investments in early stage companies.

When he first set about angel investing, Berkus made two significant contacts: one with the head of a bank and another with a VC company. From these contacts he was able to start the ball rolling. Deal flow came his way and three months later he made his first investment.

In order to professionalize his activities he founded Berkus Technology Ventures LLC. The company manages two angel investment funds which make seed capital and venture investments in internet and software businesses, primarily based in southern California.

Investments are made in companies which demonstrate an opportunity to become a dominant player within a vertical market, or in the internet, communications or multimedia niches:

❝ I do this full time and I have turned it into an organization rather than an individual effort – that would define the term professionalized angel. Most of the angels I have met are investing because they are putting money back into industries that they usually understand, from money they were able to see from the sale of their company. So many of them are former entrepreneurs, and many of them do this part time. The TechCoast Angels, for example, is made up of over 130 people and I think only three or four of us can be classed as professionalized angels. The rest have other focuses. ❞

Berkus is board chairman or board member for numerous public and private internet and software companies. These include: GameSpy Industries Inc; EPC International Inc; Hotelware Corporation; C.View Technologies Inc; Sonic Desktop Software Inc; Word-Of-Net Inc; and Apogee Broadcasting Corporation. Recent mergers or sales of BTV companies have led to BTV investments in National

Computer Systems Inc (NASDAQ: NCLS); Electrax Systems Inc (NASDAQ: ELTRAX); and Web Interactive Services Inc (NASDAQ: WEBB).

Prior to his career as an angel investor he ran two companies. The first, which was in the record manufacturing industry, he founded at the age of 13 going on to take it public at the age of 33. He was an early pioneer in the mini-computer industry, founding his second company, Computerized Lodging Systems Inc, which for two consecutive years was featured in the *Inc.500* list of America's fastest growing companies. In 1990 he sold the company, running it for a further three years before embarking on a career as an angel investor.

He is co-author of *Better Than Money* (quoted in this book on pages 279–80) a book for software companies addressing the issues resulting from rapid growth. In the investment community, he is the Managing Partner of Patina LLC and of Kodiak Ventures LP, both seed capital investment funds, and an active member of the TechCoast Angels, a group of early-stage venture investors.

Dave is a graduate of Occidental College where he currently serves as a Trustee of the College.

Email: dberkus@berkus.com

Richard Morley

Dick Morley, co-founder of the Nashua Breakfast Club, has invested in over 70 high-tech start-up companies. He tends to take on the role of a "silent investor," with minimal interaction following an investment decision.

Dick Morley is one of the founders of the Nashua Breakfast Club, which he describes as, *"An ad-hoc arrangement of, what started with two people and then became a core group of four with a further 22 individuals that we fax information about deals to."*

Dick Morley is probably best known as the father of the program-mable controller and is the leading visionary in the field of advanced technological development. He is also an entrepreneur whose consistent successes in the founding of high-technology companies has been demonstrated through more than three decades of revolutionary *Richard Morley* achievements. Morley is the recipient of the Franklin Institute's prestigious Howard N. Potts Award and is an inductee of the Automation Hall of Fame. He holds more than 20 US and foreign patents, including those for the parallel inference machine, the hand-held terminal, the programmable logic controller and magnetic thin film.

With his technical background in mind, he says:

❝ What I do typically is to have one meeting, possibly, before the investment decision, and my job is to analyze whether or not the technology is feasible at a maximum of three times the entrepreneur's estimate. They spend triple what they think they will, but we of course don't tell them that. The question I get asked by the Breakfast Club and other professional investors is: is this technology feasible in the time scale and the money scale? I either say yes or no, and most of the time I say yes, because technology today is easy. The second question they ask is: if they don't deliver do you know people, or can you yourself deliver, the technology? And then I usually attend one meeting. I am almost always not on the board. And then I never see them again. Some of the people in the Breakfast Club, who are financially orientated, will take a seat on the board, if asked, and stay on the board. Then I hear from those guys: hey, Dick, they've got a problem here or there. But generally I don't follow it. ""

He doesn't monitor his investments at all, and says, *"I'm just as surprised as they are when they make it."*

Further information: www.barn.org

Mitch Kapor

Founder of Lotus Development Corporation, Mitch Kapor has been an active and high-profile angel for over 20 years. He has made around 25 investments, often taking a lead and advisory role, and is now a partner with the VC firm, Accel Partners.

Mitch Kapor

Mitch Kapor, 49, is the founder of Lotus Development Corporation and the designer of Lotus 1-2-3, the desktop productivity tool which led the way to the ubiquitous adoption of the personal computer as a business tool in the 1980s. For 20 years he has been at the forefront of the IT revolution as an entrepreneur, investor, social activist, philanthropist and most recently, venture capitalist with Accel. He has been an angel investor in high-technology start-ups since the early 1980s. Following his success with Lotus, Mitch Kapor was very much in the spotlight and received a great deal of public attention. He says, *"I was just in the flow of things, meeting people, knowing people."* Entrepreneurs began approaching him for advice and financing. *"I started to invest in what is now called angel investing, it wasn't called that then, it didn't really have a name."*

He has made around 25 angel-type investments, focusing on the IT industry sector. He was the founding and lead investor in several hugely successful start-ups, including UUNET Technology and RealNetworks. He says about RealNetworks:

"" The valuation was at $12m, but I put in $1m on that round. There was a VC round later, where the pre-money valuation was into the 40s, which was kind of a record breaker at the time, in 1995. Now when you look at RealNetworks today, with a market cap of $5–6 bn, it looks like a pretty good investment. ""

Mr Kapor also talks about deals that weren't so successful: "*I probably learnt more from my failures, like GoCorporation, than from my successes, at least as much.*" Initially, the deals that would get his attention were technology projects that could be used to make some sort of difference and have a positive impact on the user experience:

❝ I wasn't primarily driven at all by what was going to produce an attractive return, I was driven by what I thought was interesting to work on and be a part of. That also led to some failures in screening, where I would sometimes fall in love with projects and not see some of the obvious problems from the management point of view. ❞

Mitch Kapor developed an investment style in the 1990s that worked well for him:

❝ I am kind of a softie in terms of negotiating and so, to protect myself, I sometimes wound up structuring deals that anticipated subsequent VC rounds. I would essentially get a ride along on whatever they agreed to in the venture. So that saved having to work out lots of issues twice, since I knew various subsidiary terms would be thrashed out in a venture round. In fact, I personally came to the conclusion that what worked for me and this is a style which I used in several deals in the 1990s (including a couple that were very successful, UUNET and RealNetworks) was to be the first money in the seed round, as opposed to co-investing with a VC. I would work closely with the entrepreneur, with the intent of raising venture capital. In fact, in several cases the entrepreneurs were not sure they wanted to go down this route, for example, Adams at UUNET, Rob Glaser who was putting some of his own money into the company, and Ray Ozzie at Groove Networks. But, bringing in venture investors always struck me, if it was the right one, as the right thing to do for a lot of projects. ❞

In 1971 Mitch Kapor graduated from Yale with a BA in linguistics and psychology. He also attended MIT's Sloan School of Management. In 1990 he co-founded Electronic Frontier Foundation, and served as chairman until 1994. In January 1999, Kapor joined Accel Partners, a leading VC firm in Palo Alto, California. "*My going to Accel last January, in part, was the result of seeing the excellent work that Accel did with UUNET and RealNetworks.*"

He concludes by saying:

❝ Angel investing is fun, and I encourage people who are in a position to do it, to do it. I think the angels are now an important part of the ecology of growing, high-tech companies. I've seen companies now coming to Accel that have already raised one, two, or in some cases three million dollars from angels, and then we come in and do the next round, which we call early-stage. ❞

Darryl Wash

Investment banker turned Angel, Darryl Wash, co-founder of Ascend Venture Group, has backed 20 early-stage companies, including successful companies, such as StarMedia Network and Kozmo.com. His focus is on technology companies. He takes on the role of a venture angel, positioning himself half-way between traditional angel investing and VC firms.

Darryl Wash

Darryl Wash co-founded Ascend Venture Group, LLC, in January 2000, which focuses on investing in early-stage technology companies via a strategy of leveraging minority networks and working with women entrepreneurs to identify unique, attractive investment opportunities:

❝ I originally decided, together with my partners, that I didn't want to invest every dollar I had in private companies. I believe that private investing in any stage company should only be done with a portion of one's wealth into a diversified portfolio. As a result, I felt that I needed more capital to make these investments. So I sought out four of my very close friends, all of who are minorities from Goldman Sachs, and suggested that we band together to form an investment partnership vehicle, investing on the side while still continuing to work. Over five years this has evolved into Ascend Venture Group – a full-time activity for us. ❞

Ascend occupies an interesting space, in between the angels and the VCs. They help position the companies for the next VC round. They focus on the companies' need to have the right terms, the right valuations for the stage they are at, the right people, and to have identified the milestones that need to be achieved and the process by which they will be achieved.

Darryl Wash, together with three of the angels he has co-invested with over the past four years (who are now his partners at Ascend), has invested just under $8m in 20 early-stage companies. The investments in aggregate have returned well over $22m so far, and he expects the portfolio's value to increase threefold in two years. StarMedia Network, Inc, is the biggest confirmed success so far in terms of liquidity. Originally, they invested $145,000 in common stock, at a pre-money valuation of $4.6m. In the subsequent three rounds they invested a further $252,000. The company is now publicly traded, and has a market capitalization in excess of $1bn.

He describes the support that he provides as *"non-intrusive, non-invasive."* He says:

❝ There are enough tasks to perform and challenges that entrepreneurs have to face in building a business, they don't need angels showing up and asking questions. What they really need is for angels to be value added. So, we will maybe fire off an email saying "Hey, did you think about offering this?," or "Hey, I know this person, would you like an introduction?" and quite honestly, if they don't respond, it is because they are doing something that is hopefully more important for the company, and we are not able to make those decisions. I need to count on managers to make them. ❞

Prior to Ascend, Mr Wash gained 11 years' investment banking experience with Goldman, Sachs & Co and Peter J. Solomon Company. He obtained a Masters in Business Administration at Stanford University School of Business (Arjay Miller Scholar – top 10%) and a Bachelor of Arts in Economics, University of California at Berkeley (highest distinction in General Scholarship (top 3%) and Phi Beta Kappa). He currently sits on the boards of several investee companies, including: B2Emarkets, Inc and Pennoyer Capital Management.

Further information: Ascend Venture Group, 1500 Broadway, 14th Floor, New York, NY 10036. Tel: (001) 212.324.2225. Email: dwash@ascendventures.com

Frank Levy

Frank Levy, founder of the Wasabi Fund, LP, became involved in angel investments during a hiatus between start-ups. With 23 partners, he made 18 early-stage internet investments between April 1999 and March 2000. He is a relatively new angel with a unique approach. He generally plays a "reserve force" role.

Frank explains how he became involved in angel investing:

Frank Levy

❝ PlanetAll, where I had been an early employee, had been purchased by Amazon about six months earlier, and it was the right time for me to move on. I wanted to join or co-found another start-up. To kick off my search, I wrote an email to the president of the hi-tech club at HBS basically introducing myself as an alum with some internet experience looking to get involved with another start-up. The note was forwarded to the entire graduating class. The response from students who intended to turn their field study projects into start-ups upon graduation was overwhelming. I started speaking with lots of students on the phone, and their businesses sounded very exciting. None of them were quite the right fit for me to join, but several seemed like promising investments. My PlanetAll stock was worth about $1m at the time, so I figured that I would allocate $250,000 for angel investments. The minimum investment in most of the companies I was talking to was around $50,000. If I invested alone, I'd only be able to do five deals, and this didn't seem diversified enough. Thus, I called Warren Adams and some other friends and they agreed to pitch in. Within about a month, I had raised my goal of $1m and formally organized the Wasabi Fund, LP. Since the fund was so tiny, and since it was my first foray into investing, I just charged a minimal management fee and 10% carried interest. ❞

It took Frank about nine months to invest the Wasabi Fund. In parallel with this effort, he was working on a business plan of his own for FairAir.com, a firm he ultimately co-founded in January 2000. He spends about 10 hours a month on Wasabi Fund-related matters while spending most of his time running FairAir.com:

❝ Evaluating and investing in start-ups was excellent preparation for founding a firm of my own. It focused me on what investors would be looking for and introduced me to other angel investors. I raised $1.3m for FairAir in about two weeks, largely from the same circle of people who were partners in the Wasabi Fund. ❞

Frank is a hands-off investor. Because the amount of his investments has been so small, the Wasabi Fund has only gained board representation in one deal. Frank's involvement generally consists of helping make introductions to other potential investors and generating business development leads by phone and email.

Frank served in business development, operations, and product development roles at PlanetAll from 1996–1999. He graduated from the Harvard Business School in 1995 and Yale University in 1989. Between college and business school he worked in management consulting.

Email: franklevy@wasabifund.com

Tony Morris

Tony Morris has made 19 investments, of which one (idealab!) has grown by several hundred times and only one failed. He is a resource to the start-ups and a "coach angel." His focus is on the internet and IT industry sectors.

Tony Morris has been an active angel investor since 1989. He set up Morris & Associates in 1987 (a Boston-based management consulting and financial advisory firm for IT companies and investors). He is a well-known PC industry pioneer, having founded Morris Decision Systems Inc, one of the nation's first value-added PC reselling and services organizations, focusing exclusively on the corporate marketplace.

His angel activity is focused on emerging IT and internet ventures. Most of his deals come to him via his personal network, and this is augmented by his membership in Walnut Venture Associates, a group of 21 active angel investors in Boston. Over time he has developed an effective screen for deal flow that comes his way:

1 Is it a game changer somehow?

2 Is the deal big enough to attract real venture capital?

3 Can I bring something to the table?

4 Do I have a good feeling about the management?

5 Am I following a winner?

He has made 19 investments to date, and of these there has only been one "loser." He says, *"I made the investment in September 1993 and by March 1994 it was toast."* He explained that he did not apply one of his screens: he didn't have a great feeling about the management.

His biggest win to date has generated a return of several hundred times. The company is idealab! He says it was an extraordinary situation, where he was incredibly lucky:

❝ I am a so-called idealab! resource, so I have worked on a variety of idealab! companies. In exchange for that work I was permitted to be an original investor in the company and some other stock was made available to me, common stock, at a nominal cost. So I am extraordinarily lucky to be investing next to Bill Gross. He's different from you and me. ❞

Morris acknowledges his good fortune with idealab! but spends much more time focusing on understanding the approaches and strategies that have worked in his portfolio as a whole and can be used again. *"I'm concerned with what's replicable. I'm happy to be lucky, but I'd rather bet on what can be repeated."*

The five screens he mentions apply to all his successful deals. In his portfolio he is currently excited about deals such as Interact Commerce Corporation and Event Zero and regards these as big wins where he has had a definable impact on the outcome.

His involvement with a company varies, but in general the younger the company the broader the role he plays. Usually he acts as a mentor to the CEO, providing seasoned advice, and as the company grows and brings on its own management team, he is frequently augmented by the VCs, so the need for his input declines, i.e. there is a natural period where he is actively involved and a natural period where he is not. He says:

❝ I'm a strategy consultant, so I'm eager to be involved. I'm on three boards of directors and on two boards of advisors. I think I would go on a board of advisors almost anytime, but I'm reluctant to go on the boards of directors for more than three or four companies. The fiduciary obligation really limits your freedom, so I don't go on boards without taking compensation: The support you provide is one of the primary values you can bring to the table, and it is one of the reasons that the VCs let me invest next to them. They know I'm a friend of the company and I'm willing to invest as well, and, gee, this makes them feel great. ❞

Manny Villafana

Serial entrepreneur turned investor, he has backed over 50 start-ups in the medi-tech sector. An influential investor in the Minneapolis region, he sticks religiously to his area of expertise and is regarded as the "make or break" ingredient of medi-tech start-up companies.

Manny Villafana, 60, has over the past 28 years been actively involved in the medi-tech industry both as an entrepreneur and later as an angel investor. He is the founder of two multi-billion dollar, publicly held companies. His entrepreneurial track record includes founding: Cardiac Pacemakers, Inc in 1972, St Jude Medical, Inc in 1976, GV Medical, Inc in 1982, and ATS Medical, Inc in 1987.

Manny Villafana

In his angel activities he sticks to what he knows: *"I only do medical deals."* He focuses on businesses in the Minnesota region, where he is based, which he describes as a very fertile area: *"I have to lock the door at times."* His reputation goes before him, and sourcing deals is not an issue, they come looking for him. His evaluation process involves various screens in three main areas: the team, the market, the technology. This is often spread out between the angels in the deal, but he personally likes to evaluate the technology. He is reluctant to take a seat on the board.

Lucius Cary

Lucius Cary has experience of raising capital, investing capital, and matching angels and entrepreneurs. He has made over 50 investments to date, predominately in high-tech businesses located within an hour's drive of Oxford, England. He takes a very hands on role, and is a "coach angel."

Lucius Cary

❝One might imagine that the process of raising and investing capital would be relatively straightforward, given the stated desire to raise capital on the one hand and the stated desire to invest capital on the other: Nothing could be further from the truth. The whole process is often traumatic for both parties and the fear of the unknown is rarely far beneath the surface.❞

Lucius Cary began his entrepreneurial career by raising £26,000 from four business angels in 1972 to found his own first business, an American hamburger restaurant. By 1978 there were three restaurants in the chain and 50 employees, all funded from the original investment and without bank borrowing. To begin with, he cooked, cleaned, waited at table, etc., but by 1978, each of the restaurants had its own manager, and he had an income and had all but done himself out of a job. The investors had been repaid all but £1,000 of their investment and had received directors' fees, and continued to own 49% of the business so that everyone was happy.

But he had had great difficulty in raising the start-up capital in 1972, and was turned down by all the venture capital companies he approached. He eventually found capital from four business angels who answered small classified advertisements in the *FT* and *Daily Telegraph*. Looking back, it seemed a very slender thread on which to have depended for founding a business which had been reasonably successful. He felt that what he had needed himself, in 1972, was a mechanism for presenting his plan in detail to several hundred business angel investors, rather than trying to reach them by means of a small classified advertisement.

While continuing to be the managing director of the restaurant business, he therefore founded the monthly publication Venture Capital Report (VCR) in 1978, which enables entrepreneurs to present their business plans in some detail to potential investors. This quickly came to absorb all his time and he sold the restaurants in order to concentrate full time on VCR, of which he was the managing director for 18 years until 1996, when he became chairman. VCR has several hundred business angel subscribers. The cost of a subscription is £350. For subscribers it thus provides a cost-effective way of looking at around 100 business opportunities per year, each of which is covered by a concise article with financial data and the name and address of the entrepreneur.

As a result of running VCR, it became clear that those entrepreneurs who find it most difficult to raise venture capital are those seeking seed capital, i.e. relatively small sums for very early-stage projects. Therefore, in 1983, he founded Seed Capital Ltd, and has run this in parallel with VCR ever since. Seed Capital has managed a succession of seed capital funds – Seedcorn Capital (1983), Seed Investments (1986), Seed Investments II (1988), Seed Investments III (1991), Seed Investments IV (1995) and Oxford Technology VCT (1997). The latest fund to which Seed Capital is investment advisor is Oxford Technology 2 VCT, which raised £6m in April 2000 with the aim of investing this capital in 15–20 early-stage and start-up technology companies within a 60 mile radius of Oxford.

He was educated at Eton and then spent one year serving an engineering apprenticeship at the Atomic Energy Research Establishment, Harwell, before reading Engineering Science and Economics at Trinity College, Oxford. He later spent two years obtaining an MBA at Harvard Business School.

John Hime

John Hime has made 29 angel investments in early-stage technology companies located in the Texas region. He is often the first angel investor in a deal, and generally participates as a reserve force and angel.

John Hime has been investing in early-stage technology companies since 1991. He currently focuses on emerging internet opportunities for software products, networking, e-commerce and services. He has served on four boards of directors and acts in an advisory role to a variety of entities. Investments are funded through Hime's family partnership, Curly H Ventures, Ltd.

John Hime

John Hime has developed a reputation of being the "good guy" for entrepreneurs to call. He tries to help out anyone who contacts him, even if he isn't going to invest. He helps by pointing them to other funding sources and giving them feedback on their plan. Based on the reputation which he has developed as a result of this approach, he doesn't have to actively source deals.

He uses an efficient screening process: he replies to approaches with a request for an executive summary using a standard form letter (see page 130) which clearly outlines what he is looking for by summarizing in bullet points: his typical deal, must haves, and how he can add value. This way the entrepreneur will be able to carry out a self-screen, filtering the quality and reducing the number of deals Hime receives. For those executive summaries that match his criteria, he schedules a face-to-face meeting. For those that don't, he replies with feedback and a list of other potential investors to contact.

He participates in deals as a reserve force angel, and is, *"Always available for specific projects or problems. This ends up being about four hours per company per month, with notable exceptions."* His best deal to date returned 40 times the original investment value in the space of 15 months. The company was sold to a public company, and he says: *"The bad news is that I was so delighted that I sold the stock as soon as possible, and it then almost immediately doubled. I could have made 80 times my original investment had I been more patient."*

Hime has 25 years of experience in leading computer systems and software manufacturers. During this time he developed expertise in software development, marketing, business strategy and people management. He was the Vice President of Marketing at Tivoli Systems during its start-up phase. Prior to joining Tivoli, he spent 10 years in Silicon Valley start-up companies, where he was the first Vice President and General Manager of MIPS Computer's Systems Business Unit, the first Vice President of Marketing at Frame Technology, the first Director of Marketing at Sun Microsystems, and the first Director of Product Marketing at Pyramid Technology. He participated in preparing the initial public stock offerings at MIPS and Sun, and in obtaining venture capital funding for all of these companies in their early stages.

He received his BA degree in Mathematics from the University of Texas, Austin (1970), and completed graduate coursework in Computer Science and Electrical Engineering. He is fluent in French, German, and Spanish. John is married, and has two grown sons and two teenage daughters. He is an avid shooter and hunter. He also owns and operates a cattle ranch near Blanco, TX.

Denis Payre

In 1990 Denis Payre co-founded Business Objects in Paris, which at the time of IPO was valued at $230m and is now valued at $3bn. Since 1997 he has invested in 10 start-up companies and sits on the board of six. He is a coach angel, who is able to give first-hand advice and support to the companies he backs.

Denis Payre, 37, co-founded Business Objects in 1990, which was the first European software company to go public on NASDAQ, and was quoted in the *Wall Street Journal* as being the most successful IPO of 1994. The angel in his company had a total ROI of several hundred times. The enthusiasm and interest this generated resulted in a lot of calls: *"We were viewed as the model to emulate."* After six years of exhaustive hours and commitment to Business Objects, he retired and became an angel investor: *"I felt it was interesting to share this experience with other European entrepreneurs."*

Denis Payne

He has made 10 investments in the last three years. Prolin, a software company based in Holland, is the first of his deals to liquidate. It was acquired by Hewlett-Packard eight months after his investment, generating a return of seven times his original investment. The second was Emme, which went public in France. He says: *"It is actually quite an unusual investment for me, because it is more of a consumer product-type company that does cultural CD ROMs and software, but I just liked the entrepreneurs, so decided to do it."* He says he didn't spend much time on this deal, and made probably two times his investment. He believes two of his remaining eight deals will float before the end of the year. His investments are spread out across Benelux (Belgium, Holland, and Luxembourg), France and England. He is

French, but lives in Belgium; one of the reasons for moving to Belgium was that *"I really could not stand the wealth tax in France any more, which is a big issue."*

He takes on the role of a coach angel, and believes the entrepreneurs value him as an investor because:

❝ I have the credibility of a guy who has been there, who has done it successfully, who has taken a Europe-based technology and made it a global success. They say, "If he tells us to do that, we probably should. ❞

Andrew (Flip) Filipowski

Angel investor based in Chicago and the Carolinas and founder of PLATINUM technology, inc, which sold for over $3.6bn. In 1999, he founded divine interVentures, inc, an internet holding company composed of 70 infrastructure e-commerce companies. He has made dozens of angel-type investments and usually takes on the role of "advisor."

Andrew Filipowski, better known as Flip, founded and built PLATINUM technology into one of the top 10 global software companies. He sold the company in 1999 for over $3.6 bn to Computer Associates (at the time, the single largest software transaction in history).

He now devotes his energy and expertise to new internet enterprises via divine interVentures, which he founded in 1999. divine is an internet holding company actively engaged in infrastructure e-commerce through a community of associated companies. Flip describes divine as

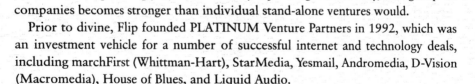

Andrew Filipowski

"a company that partners with entrepreneurs and brick-and-mortar businesses to build the hybrid market leaders for the new digital economy." divine's strategy is based on an internet Zaibatsu™ model, where all the start-up companies backed by divine can form mutual strategic relationships with each other. Flip strongly believes that by operating in this way, the group of companies becomes stronger than individual stand-alone ventures would.

Prior to divine, Flip founded PLATINUM Venture Partners in 1992, which was an investment vehicle for a number of successful internet and technology deals, including marchFirst (Whittman-Hart), StarMedia, Yesmail, Andromedia, D-Vision (Macromedia), House of Blues, and Liquid Audio.

In total he has made dozens of angel investments during the 1990s, with BlueRhino standing out as a major win. He believes there is still a lot of art involved in investing in start-up companies. He focuses on the management team, seeing the entrepreneur behind the deal as the key to a successful deal: *"Find a good CEO and build a company around them."*

Tel: (001) 630.799.7500, Fax: (001) 630.799.7501.

Further information:www.divine.com

divine interVentures, inc, 4225 Naperville Rd, Lisle, Illinois 60532.

Bert Twaalfhoven

Bert Twaalfhoven has invested in 23 angel deals, with an average investment size of $200,000. He has been involved in a total of 50 start-ups, and takes on varying roles within the companies he backs, which range from reserve force to controlling to coaching. He is often the primary entrepreneur as well. "I used to be hands-on with my investments, now I tend to support the entrepreneur from afar or have a manager who keeps on top of them," he says.

Dr. Twaalfhoven's entrepreneurial, angel, and venture capital activities have taken him from Holland to Texas to China and include such diverse industries as airplane manufacturing parts, laundromats, and venture capital. He is the founder of Indivers, which is the majority shareholder of the Interturbine Group of companies as well as Reynolds Aluminium, among others.

He is personally interested in promoting entrepreneurship in Europe and especially Eastern Europe where he feels substantial work is

Bert Twaalfhoven

needed. He is the founder of the European Foundation for Entrepreneurship Research (EFER) as well as a founding member of Europe's 500 and an initiator of EASDAQ.

His activities with start-ups are twofold. He has invested as an individual angel in 23 deals, and has started another 27 companies independently or with members of his extended family (there are seven Twaalfhoven children, most of whom are involved in one of the businesses).

Dr. Twaalfhoven earned his BSc at Fordham University (1952) and his MBA from Harvard Business School (1954). In 1993, Dr. Twaalfhoven received an honorary doctorate from Fordham University for his achievements in the area of education and as an international entrepreneur.

Randy Komisar

Randy Komisar takes on the mentoring role of "Virtual CEO," and invests time or "sweat equity" into seed-stage deals, with follow-on financing where needed. He has backed over a dozen deals, including WebTV which was acquired by Microsoft for $425m less than three years after it was founded, and TiVo which went to IPO within two years of being founded, and currently has a market capitalization of approximaely $1.8bn.

Each year he works with one or two new start-ups as the Virtual CEO and, in addition, takes on a less intensive advisory role with three to four companies. He receives pitches from as many as 10 entrepreneurs a week. He has a *"symbiotic relationship with the VCs that helps in the screening and filtering process. When I have a deal that I think is ready for financing, I will vet it against a set of VCs and use them as my screen. They often call me to review deals for them or to mentor early-stage teams. So, it is symbiotic, I'm a source and a screen to them, and they*

Randy Komisar

are a source and screen to me."

He explained to us how he has turned the traditional angel investing model around, and generally invests his experience as a Virtual CEO: *"I don't invest for the privilege of helping the company, the company pays me for my help. So, I generally get a carry."* His investing strategy is quite different from many angels, and essentially he invests management experience:

❝ I tend to invest my capital with the professionals and I tend to work my deals up through the VCs as part of my screening process... I've invested my time in companies at a stage where if I was investing cash it would be extremely risky, but investing time and spreading the risk the way I do it actually works out quite well, affording me the opportunity to get involved with ideas and people that may not be suitable for funding quite yet. ❞

Putting a price on his involvement in seed-stage deals varies, depending on the role he plays. For example, he says:

❝ I'll take five points of a seed-stage business for a year's worth of my time, at an average of a day a week. I can't get that sort of leverage in a business where the risk is already taken out. So I go in and invest my time to remove the risk that I know how to remove. Then I pass it on to the operating guys to take out the next level of risk. ❞

WebTV was the first deal that he invested in as a Virtual CEO. Originally he was asked to be the CEO, which he declined, but agreed to help the founders as a team mate, *"which involved my being an advisor, later a board member, and then I actually started coming in and spending a day or so a week with the team."* He helped to hire the team, structure and strategize the deals with critical partners (e.g. Sony and Philips), make appearances where it helped add credibility, and assisted in closing the VC round:

❝ I would be a sounding board for Steve, the founding CEO, as he wrestled with issues of building the company that were completely new to him. My role moved from being an advisor, to being director, to bridging the company at a point when it was between angel and VC financing, to coming on board and actually rolling up my sleeves and helping to restructure the company just prior to purchase by Microsoft...

I don't think about the way I invest my time or money in the way that an angel or a professional investor would, I think about it much more like an entrepreneur... I don't sit around contemplating IRRs and I really am not that concerned about whether a venture is addressing a big or small market. I decide what and who excites me and figure out if I can actually help them and have impact. My sourcing and screening is different from most. I decided upfront that I wouldn't take cash because that enables me to apply my screen rather than using their screen in evaluating what deals I'm going to do. I don't have to look for those companies that can afford to pay me, or those companies that value their cash more or less than others. I can work instead as a junior founder with these early teams, with the principal goal of determining whether there is a business model behind the idea and mentoring the team to get to what I call a Phase II company (i.e. starting to build the organization and underlying foundation for a revenue stream) and help structure the company and the strategy and business model to prepare for becoming a true operating company. ❞

Komisar is a graduate of Harvard Law School. He was Senior Counsel at Apple and later went on be a co-founder of Claris Corporation. He served as CFO and Vice President of "Go" Corporation and, following its sale to AT&T, went on to become CEO and President of LucusArts and Entertainment and later the CEO of video-game company, Crystal Dynamics.

He is the author of *The Monk and the Riddle, The Education of a Silicon Valley Entrepreneur*, published by Harvard Business School Press, and *Goodbye Career, Hello Success*, published in the March/April 2000 edition of *HBR*.

Esther Dyson

Esther Dyson has made over 40 investments in early-stage technology companies in the US, UK, Sweden, and emerging markets, such as Eastern Europe. She takes on a "reserve force" role, with varying levels of activity. She is chairman of EDventure Holdings, which actively invests in US and European start-ups, and she is the Editor-in-chief of Release 1.0.

Esther Dyson

Esther Dyson, 48, is a prolific angel investor, based in New York, who concentrates her activities on three intersecting focuses: emerging technologies (groupware, artificial intelligence, the internet, wireless applications); emerging markets (Eastern Europe); and emerging companies.

Her expertise in these areas give her a *"competitive advantage."* In 1994 she was one of the first to explore the impact of the net on intellectual property. In 1997 she wrote a book on the impact of the net on individual lives, *Release 2.0: A design for living in the digital age*. She is the Chairman of EDventure Holdings which publishes the influential monthly computer industry newsletter, *Release 1.0*, and sponsors two industry conferences: PC Forum in the US and EDventure's High-Tech Forum in Europe.

After graduating from Harvard with a BA in Economics, she worked for *Forbes* as a reporter and, in 1977, joined New Court Securities where she researched and followed start-ups, such as Federal Express. After a stint at Oppenheimer covering software companies, she moved to Rosen Research and in 1983 bought the company from her employer, Ben Rosen, and renamed it EDventure Holdings. *"I was writing a newsletter for the industry, so I knew all these companies and finally decided there were some opportunities that were too good to pass up."*

Esther says: *"I have devoted my life to discovering the inevitable and promoting the possible."* She focuses as an angel investor and a commentator on emerging technologies. When screening these types of deals, she goes by the same criteria that apply to all business types, and emphasizes that some investors have lost sight of these basic principles: *"Good people; reasonable idea; honesty."* She goes on to say: *"Are these people that you want to work with when things go wrong? What are they creating that is of value and unique? Fundamentally, those are the questions."*

She supports the entrepreneur in whatever capacity is needed, with contributions varying from helping with hiring to editing product brochures, on occasions. Typically she will help to raise follow-on financing and with strategic issues.

The number of deals she is involved with at any one time varies enormously: *"Sort of like the weather, you have eruptions here and there."* She may have four deals where she is very active, and 10 or so where she is involved peripherally.

One of her recent successes is an investment in Orchestream. She put in $260,000 and was very involved at times. At one point she went on a ski trip to Aspen with a small group, including Charles Muirhead, one of the founders. There they could spend time together focusing on the company (*"obviously it wasn't all business"*) and it served as a wonderful opportunity to dig deep into the issues of the business. The company eventually went public with a valuation of $300–400m, generating a *"10-bagger return on investment"* in less than two years.

Email: edyson@edventure.com

David Amis

David Amis, who has made 15 angel investments, previously served as the Managing Director of Venture Capital Report Ltd, which has matched over 300 entrepreneurs with angels. As a reserve force or silent angel, he invests individually and through StartUpFund I, where he serves as the Managing Partner. As an entrepreneur, he has also raised over $10m from more than 100 individual investors.

David Amis, 34, is the founder of Capitalyst which provides co-investment opportunities to angels and capital-raising support to entrepreneurs. He launched the first StartUpFund in order to provide an institutional platform for non-angels wanting to participate in the early-stage capital arena. Through StartUpFund I and individually, his early-stage activities cover a wide variety of industries, *"We invest in great entrepreneurs, with fundamentally sound business models that will make money,"* he says. *"We also create and support Capitalyst Angel Groups which provide deal flow and angel training to their members."*

David Amis

With Howard Stevenson, he is a co-author of *Winning Angels*. David enjoys speaking to audiences of both entrepreneurs and angel investors and has done so throughout the US and Europe.

In 1996 he joined Venture Capital Report (VCR), based in the UK, as the Managing Director. VCR produces a monthly publication which features detailed articles about entrepreneurs seeking start-up capital and offers a forum for entrepreneurs to give investment presentations to active angels. It processed 2,000 entrepreneurs annually to identify 200 for introduction to a closed-distribution base of 800 angel investors. During his tenure, VCR increased its subscriber sales by 100% and completed 25 early-stage transactions.

David focused on entrepreneurship and entrepreneurial finance at both the University of Southern California (1989) and Harvard Business School (1994) where he won several business plan awards and earned honors grades in his entrepreneurial-related classes. He led an award-winning field study team at HBS on seed capital networks funded by the Kaufman Foundation and supervised by Jeff Timmons.

Additional information on David's activities can be found at www.WinningAngels.com.

Howard Stevenson

Howard Stevenson, who has made over 80 angel investments, headed the Entrepreneur Management Unit at Harvard Business School for 18 years. He is generally a reserve force or silent angel but has participated in virtually every role, including that of founder, member of the management team, and board member. Howard has authored numerous books, articles, and cases and is a leading thinker in the areas of entrepreneurship and angel investing.

Howard Stevenson

Some of the companies which Howard has backed include: PlanetAll, ZipDirect, Medivation, Advanced Cell Technology, and Road Rescue. A typical investment ranges from $25k to $200k and he prefers to stick to pre-money valuations that are below $5m. Howard says that *"sourcing is evaluation"* and he has found that his ex-students provide a good source of interesting opportunities.

Howard developed the Entrepreneurial Management course at Harvard Business School. He is Sarofim-Rock Professor of Business Administration – The Sarofim-Rock Chair was established in 1982 to provide a continuing base for research and teaching in the field of entrepreneurship. He has authored, edited or co-authored six books and 43 articles. He has also authored, co-authored or supervised 150 cases at Harvard Business School. His latest popular book is *Do Lunch or Be Lunch: The Power of Predictability in Creating Your Future*, published by HBS Press.

He was a founder and first President of the Baupost Group, Inc, which manages partnerships investing in liquid securities for wealthy families. When he resigned from active management, Baupost assets had grown to over $400m. He is now Chairman of the Baupost Fund, a registered investment company. From 1978 to 1982, Professor Stevenson was Vice President of Finance and Administration and a Director of Preco Corporation, a large privately held manufacturing company. In addition, from 1970 to 1971 he served as Vice President of Simmons Associates, a small investment banking firm specializing in venture financing. He is currently a director of Bessemer Securities Corporation, Camp Dresser & McKee, Landmark Communications, Sheffield Steel, Market Insight, and The Baupost Group, Inc, as well as a trustee for several private trusts and foundations.

Howard received his BS in Mathematics, with distinction, from Stanford and his MBA, with high distinction, and DBA degrees from Harvard University.

Additional information on Howard's activities can be found at www.WinningAngels.com.

Contact details

Please try our site www.WinningAngels.com if you are interested in additional learning opportunities or information on specific issues:

- Winning Angels workshops.
- Winning Angels newsletter.
- Future books.

Capitalyst LLC

Please contact Capitalyst through its site: www.capitalyst.com if you are interested in investing in a diversified start-up fund.

BIBLIOGRAPHY

Berkus, Dave and Bob Kelley. *Better Than Money!* Santa Barbara, CA: Synergy Communications Press, 1994.

Bhidé, Amar. *The Origin and Evolution of New Businesses*. Oxford University Press, 2000.

Gladstone, David. *Venture Capital Investing*. Englewood Cliffs, NJ: Prentice-Hall, 1988.

Kawasaki, Guy. *Selling the Dream: How to Promote Your Product, Company or Ideas – And Make a Difference – Using Everyday Evangelism*. HarperBusiness, 1992.

Landrum, Gene N. *Profiles of Genius: Thirteen Creative Men Who Changed the World*. Buffalo, NY: Prometheus Books, 1993.

Lax, D.A. and Sebenius, J.K. *The Manager as Negotiator*. New York: The Free Press, 1986.

Porter, Michael E. *Competitive Strategy: Techniques for Analyzing Industries and Competitors*. New York: The Free Press, 1998.

Sahlman, William A., Howard H. Stevenson, Michael J. Roberts and Amar Bhidé. *The Entrepreneurial Venture*. Boston, MA: Harvard Business School Press, 1983.

Sahlman, William A. "How to Write a Great Business Plan." *Harvard Business Review*, July 1997.

Stevenson, Howard H. and Michael J. Roberts. "The Start-Up Process." Harvard Business School Case, December 1983.

Stevenson, Howard H., Roberts, Michael J. and Grousbeck, H. Irving. *New Business Ventures and the Entrepreneur* (4th edn). Richard D. Irwin, Inc, New York: 1974.

Van Osnabrugge, Mark and Robinson, Robert J. *Angel Investing: Matching Start-Up Funds With Start-Up Companies*. San Francisco: Jossey-Bass, 2000.

Accredited investor   An accredited investor is one identified by the Securities and Exchange Commission as able to make investment decisions concerning certain private placement offerings, which are the preference of entrepreneurs. An accredited investor is defined as having an annual income of $200k or greater for three years or a net worth of $1m or more.

Angel investor   An investor who provides capital and support (through advice, contacts, or hands-on work) to an early-stage company. Angels are commonly ex-entrepreneurs or business managers themselves. The use of the word "angel" dates back to patron angels who were major benefactors to the theater and arts more broadly. The term was brought to prominence in the USA by William Wetzel, when he described angels in his *Sloan Management Review* article of 1983 as: "A diverse, dispersed population of individuals of means; many of whom have created their own successful ventures and will invest their experience as well as their capital in ventures they support."

AIM   Alternative Investment Market. A stock market regulated by the London Stock Exchange.

BATNA   Acronym for best alternative to a negotiated agreement.

Bio-tech   Biotechnology is the manipulation of micro-organic plant and animal cells to produce materials/products which can be used in daily life.

Break-even   When the cash revenues and the operating costs of a company are equal. In other words, the point at which a company begins to cover its costs through sales and does not need outside capital to survive.

Bridge financing   A short-term loan intended to provide or extend financing until a more permanent arrangement is made.

Burn rate   The rate at which a company is losing cash, typically expressed as a monthly rate.

Business angel   The British term for an angel investor.

Business model   The combination of factors that describe the business, including the market the business will serve, the perceived value delivered to the customer which determines profitability per unit of sale, and the sustaining factors which will allow the company to thrive over the long term.

Business plan   A document that lays out the key components of the business, which is used internally and as a capital-raising tool. It should include: executive summary, product or service description, market and competition overview, production/operations, management team, financial data/projections, financial structure.

Capital gains   The difference between the price paid for shares and the price at which they are sold.

Capital matchmaker   An organization (profit or non-profit) which matches entrepreneurs and angels to do early-stage deals. They usually charge both parties a fee and then publish a summary of the entrepreneur's plans to the angel investors.

Cash flow   The flow of cash in and out of a company. A company with negative cash flow can still be a profitable company. Start-up and entrepreneurial companies need to pay particular attention to cash flow management.

Coach angel   An angel investor who meets with the entrepreneur regularly and provides support, advice, and any assistance as needed and requested by the entrepreneur. Considerable experience in angel investing is a must. However, even a new angel could have impact if they remember to act as a coach. Remember that coaches stay on the sidelines.

Controlling angel   An angel investor who takes on a direct management role in an investee company, and who really becomes the entrepreneur by taking control (outright or through conventions) and manages the company.

Convertible note   A financial debt instrument that can be converted into another financial instrument, such as common or preferred stock.

Co-opetition   Describes the thinking of many angel investors on competing for deals; they are as likely to cooperate as compete and it is often possible to do this by investing together and sharing the risks.

Current assets   Assets of a company, such as cash, inventory, and accounts receivable, which can be converted into cash in less than one year.

Deal flow   Refers to the quantity and quality of investment opportunities available to an investor.

Deal terms   The legal terms upon which the investment is made (e.g. common shares with pre-emptive right).

Debt/loan capital   Capital that is invested in a business in exchange for the legal requirement to pay a certain sum as interest each year on the loan capital provided, and possibly also to repay some of the capital according to an agreed schedule. Debt will usually be secured against assets.

Development capital   Also known as "growth capital," development capital provides a company with resources to expand and grow, as opposed to the seed capital which may be used to build a prototype, for example.

Dilution   A decrease in the equity position of a shareholder when additional shares are issued.

Diversification   An investment strategy which includes making many investments in order to narrow the variability of returns. Investors in the stock market will typically invest in 20 or more companies and industries so that any one company failure or industry downturn will be mitigated by their other investments. In early-stage investing, the variability of returns is extreme since the likelihood of failure in each investment is high.

Due diligence Investigation and research carried out in order to evaluate an investment proposition and determine whether to commit funds. This process includes reviewing: management team, market, competition, track record, finances, etc.

Early stage Refers to a young company which may or may not have a management team, a product, sales, or money in the bank, but is endeavoring to garner these things. A company is past early stage when it no longer needs equity capital to maximize its growth.

Empire builder An entrepreneur who grows and controls several businesses all through one primary organization. These entrepreneurs may be paranoid about giving up control, although most entrepreneurs are paranoid (Dave included).

Entrepreneur A term often used to describe an owner/founder of an unquoted business. It often relates to an enterprising person setting up or growing a new company which requires capital.

Equity Ownership stake in a company. Equity or share capital is the risk capital provided to finance a business.

Exit The way investors get their money out of a deal (e.g. selling shares to the public market after an IPO).

Follow-on investor An angel investor who follows an other investor into a deal.

Harvard framework The Harvard framework provides a way of evaluating an investment opportunity. Rather than judging entrepreneurs or their business plans as winners or losers, it is most productive to look at the investment opportunity, and deal. The right combination, which is often manageable, means a high-potential opportunity. A bad combination, or the lack of any single element, is a recipe for failure.

Harvesting The process or act of extracting one's capital gains from an investment (e.g. supporting a strategic sale which results in the sale of all company shares, including those of the investor). In most cases, the investor cannot effect a harvest but rather, is dependent on the entrepreneurial management team to do so.

Informal venture capital market Essential the total capital invested by angels. This market is considered to be informal because there is no overall organization to its placement. It is estimated that $20bn–30bn is invested annually in the US.

Internal public offering (IPO) A company's first offer to sell stock to the public.

Intellectual property Intangible assets, such as knowledge, brand names or patents, etc.

Internal rate of return (IRR) Equivalent to the compound rate of return of an investment.

Lead investor An investor who is either the first investor in, the largest investor, or the most visible and active investor in an early-stage deal. The lead investor often influences the investment decisions of many other investors, sometimes unintentionally.

Lifestyle entrepreneur An entrepreneur who creates a lifestyle for him or herself through entrepreneurship. For example, an entrepreneur who starts a boat company because he wants to make boats not because he wants to generate wealth.

Liquidation Terminating a business operation, involving the sale of a company's assets, for distribution to creditors and shareholders in order to priority.

Liquidity event Another term to describe an exit or harvest event.

Listing When a company trades its stock on a stock market.

Living dead A company that is just able to keep going, and is unlikely to generate investor returns.

Loan capital A form of debt which has to be repaid at a specified time in the future.

Management buy-out (MBO) When existing management of a company raises capital to buy the business from the owners.

Matchmaker services Organizations that serve as a link between entrepreneurs seeking capital and investors seeking investment opportunities.

NASDAQ Acronym for National Association of Securities Dealers Automated Quotations system. A computerized system to facilitate trading by providing broker/dealers with current bid and ask price quotes on over-the-counter stocks and some listed stocks.

Negative harvests Harvest events where the loss of capital or gains is finalized but a saving of time or liability may be the positive result.

Net present value The current value of future cash flows discounted back to today's date using a stated discount rate.

Networking In angel investing, networking is the process of meeting people in order to create deal flow, identify co-investors, or meet more people.

Options/stock options Financial instrument which gives the holder the right to buy an underlying instrument (e.g. common stock) at an agreed amount.

POA Plan of action.

Post-money valuation The valuation or total price of an early-stage company after the investors have placed their capital in the business. See also **pre-money valuation**.

Preferred stock Shares with preferential rights over common stock. For example, the preference shares may have rights in the form of divided rights, board rights, or information rights.

Pre-money valuation The valuation or total price of an early-stage company before the investment occurs. A "$3m pre-money valuation" values the company at $3m before the investors put their capital in. If investors then placed $500k into the company, the post-money valuation would be $3.5m. This is important because the percentage of the company provided to the investors is based on the post-money valuation. In the above example, $500k/$3.5m=14%. So the investors own 14% of the company after they invest.

Price   In early-stage deals, refers to the price of the shares that an investor pays when she invests.

Redeemable preference shares   British angels can invest using redeemable preference shares. In this situation an angel may split an investment of $100,000 as follows: $100 as common stock for 6% of the company and $99,900 as redeemable preference shares. If the investee company does well and achieves cumulative profits, then it is legally entitled to repay the redeemable preference shares, and the investor maintains his equity stake of 6%. If the company fails, then just as with common stock, the investor is likely to lose the capital invested.

Return on investment (ROI)   Normally refers to the annual return on capital, i.e. if your savings account pays 4.1% interest, that is the ROI. If $100 were invested and earned 50% over two years, it would then be worth $225. Total ROI is the total percentage increase over the life of the investment.

Rescue capital   Capital which will be used to help a company turn around and get out of a troubled situation, and set it back on course to profitability.

Reserve force   Contribute as required, e.g. make an introduction, refer additional investors, work for one day on a key company issues, spend an hour on the phone giving advice in a particular area of expertise.

ROI   see **Return on investment**

Seed capital   Capital which will finance a company at the conceptual stage.

Seed stage   A company very early in its development, typically with one or more of the following: an inventor/entrepreneur, a business concept, or a patent.

Serial investor   An angel investor who makes many early-stage investments.

Silent investor   An angel investor who takes no active involvement in the company.

Spin-out   Emergence of a company in its own right from a large business.

Start-up   An early-stage company, typically with two or more of the following: a management team, equity capital, a prototype, or a sale.

Sweat equity   Equity which is earned in recognition of time, energy and commitment to those involved in the seed and start-ups stages of a company.

Syndicate   A group of co-investors in a deal.

Team member angel   Takes on a full-time role, perhaps VP of sales, special projects, or board member working on the IPO.

Trade sales   Sale of a company to another company, as a form of exit.

Underwrite   An institution will underwrite the risk of a company not receiving committed funds. This agreement will cover any shortfall if investors change their minds.

Valuation   The total determined value of a company, usually resulting from the price paid by new investors. The total valuation is essentially the price one would pay to buy the whole company, if that were their interest.

Value-added investor   An investor who brings strategic or other benefits aside from the capital provided.

Value event   An event in the life of a company which drastically increases its perceived or real value. Examples include: closing the first sale, achieving cash flow break-even, or recruiting a management team.

Value proposition   The fundamental proposition for customers of the early-stage company; what they will get for their money. If customers are willing to pay more for the product than it costs the company to make it, the value proposition is real.

Venture capital   Institutional investors in entrepreneurial companies, usually investing no less than $2m and coming in after the angel investors.

Venture capitalist   A professional who invests capital in high-growth potential companies on behalf of a fund.

Vulture capital   A description of venture capital used by those who believe that venture capitalists take too much and offer too little when they invest.

Working capital   Capital that finances the ordinary activities of a company.

INDEX

ability to win 89
academic/investment banker valuation
    method 146, 148, 152–3
Accel Partners 132, 133, 309, 329,
    338, 339
accountants 49
accredited investors 355
Adams, Warren 156, 198, 315, 316
adding value 118–19, 123
    and negotiation 230
admin assistants 88
administrative costs, CommonAngels
    212
Advanced Cell Technology 352
advertising 61
advice for new angels 24–5
advisors 77
    cost of counsel 212
    finding and using 273
    start-up advisors 118–19, 123, 253
        method of valuation 154–5
Aero Design and Engineering 258
AIM 355
Alberg, Tom 67, 95, 135–6, 173–4,
    327
almost-there entrepreneurs 139
Amazon.com 67, 68, 94, 95, 99,
        135–6, 173–4, 257, 287
    funding steps 200
    and IPOs 295
    and PlanetAll 298, 316
    value events 263
America OnLine (AOL) 76
Amis, David 26, 61, 111, 120, 168,
        205
    and the 2x rule 272
    and Amis Ventures 318
    in-depth profile of 351–2

interview with Bill Sahlman 213
monthly meetings 273
and negotiation 233
and networks 42, 44
reserve force role 249–50
and strategic partnerships 303
see also Winning Angels Study
Amis, Fred 94
Amis, R.T. 294
Amis Ventures 318
angel conferences 4
angel groups 3, 4, 39, 62, 107
    forming small groups 107–8
    of three 125
angel investors 355
anti-dilution 187, 211, 217
AOL (America OnLine) 76
Apple Computer 47, 67, 95, 173, 258
    and IPOs 295
Ascend Venture Group 334, 340
asking questions 116–18, 120
Atkins, Betsy 40, 54, 63–4, 107, 121,
        122–3, 327
    and negotiation 236, 237
    on sourcing 121
    supporting roles 250, 266, 268, 273,
        278
    on valuation 171
ATS Medical Inc 333

B2B 52
bankers, personal meetings with 38
bankruptcy 291
    planning for the ultimate exit 317,
        318
    reorganization bankruptcies
        299–300
    resource bankruptcies 279–80

bargaindog.com 173
Barnes&Noble.com 95, 135
BATNA 355
Baucom, Larry 62
Baupost Group 352
Belton, Tim 90
Ben-Meir, Jake 118
Berkus, David 14, 38, 66, 69–70, 327
    failed harvest story 319–20
    in-depth profile of 336–7
    on resource bankruptcies 279–80
    on structure 209
    supporting roles 268, 269, 277, 278
    valuation method 146, 150, 158,
        160, 170, 172
Berkus Technology Ventures 327, 336
Berndorf AG 332
Berwind Railway Service Company
    297
Bezos, Jeff 67, 135–6
Bhidé, Amar 93, 131–2
bio-tech 355
Blaak, Jaap 53, 247, 250, 328
Blair, Andrew 41, 52, 114, 123, 328
    on harvesting 289
    on losing investments 140
    on mentors 245
    on structure 208
    supporting roles 249, 278
    on valuation 152
Blockbuster 261
board of directors 203
    CommonAngels 211
    Draper Fisher Jurvetson (DFJ) 219
    taking a board seat 268, 269–70
    and VCs 306
board rights 186
Body Shop 174, 261
brand names 304
break-even 355
bridge financing 355
Brightstone Capital Ltd 330
Brown, Alex 76
Bryant, Tarby 172, 328
Buffet, Warren 260
burn rate 355
Burr, Craig 53, 82, 103, 110, 328

lead investor role 251
on negotiation 229
on valuation 167, 173
Burr Egan Deleage & Corporation 328
business angels 355
Business Angels International 328
business experience see experience
business models 91, 92–3, 355
Business Objects 59, 346
business opportunity 75, 77, 79, 91–9
    company growth 98–9
    competitors 103
    context 99–103
    customers 91, 93–4
    deal price and structure 104
    Harvard framework 75, 77–8, 357
    model 91, 92–3
    products and markets 91–2
    scale and scope 98–9
    size of 91, 96–8
    stages of development 125–6
    timing 91, 94–6
    value proposition 94
business plans 253, 355
    reading 115–18, 120
business process patents 103

capital
    low capital requirements 169
    raising 269
        e-businesses 263
        retail businesses 261
        service businesses 259, 260
    significant, and negotiation 229
    starting 21
capital gains 356
Capital Investors 124, 334
capital matchmakers 356
capitalization, DFJ 215
Capitalyst 16–18, 78, 87, 108, 118,
    248, 249–50, 351
    contact details 353
    preferred deal terms 214
    value events 260
career changes, planning the ultimate
    exit 317, 318
Carnegie, Andrew 81, 85, 87

Cary, Lucius 14, 41, 62, 66, 328
  on asking questions 116
  on evaluating entrepreneurs 122, 124
  in-depth profile of 344–5
  on negotiation 230, 237
  size of investment 21
  on structure 205, 207
  supporting roles 268, 269, 271, 272,
    277
  on valuation 150, 169, 171
cash flow 356
  break-even 303
  service businesses 260
cash requirements 166
CCBN (Corporate Communications
    Broadcast Network) 332
CEOs
  finding a good CEO 62
  and harvesting 307
  virtual 253, 348–9
chance encounters 62
Changemyaddress.com 303
Chapter 7 299, 300–2
Chapter 11 299–300
cheerleaders 273
Chen, Jack 71, 134
chief financial officers 88
Churchill, Winston 81
Cisco Systems 262
Civilization 12
co-investment 50, 54, 63–4, 123–4
  following the leader 64
  and negotiation 234
  see also angel groups
co-opetition 356
co-sale agreements
  CommonAngels 212
  DFJ 220
coach angels 13, 119, 183, 250, 251,
    265, 268, 356
Coca-Cola 96
commitment, from the management
    team 88–9
CommonAngels 210–13, 331, 332
compensation limits 187, 204, 216
competition 103
  non-competition agreements 185, 212

competitive risk 105
Computerized Lodging Systems Inc.
    337
conditions to investment,
    CommonAngels 213
consent rights 187–8, 202–3
constructive criticism 113
Contact Software International 133
controlling angels 13, 181, 183, 250,
    251, 265, 268, 356
controlling managers 119
conversion rights 186, 217
convertible notes 186, 193–6, 196,
    214, 356
corporate action, efficient 202–3
Costner, Kevin 303
costs, CommonAngels standard term
    sheet 212
Curly H Ventures Ltd 329, 345
current assets 356
The Custom Shop 90
customers, and business opportunity
    91, 93–4

deal flow 356
  generating 35–6
  initiating 69–70
  quantity and quality 56–8
  rates of 66–7
  screened 41
  unique source 63
  and venture capitalists 65
deal price 104, 163–4
deal sifter 34
deal size 21
deal structure 78, 104, 179–222
  allied interests in 309–10
  characteristics of sensible deals 182
  common shares 185, 190–1, 196,
    211, 214, 216
  convertible notes 186, 193–6, 196,
    214, 356
  and financial returns 163
  and future round finance 198–201
  ideas on failure 197
  importance of 181, 183
  and negotiation 236

preferred shares 186, 191–3, 196, 210–13, 214, 216–17, 219–20
   term sheets 181, 210–21
protection agreements 189
reporting built into 207
seen as irrelevant 183–4
and VCs 181, 191, 192, 202–4, 306
winning tools and tactics 207
see also dilution
deal terms 356
death, planning for the ultimate exit 317, 318
debt/loan capital 356
Dell Computer 96, 257, 261
Demon Internet 63, 333
development capital 356
dilution 165, 356
   anti-dilution 187, 211, 217
discounted cash flow method of valuation 146, 152–3, 158, 160
diversification 356–7
dividend rights 186
   CommonAngels 210
   DFJ 216
divine interVentures 328
Doerr, John 213
Dollinger, Steve 297
Doriot, General George 80, 121, 183
DoubleClick.com 281, 282
Draper Fisher Jurvetson (DFJ) 198, 215–21
Draper, Tim 215, 306
   on future rounds 198
   on support 247, 267
   on term sheets 214
   on valuation 155
Drumlin Ventures 331
due diligence 357
Dyson, Esther 229, 328
   in-depth profile of 350

e-businesses 257, 262–3
early stage deals 56–60, 61, 266, 357
   four levers of early-stage returns 163–5
eBay 262
economic conditions 100, 101

EDventure Holdings 328, 350
Elecontronic Warfare Associates 329
electronic book publishers 99
empire builders 137, 204, 357
entrepreneurs 77, 80–6, 357
   advisors to 124
   almost-there entrepreneurs 139
   assessing 81–6, 120–4
   capabilities/track records 81, 82, 83, 84
   choice of ventures 131–2
   compensation limits 187
   conflicts with 206
   egos 121
   empire builders 137, 205, 357
   ethics 122
   experiential assets 264
   failing right 280–1
   five-star 58–9
   focusing on 206
   goals of 81, 82, 83
   and greed 176, 236
   and harvesting 311, 312
   high-potential entrepreneurs 138–9
   John Hime's letter to 109, 130
   knowledge of opportunities 81, 82, 83
   lifestyle entrepreneurs 137–8, 205–6, 358
   meeting 120
   and negotiation 232–8
   options on the entrepreneur 166
   personality characteristics 84, 86
   red flags 125
   rejecting 110–13
   responding to 109
   screening entrepreneurs 130
   serial 137, 205
   and structure 183
   studying or teaching entrepreneurship 4, 35, 46
   and support 271
   types of 137–9, 205
   wanna-be entrepreneurs 139
   winning investors 120–4
Epinions 134
equity 357

Equity Growth Management 329
Espuleas, Fernando 134
Estée Lauder 90
Etienne, Larry 85
etoys.com 295
European Technology Ventures 332
EV (expected value) 18–21, 166
evaluation 26, 73–141
    adding value to a deal 118–19
    expanded framework 79–104
    Harvard framework 75, 77–8
    and harvesting 310
    IT/Internet start-ups 128
    macro-situation (context) 78
    medical start-ups 127
    people 77, 80–90
    questions to ask 116–18, 120
    reading business plans 115–18
    rejection 110–13
    risk 105–6
    sharing the evaluation process
        107–8
    and sourcing 33, 34, 35, 76,
        120–1
    time management 114–15, 124
    winning tools and tactics 125–6
    see also business opportunity; deal
        structure; entrepreneurs
exit 122, 357
    low exit costs 131
    structure and exit impact 189, 190,
        192
    see also harvesting
expanded framework 79–104
expected value (EV) 18–21, 166
expenses see costs
experience 7, 14
experiential assets 264
exposure capabilities see financial
        inventory
Express Custom Tailors 90

failure
    failed harvest story 319–20
    failed investments 109
    how to fail 280–1
    preparing for failure in a deal 197

FairAir.com 94, 263, 341
family events, planning for the ultimate
        exit 317, 318
family support 6, 11–12, 14
fees see costs
Filipowski, Andrew 62, 172, 272, 328
    in-depth profile of 347
financial inventory 9–11, 13–14
    nest egg chart 9–10
    size of initial investment 21
financial officers 88
financial sales 290, 291, 296–7, 323
financial troubles, planning the
        ultimate exit 317, 318
financial value events 255
financing risk 105
first offer rights, DFJ 219
first refusal rights 188
    CommonAngels 212
focus activities 35, 36, 51–5
    acting in a syndicate 54
    industry focus 52, 53
    network focus 51, 53
    target preferences 55
follow-on finance 188, 212
    CommonAngels 212
follow-on investors 357
founder stock 204
friends, discussions with 120
future price conversion 187
future round finance 198–201

Garage.com 108
Gates, Bill 84
The Gathering of Angels 328
Gladstone, David 37, 116–17
Glazer, Harry 101
GoCorporation 132, 140, 339
Goulder, Morton 89, 251
greed 176
    and negotiation 236
Green, Josh 88, 116, 121, 134, 329
Gross, Bill 128, 133
groups see angel groups
Growth Plus 333
Guererri, Carl 20, 38, 66, 152, 207,
        329

and negotiation 228, 235
  supporting roles 268, 269, 272

Harvard framework 75, 77–8, 357
harvesting 285–323
  bankruptcy 291
  factors contributing to successful
      302
  failed harvest story 319–20
  financial sales 290, 291, 296–7, 323
  initial public offerings (IPOs) 290,
      294–6, 303, 306, 323, 357
  and minority shareholders 307
  negative harvests 287, 299–302,
      323, 358
  opposing forms of 288
  partial sales 290, 291, 293–4
  planning for the ultimate exit
      317–18
  positive harvests 287, 289–98
  strategic sales 287, 291, 297–8, 303,
      323
  successful harvest story
      (LifeMinders) 320–1
  taking the company public 312
  value events 303–5
  and VCs 296, 303, 304, 306–8, 309,
      310, 323
  walking harvest 289–92
  winning tools and tactics 311–12
Heinrich von Liechtenstein, Prince
      118, 121, 206, 333
Hewlett-Packard 304
high-potential entrepreneurs 138–9
Hime, John 14, 24, 37, 49, 67, 124, 329
  on convertible notes 193
  dealing with rejection 110
  entrepreneur letter 109, 130
  evaluation process 124
  on harvesting 314
  in-depth profile of 345–6
  investment criteria summary 70
  and negotiation 226–7, 228, 236, 238
  supporting roles 269, 278
  on valuation 171
Horey, Brian 329
  on harvesting 313

  losing investments 140
  on negotiation 239
  on sourcing 121
  on structure 209
  on supporting roles 276, 278
  on valuation 151

IBM 96
idealab! 128, 133
implementation practices 253
Individers BV 333
industry stage 102
informal venture capital market 357
information rights 186
  CommonAngels 211
initial public offerings (IPOs) 290, 291,
      294–6, 303, 323, 357
Intel 101, 116, 258, 321–2
intellectual property 357
Inter Turbine Logistics 68–9
Interelate 157–62
  funding steps 198
  value events 256, 260
interest payments 198
interest-driven bargaining 241
internal rate of return (IRR) 357
Internet 52
  building your own website 109
  and business opportunity 99, 101
  e-businesses 257, 262–3
  and profitability 303
  start-ups 128
  $2m–$10m internet standard 146,
      151, 159
InterVentures 347
Intranets.com 128
intuition 122
IPA Services 332
IPOs (initial public offerings) 290, 291,
      294–6, 303, 306, 323, 357
IRR (internal rate of return) 357

Jackson, Samuel 231
Jobs, Steve 85

Kapor, Mitch 24, 50, 84, 116, 132–3,
      329

on entrepreneurs 122
on harvesting 309
in-depth profile of 338–9
losing investments 140
and negotiation 227, 229, 240
on valuation 167, 171, 173
Kaufman Foundation 306, 336
Kawasaki, Guy 41, 47
Kelly, Peter 137
Kempka, Uday 316
Kennedy, John F. 300
Kline, George 66, 123, 172, 205, 273, 330
on negotiation 226, 235, 237
knowing other angels 8
see also angel groups
Kok, Frans 68, 76, 296, 330
on harvesting 311
on LifeMinders 320–1
and negotiation 230, 238
Komisar, Randy 24, 44, 105, 264, 330
in-depth profile of 348–50
three stages 125–6
on valuation 154, 171
on VC relationships 273, 310
Kozmo.com 68
Kramlich, Richard 67–8, 173, 247, 330

Ladder of Time 114
Landrum, Gene N., *Profiles of Genius* 85, 86
lawyers 38, 49
and negotiation 237
lead investors 251–2, 358
monthly meetings 273–4
Lear, William 85
learning curve 3–4
legal documents 253
see also deal structure
legal fees and expenses 220
Lerner, John 315
Levy, Frank 19, 94, 229, 315, 330
in-depth profile of 341–2
LifeMinders.com 68, 320–1, 330
lifestyle entrepreneurs 137–8, 205–6, 358

liquidation 358
preference 211, 216
liquidation rights 186
liquidity event 358
listing 358
living dead 301–2, 358
loan capital 358
losing investments 140–1
Lotus 83, 338
Lovet-Turner, Nigel 330
Low, Rob 51, 62, 125
Lu, Amos 62

McCallion, John 121, 169, 206, 331
and negotiation 236
McGeady, Steve 101, 275, 277, 321–2, 331
McGlinn, Ian 174
MacLean, Audrey 41, 43, 46, 49, 62, 77, 123, 331
on business opportunity 95
on harvesting 313
in-depth profile of 335–6
and negotiation 229
on sourcing 121
on structure 208
on supporting roles 276
on valuation 151, 171
on VC relationships 273
Madrona Investment Group 135, 327
management by-out (MBO) 358
management teams 80, 87–9
retail businesses 261
service businesses 260
managers, and product businesses 258
market risk 105
marketing 253
value events in 254, 259
matchmakers 41, 108, 358
MBAs, hiring to do initial screening 108
MBO (management by-out) 358
medical start-ups 127, 343
Medivation 352
meetings 273–4
Meier, Sid 12
mentors 64, 245

Merlin Investments 331
Microsoft 83, 174, 322, 348, 349
    Word 99, 103
minority shareholders, impact on
        harvesting 308
Missouri Valley Machinery Company
        294
monthly meetings 273–4
Morley, Richard 14, 16, 24, 39, 48,
        50, 67, 331
    on business opportunity 98
    on harvesting 314
    in-depth profile of 337–8
    on investing in three rounds 283
    and monitoring 268
  · on supporting roles 266, 269, 278
    on valuation 172
Mornell, Pierre 89
Morris & Associates 331, 342
Morris, Anthony 331
Morris, Tony 67, 102
    in-depth profile of 342–3
    IT or Internet start-ups 128
    losing investments 140–1
    on sitting on boards 270
    on structure 183, 189, 191, 209
    on supporting roles 276
    valuation methods 149
    winning deals 133
multiplier method of valuation 146,
        152, 157, 160
must do 129
Myers, Wade 87, 94

NASDAQ 78, 358
Nashua Breakfast Club 251, 283, 331,
        337
National Venture Capital Association
        306
negative covenants, CommonAngels
        212
negative harvests 287, 299–302, 323,
        358
    Chapter 7 299, 300–2
    Chapter 11 299–300
    living dead 301–2, 358
negotiation 26, 223–44
    and alternatives 241–2
    away from the table strategies 242–3
    best case scenario 234
    and evaluation 76
    front men 238
    having "big wings" 229, 231
    interest-driven bargaining 241
    interests, issues and positions 240–1
    issues 232–4
    objectives of 230
    one shot offers 237–8
    and participation roles 253
    positional bargaining 241
    refusing to negotiate 226–7
    second round 237
    winning tools and tactics 237–8
    wish list 232
Net Angels 64, 327
net present value 358
net worth see financial inventory
Netonomy 69
Network Equipment Technologies
        (NET) 335
networking activities 35, 36, 38–42,
        61, 358
    angel groups 3, 4, 39, 62, 107–8,
        125
    deal flow 57, 58
    developing a network 63–4
    educating networks 61
    focus tactics 51
    industry networking 53
    matchmakers 41, 108, 358
    personal meetings 38
    rewarding networks 42
    sharing deals with other angels 40
New Business Ventures and the
        Entrepreneur (Stevenson,
        Roberts and Grousbeck) 46
New Enterprise Associates 330
New York New Media Association 121
Newton, Jim 39, 331
nice to do 129
non-competition agreements 185,
        212
non-solicitation agreements 212
Northwest Airlines 94

one-pagers
  deal structures 207
  monthly 272
  and negotiation 237
  planning for the ultimate exit 317,
    318
  writing 36, 70
operating risk 105
operational practices 253
operational value events 255
opportunists 62
opportunity *see* business opportunity
options 358
O'Regan, Mike 62
organizational value events 255
ought to do 129

Packard, David 95–6
Palm Pilot 254, 257
Park, Joe 68
Parker, Jeff 62, 93, 122, 167, 228, 332
  controlling role 250
  issue weekends 273
  on monthly one-pagers 272
  and negotiation 237
partial sales 290, 291, 293–4
participation roles 11, 12–13, 14,
    249–53, 265
patents, business process 103
Payre, Denis 59, 69, 173, 227, 238,
    332
  in-depth profile of 346–7
Pederson, Dale 318
Pen-based computing 102
people 77, 80–90
  management team 80, 87–9
  stakeholders 79, 89–90
  see also entrepreneurs
people risk 105
Pepsi 96
personal contacts
  referrals 59–60, 61, 63
  see also networking
personal life 6, 11–12, 14
personal net worth *see* financial
    inventory
Pichler, Peter 208, 228, 332

PlanetAll 298, 315–16, 341, 352
planning
  business plans 115–18, 120, 253
  strategic planning 253
PLATINUM Technology 347
POA 358
podium effect 44
Polo Jeans 138
Porter's Five Forces 91
positional bargaining 241
positioning 253
positive harvests 287, 289–98
  financial sales 290, 291, 296–7
  initial public offering (IPO) 290,
    294–6
  partial sales 290, 291, 293–4
  strategic sales 287, 291, 297–8, 303
  walking harvest 289–92
post-money valuation 358
power of attorney 317, 318
pre-emptive rights 185, 190, 196, 206,
    232
pre-money valuation 358–9
pre-VC 266
preferred stock 358
preparation activities 35, 36, 37
presentation materials 253
price 104, 359
price conversion 187
Priceline.com 103
Private Investor's Network (PIN) 62
product businesses 257, 258
product/service risk 105
production value events 255
products, demonstration of new 304
profitability 303
prototypes 258
public relations 62
Pümpin, Cuno 44, 249, 267, 332
purchase agreements
  CommonAngels 212–13
  DFJ 220

questions to ask 116–18, 120

R Morley, Inc 331
reading business plans 115–18, 120

RealNetworks 83, 173, 309, 338
red flags 125
Redbus Investments 63, 333
redeemable preference shares 359
redemption rights 186
   CommonAngels 211
referrals 59–60, 61, 110
Reg Valin 333
registration rights 186, 217–18
   CommonAngels 211–12
regulation 102–3
rejection 110–13
   approaches 111–13
   the good, the bad and the ugly 111–12
reorganization bankruptcies 299–300
reputation, risk of losing 197
rescue capital 359
reserve force angels 12, 118–19, 183,
   249–50, 251, 265, 267, 359
resource bankruptcies 279–80
restrictions and limitations (DFJ) 220
retail businesses 257, 261–2
returns
   in harvesting
     Chapter 7 301
     Chapter 11 300
     financial sales 296
     IPO 295
     partial sales 294
     strategic sales 298
     walking harvest 292
revenue model development 253
Rigby, Martin 61, 236
risk 105–6
   acceptance 8–9, 12, 15
   in harvesting
     Chapter 7 301
     Chapter 11 300
     financial sales 294, 296
     IPO 295
     partial sales 294
     strategic sales 298
     walking harvest 292
   moving or dividing 106
   reducing 106
   visualizing risk and reward 174–5
Road Rescue 68, 352

Robinson, Robert 46, 232, 240
Rock, Arthur 67, 82, 231
ROI (return on investment) 163–4,
   165, 359
   and negotiation 225, 241
   and venture capital investments 309
Rollerblade 102
Ronnick, David 138
royalty rights 186
Russo, Carl 134

Sachnoff & Weaver Ltd 334
Sahlman, William 3, 14, 24, 54, 134,
   179, 332
   business plans 116
   Harvard framework 75, 77
   on lead investors 251
   on the living dead 301
   and PlanetAll 315
   on structure 182, 197, 213
   on valuation 168, 174
sales ability of entrepreneurs 84
sales risk 105
SalesLogix 133
Sanders, Colonel 84
scale production 258
scaling out 311
Schwarz, Ryan 185, 202
screening 108
   hiring your own screener 124
search activities, deal flow 58
Seed Capital 328, 344–5
seed stage deals 266, 359
selective industry targeting 52
Selling the Dream (Kawasaki) 47
serial entrepreneurs 137, 205
serial investors 359
service businesses 257, 259–60
services, demonstration of a new
   service 304
sharing the evaluation process 107–8
Shaw, George Bernard 299
silent investors 12, 118, 183, 249, 267,
   359
small groups of angels, forming 107–8
Smith, Fred 85, 231
Softbank 68

Solomont, David 39, 40, 41, 53, 62, 223, 332
  full-time associate of 124
  on negotiation 229
  on sitting on boards 269
  on structure 210
  on valuation 151, 166
sourcing projects 26, 31–60
  advertising 61
  chance encounters 62
  deal flow quantity/quality 56–8
  deal sifter 34
  focus activities 35
  generating deal flow 35–6
  networking activities 35, 36, 38–42, 61
  preparation activities 35, 36, 37
  referrals 59–60, 61
  takeaways from sourcing 71
  visibility activities 35, 36, 43–50
specialities, developing 108
speed reading 108
spin-out 359
stage of industry 102
stakeholders 79, 89–90
Stanford, Cliff 63, 333
StarMedia Network 35, 68, 83, 89, 134, 173, 239, 272, 340
  funding steps 199
  and harvesting 313
  and IPOs 295
  value events 263
start-up 359
start-up advisors 118–19, 123, 253
  method of valuation 154–5
starting capital 21
StartUpFund I 252, 351
statistical significance theory 15–18, 21
Steve Walker & Associates 334
Stevenson, Dorothy 89
Stevenson, Howard 75, 77, 83, 120–1, 122, 149
  and harvesting 287, 292, 295
  in-depth profile of 352–3
  and networks 44
  silent investor role 249
  and sourcing 61, 68

stock options 358
strategic partners 263, 275, 303
strategic planning 253
strategic sales 287, 291, 297–8, 303, 323
strategic support 263, 271
strategic value events 255
strategies for winning and speed 107–9
strategy creation 5–23
  expected value (EV) 18–21
  fundamentals 21–2
  knowing yourself 5–15
  portfolios of investments 15–18
  sample strategies 22–3
structural incentives, creating 311
structuring see deal structure
successful harvest story (LifeMinders) 320–1
Sun Microsystems 116
supporting roles 245–93
  best fit 265–6
  board membership 268, 269–70
  coaches 13, 119, 183, 250, 251, 265, 268, 356
  contributing to 264–8
  controlling investors 13, 181, 183, 250, 251, 265, 268, 356
  experiential assets 264
  investor update 274
  lead investors 251–2, 358
  mentors 64, 245
  monitoring 268
  participation roles 11, 12–13, 14, 249–53, 265
  reserve force 12, 118–19, 183, 249–50, 251, 265, 267, 359
  resource bankruptcies 279–80
  silent investors 12, 118, 183, 249, 267, 359
  start-up advisors 118–19, 123, 154–5, 253
  strategic support 263, 271
  team members 13, 77, 119, 250, 262, 265, 266, 267, 272
  three hurdles management 274
  time management 278
  and types of start–ups 257–63

see also value events
sweat equity 359
syndicates 359
    see also co–investment

tag-along rights 185, 190, 196, 232
Tailwind BV (Netherlands) 328
team members 13, 77, 119, 250, 265,
        267, 272, 359
    and best fit 265, 266
    creation of a great team 305
    e-businesses 262
    see also management teams
Tech Coast Angels 69–70
technological risk 105
technology deals 124
technology development 100, 101–2
Telemex 287
Tellme Networks 134
3i 65
three hurdles management 274
three round financing rule 283
three stages of company development
        125–6
time commitments 7, 12, 14
time management 114–15, 124, 278
Timmons, Jeff 352
Tomeh, Danny 318
trade sales 359
TriState Investment Group 331
Tullman, Howard 14, 15, 115, 209,
        265, 299, 333
Twaalfhoven, Bert 25, 33, 68–9, 206,
        226, 297, 333
    in-depth profile of 348
    supporting roles 268, 269, 273
the 2x rule 272

underwriting 360
Unikel, Errol 238

Valin, Reg 41, 43, 44, 55
valuation 360
valuation methods 143–77
    academic/investment banker 146,
        148, 152–3
    Berkus method 146, 150, 158, 160,
        170, 172
    choice of method 161–2
    compensated advisor 146, 154–5
    and deal structure 163, 201, 202
    and dilution 165
    discounted cash flow 146, 152–3,
        158, 160
    feel good factor 167
    $5m limit 146, 149, 158, 160, 161,
        169–70
    and greed 176
    Interelate example 157–62
    internet companies 151
    levers of early stage returns 163–5
    multiplier method 146, 152, 157,
        160
    O.H. method 156, 160
    options on future opportunities
        166–7
    pre-VC 155, 160
    quick and easy 146, 147, 148,
        149–51
    risk and reward 174–5
    ROI (return on investment) 163–4,
        165, 177
    rule of thirds 146, 150, 159, 160
    start-up advisor 154–5
    $2m–$5m standard 146, 149, 151,
        159, 160, 161, 162, 177
    $2m–$10m standard 146, 151, 159
    value later 146, 148, 155–6
    and venture capital finance 202
    venture capitalist 146, 148, 153,
        159–60
    virtual CEO 154
    winning tools and tactics 169–70
value events 247, 254–6, 360
    and board members 269
    e-businesses 263
    harvesting 303–5
    products 258–9
    retail 261–2
    service 260
value later 146, 148, 155–6
value proposition 360
value-added investors 360
VCs *see* venture capitalists (VCs)

venture capital 360
  pre-VC valuation method 155, 160
Venture Capital Report (VCR) 108,
    344, 351
venture capitalist dance 110
venture capitalist method of valuation
    146, 148, 153, 159–60
venture capitalists (VCs) 360
  and Ascend Venture Group 340
  and convertible notes 194
  and harvesting 304, 306–8, 309,
    310, 323
    IPOs 296, 303
  making friends with 65
  and negotiation 234
  personal meetings with 38
  relationships with 273
  and structure 181, 202–4, 306
    preferred convertible 191, 192
  and supporting roles 266–7
  three round financing rule 283
Venture Law Group 329
vesting 212, 216
  schedule 216
Villafana, Manny 52, 63, 108, 124,
    333
  in-depth profile of 343
  medical start–ups 127, 343
visibility activities 35, 36, 43–50
  co-investing 39, 57, 66–7
  co-investment 50, 54, 63–5
  deal flow 57
  interviews 43
  publishing articles/books 44–5
  speeches 44–5
  teaching entrepreneurship 35, 46
  winning investments 48
  writing books 47
voting rights 187–8, 217
  CommonAngels 211

vulture capital 360

Walker, Steve 14, 44, 62, 191, 334
  and monitoring 268
  on negotiation 235
walking harvest 289–92
Walnut Venture Associates 342
wanna-be entrepreneurs 139
warranties and representations 187
warrants 188
Wasabi Fund 19–20, 341, 342
Wash, Darryl 35, 48, 67, 134, 173,
    334
  on harvesting 287, 310, 313
  in-depth profile of 340–1
  on negotiation 239
  on structure 184
  on supporting roles 276
  on valuation 152, 172
Weaver, William 43, 65, 238, 310,
    312, 334
web managers 88
WebTV 330, 348, 349
Wetzel, William 355
Wharton Consulting 334
Wharton, Tom 118, 123, 281, 334
  start-up advisor services 253
  on valuation 154
  on value events 254
Winfreestuff.com 281–2
Winning Angels Study (Amis and
    Dinnin) 26, 61, 120, 168, 205,
    235, 271, 309
working capital 360
Wozniak, Steve 68
writing one-pagers 36, 70

Yahoo! 103, 257

ZipDirect 352

THE FAST WAY TO USE THIS BOOK

Winning Angels was written to be used, and is organized so you can use it in three ways:

1 ● Pick a chapter or section that interests you and skim it for nuggets.

2 ● Use the table of contents or the index to find a specific issue that concerns you now.

3 ● Read *Winning Angels* for a comprehensive understanding of the seven fundamentals.

Here is a plan of action (POA) to get the most from this book:

1 ● *Read pages xii–xiii to see how we organized the book for your use.* Once you understand the format, you will see that *Winning Angels* is the best tool you have for making investments.

2 ● *If you are new to angel investing, complete the "Know thyself" assessment on page 5.* This will help you decide if angel investing is really for you.

3 ● *Actively participate in an investment while reading.* The most accelerated learning possible will come from making angel investments and reading *Winning Angels* at the same time.